BLACK AMERICA SERIES

PLEASANT CITY
WEST PALM BEACH

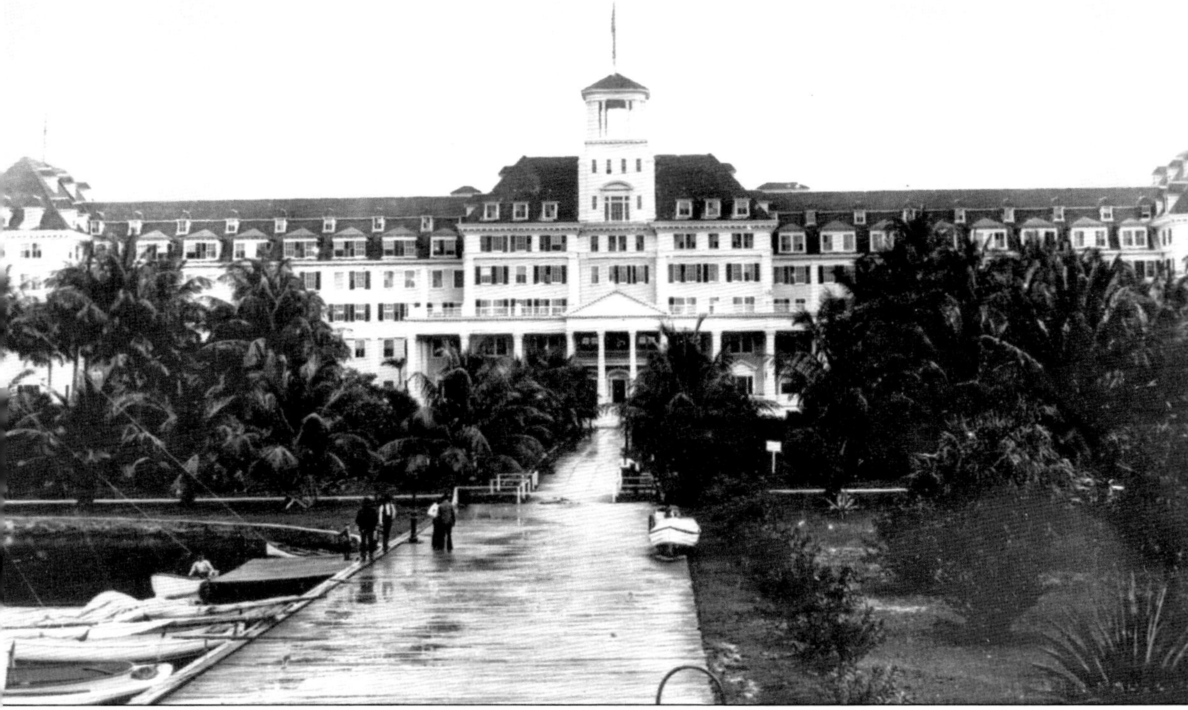

The Royal Poinciana Hotel, built in 1894, was the largest wooden structure in the world at the time. African Americans assisted in building the hotel and served there as waiters, bellhops, maids, and laundresses before the hotel burned in the 1930s. Wood from the old hotel was used to build some homes in Pleasant City. (Photo courtesy of Historical Society, Palm Beach County.)

BLACK AMERICA SERIES

PLEASANT CITY WEST PALM BEACH

Everee Jimerson Clarke

ARCADIA PUBLISHING

ISBN 978-0-7385-1758-2

Published by Arcadia Publishing
Charleston, South Carolina

Printed in the United States of America

Library of Congress Catalog Card Number: 2004115329

For all general information contact Arcadia Publishing at:
Telephone 843-853-2070
Fax 843-853-0044
E-mail sales@arcadiapublishing.com
For customer service and orders:
Toll-Free 1-888-313-2665

Visit us on the Internet at www.arcadiapublishing.com

This book is dedicated to my parents, Rev. William and Mrs. Cynthia Darthula Davis Jimerson, who were my vessels of hope and inspiration; my daughters, Renee Denise and Frances Yvette Clarke; the instructors, community leaders, and role models who shaped the lives of our many achievers, the pioneers of Pleasant City, whom time seems to have forgotten; and family and friends who share our vision and keep our great history and legacy alive.

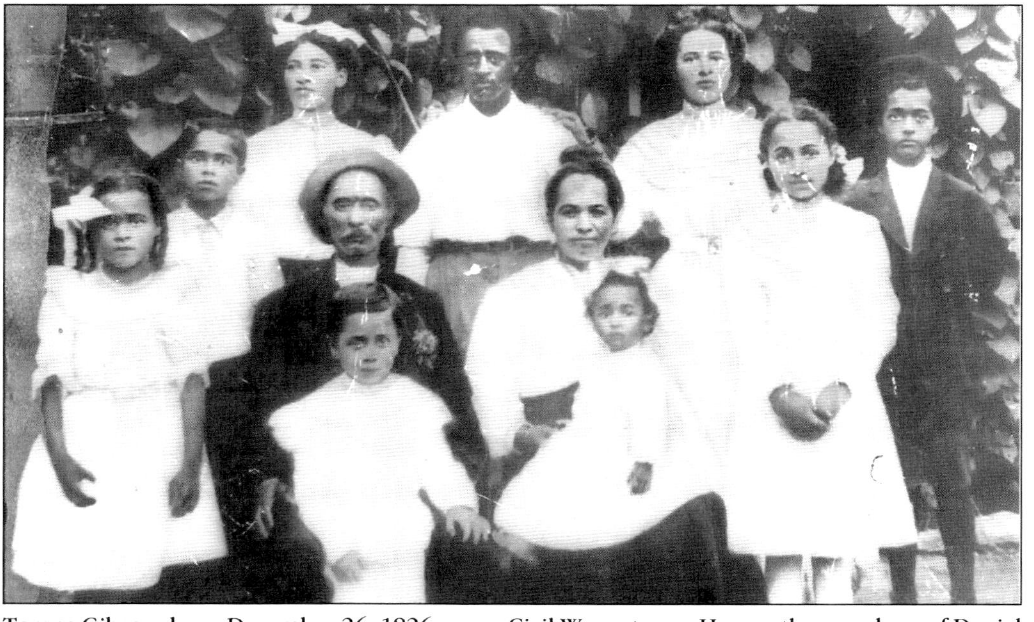

Tomps Gibson, born December 26, 1826, was a Civil War veteran. He was the grandson of Daniel Boone, fathered by Boone's son and their slave. He was originally named Tomps Calhoun Boone Gibson. Shown here are, from left to right, (seated) Tomps holding Marvin and Queen Victoria, Tomps's wife, holding Gladys; (standing) Louise, Wallace, Mariah, Roy, Queen Victoria, Ann, and Charles. (Photo by Edith Fisher-Bradberry.)

Contents

ACKNOWLEDGMENTS

The author, a native of West Palm Beach, has devoted years to researching and documenting the history of Pleasant City, the oldest African-American community in Palm Beach County. Building an awareness of the valuable contributions African Americans have made in shaping the history of Palm Beach County has been a labor of love. A debt of gratitude is owed the many families who provided history and materials to establish the Pleasant City Heritage Gallery, which opened in September 1996. Aside from being a lasting memorial to the pioneers of Pleasant City, it is a great source of historic information for the community. All of the pioneer families deserve credit for the success of this publication, but most notable are:

Anderson, John and Ophelia
Anderson, Joseph and Ethel
Anderson, Richard
Austin, Fred and Alma
Bailey, William and Ida
Bates, Thomas and Georgia
Battles, Robert and Rebecca
Bergman, Yancy and Eula
Bivens, Charles and Alice
Blatch, Moses
Blye, Wiley C. and Bernice
Bolden, George and Cora
Boneparte, Benjamin
Brown, Isadore and Jessie
Brunson, Felix and Daisy
Bullard, Albert and Diane
Burns, Elisha and George
Butler, Robert
Butler, Thomas and Ardella
Butler-Scipio, Leona
Byrd, Freddie and Mattie Bowman
Calloway, Rev. John
Carmichael, Lizzie Evans
Carter, George
Chandler, Isaac
Crocket, Jennie
Daniels, David and Rhoda
DeLancy, Felix and Annetta
Demps, Mr. and Mrs. Thomas
Denagall, Leanora Dixon
Dillard, Lizzie
Donald, James and Loreca
Downs, Mr. and Mrs. Richard
Dyett, Dr. J. Russell and Lurleen
Ellison, Rev. William and Lena
Higgins, Crawford
Ferguson, Prince and Frances
Fernandez, William and Mary
Fields, Thomas and Estella
Figger, Allen and Louise
Floyd, Richard and Idella
Fluellyn, Samuel and Inez
Foxx, Charlie and Percy
Franklin, Robert and Julia
Freeman, Harper and Lucinda
Freeman, Hattie
Fulton, William and Carolyn
Gaines, Charles and Emma
Gaines, Chester
Gildersleeve, Boise
Gildersleeve, Jacob and Mildred
Givens, Alphonso
Green, Lloyd and Clara
Griffin, William
Grisby, Earnestine
Grubbs, Johnny and Louise
Guiden, Robert and Bell
Harrell, Mr. and Mrs. C.
Henry, Rev. Thomas and Eliza
Higgins, J.D. and Margaret
Holland, William and Mamie
Hudson, Mary and Curtis
Ingram, Wil
Isaac, Rev. A.E.
Jackson, Ethel and Willis
Jefferson, George and Priscilla
Jefferson, Frank and Frances
Jimerson, Louis and Martha
Jimerson, William and Cynthia
Jones, Annie
Jones, Levi and Clarissa Rose
Jordon, John and Margaret
Jordon, John Sr.
Joseph, Daniel
Junior, Deacon and Mrs. Dora M.
Kelly, Joe and Estelle
King, George and Clara
Leary, Charles and Irene
Lovett, Charles and Inez Peppers
Lewis, Mamie
Lightbourn, Alfred and Eliza
Lovett, Mr. and Mrs. Nathaniel
Madison, Jasper and Georgia
Mack, Eva Williams
McCray, Alexander and Mamie
McIntosh, George and Laura
McQueen, John and Frances
McQueen, William and Ida
Miller, Robert Sr. and Wilhelmina
Mills, Rosa
Monroe, Susie
Moody, Wiley
Moon, Herbert Sr. and Ardie
Newbold, Samuel and

Madeline
Newbold, Thomas and Adelaide
Nottage, James and Ethel
Odum, Charlie Sr. and Addie Hall
Parson, Rev. and Mrs. Jake
Peppers, Thomas and Priscilla
Peterson, Peter and Lessie
Phillips, Fanny
Pittman, Ulysses and Jessie
Poitier, Tredwell
Preston, Eugene and Lula
Pryor, Mack and Annie
Pryor, Thomas and Patsy
Rhodes, John
Riley, Daisy
Roberts, Henry and Jane
Robinson, Amos and Bessie
Robinson, John Henry
Rogers, Frank G. and Lula
Rolle, Herbert Sr. and Florence
Romeo, Fred and Mary
Roundtree, Lloyd and Mattie
Sanchious, William
Scruggs, John and Margie
Singleton, Frank
Stepherson, Arthur
Storr, Felix and Nellie
Taggart, Shelly
Thomas, Raymond and Annie Mae
Turnquest, Lewis and Theresa
Tyson, Rev. and Mrs. Joseph
Wallace, Thomas and Lucinda
Weston, Robert
White, Edward and Carmeta
Willis, George
Witherspoon, William
Wright, Henry and Oresta

Special credit:

The Pleasant City Family Reunion Committee, Inc.
Althemese Barnes, director, Riley House, Tallahassee
Mike Browning, *Palm Beach Post*
Mary Thompson-Cleare
Tammy James
Marian Bacon White
David Preston, photographer
Henry Flagler Museum
Palm Beach County Historical Society

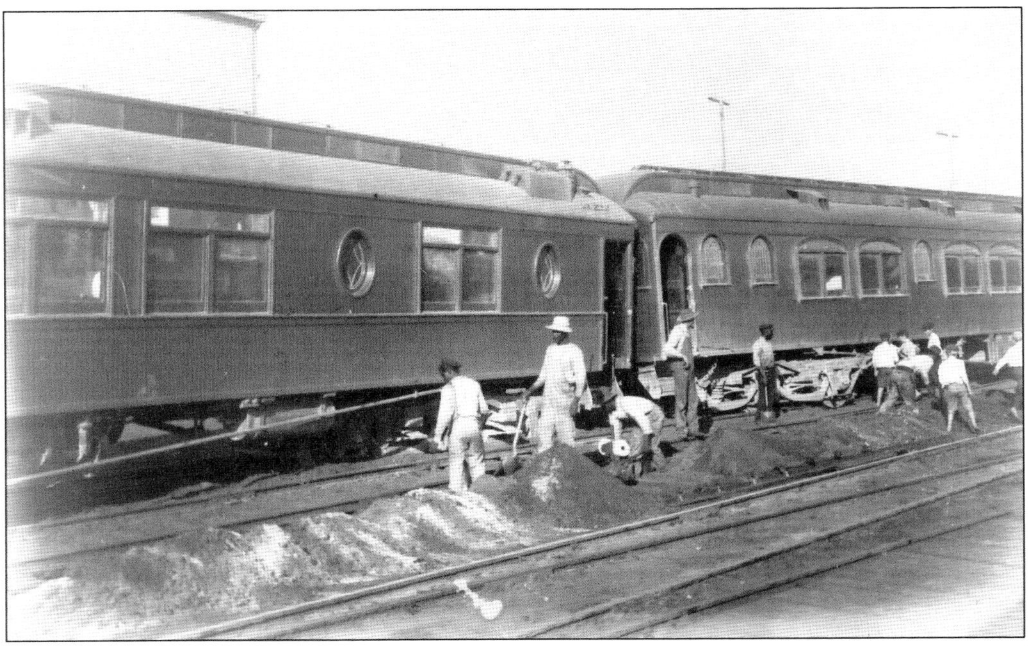

Workers extend the Florida East Coast Railroad from Juno to West Palm Beach. (Courtesy of Henry M. Flagler Museum.)

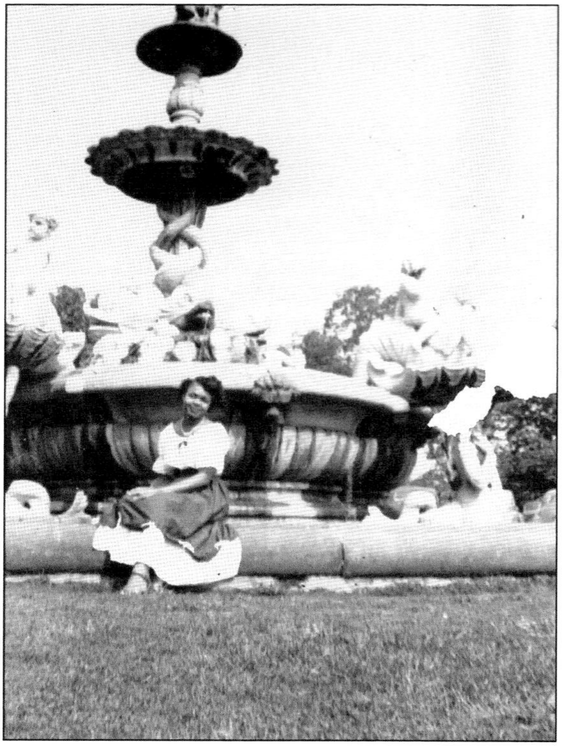

The Fountain, pictured in 1948, was just over the bridge across Lake Worth from downtown West Palm Beach.

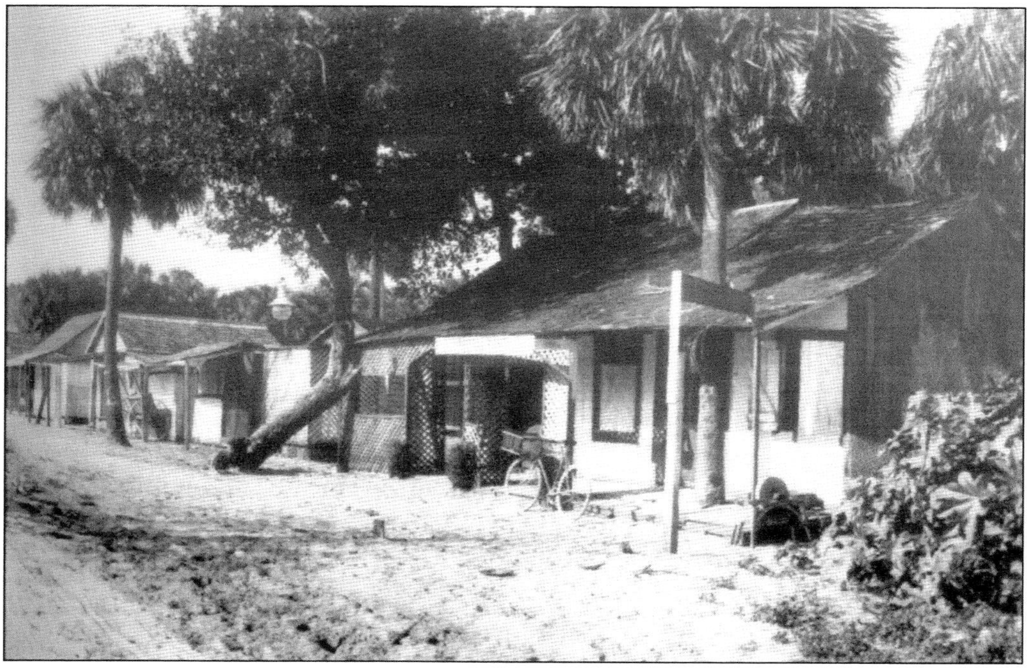

Shown here is an early view of the Styx in 1900. The Styx, located on North County Road and Sunrise Avenue in Palm Beach, was the home of more than 1,000 black workers.

INTRODUCTION

Prior to the Emancipation Proclamation, slaves who escaped from plantations in Alabama and Georgia hid in the Florida Everglades among the Seminole Indians, while others escaped to the Caribbean Islands. The Maroons, descendants of runaway slaves, fled South Carolina and other slaves states seeking protection in Florida. Many pioneers of Pleasant City, West Palm Beach, came from Georgia, Alabama, the Bahamas, and other Caribbean islands.

Black squatters were in South Florida along the southern end of Lake Worth long before Henry Morrison Flagler, Standard Oil magnate and land developer, decided to build a resort hotel on Palm Beach Island.

In 1893, almost 20 years before land developer George Curry created a subdivision on the north end of West Palm Beach and called it Pleasant City, more than 1,000 black skilled and unskilled laborers were hired by the firm of McDonald & McGuire. Their job was to extend the now East Coast Railway from Juno, north of Riviera Beach, to transport materials for the Royal Poinciana Hotel and White Hall for Henry Flagler. Many workers came by boat from Jacksonville, the "Gateway to Florida," because roads were few and automobiles were not available.

Flagler purchased land and laid out the town site of West Palm Beach in 1893 but requested that all construction workers move to the east side or to Palm Beach Island. "The Styx," a community of palmetto and driftwood shacks, boardinghouses, and shanties along a stretch of North County Road and Sunrise Avenue north of the Breakers Hotel, came into existence to provide living quarters for these black workers.

White millionaires who built their mansions on the waterfront but owned land that stretched across the island from Lake Worth to the Atlantic Ocean owned the "Styx" property. They rented their back yards at a cost of $3.00 per month. Blacks lived on the land and took care of the property while the owners went North or elsewhere in the summer. Some are said to have owned parcels of land. Along with the railroad, a footbridge was built across Lake Worth in 1896 to connect the two Palm Beaches.

The rich and famous arriving in West Palm Beach aboard the Florida East Coast train were backed over the trestle, over Lake Worth to the Royal Poinciana station, next to the hotel. Tourists came to Palm Beach for the season, arriving in the winter and leaving in the spring.

Life in the Styx was simple. Many male residents worked in the newly built hotel as waiters, bellhops, elevator operators, and guards; others worked to complete the Flagler mansion, the White Hall, by 1901. Aside from the hotel, men found employment as caddies, chauffeurs, butlers, gardeners, and wheelchair men who earned a good living. When men were off duty, they went fishing and hunted small animals such as rabbits and opossum. They also raised chickens and planted vegetables for food. The women worked as chambermaids, laundresses, cooks, and nursemaids.

Children attended school in Bethel Baptist Church in the Styx. Later they traveled over Lake Worth by ferry and walked to Lake Academy, a black school where Prof. J.W. Mickens was principal. They played stickball and ring plays, and they also jumped rope.

During their free time, adults took ferryboat rides, held family picnics, and watched baseball games. Baseball in Palm Beach County began in the Styx where teams were imported to play on local teams. Black entertainers were hired for events in the hotel.

Styx residents organized four churches: Payne Chapel and St. Paul African Methodist Episcopal Churches and Tabernacle and St. John Missionary Baptist Churches. They organized educational, fraternal, and business institutions and developed a colorful lifestyle that continued in Pleasant City.

Medical needs were met by Dr. Thomas Leroy Jefferson, one of the first black doctors, and Millie Gildersleeve, the first nurse and midwife in Palm Beach County.

Bicycles were the mode of transportation. Travelers rode their bicycles to the ferryboat, placed them on board, and for only 5¢ sailed across Lake Worth before continuing their trip on their bicycle or wheelchair.

Many Styx residents had staked out property on the west side of Lake Worth before George Curry's subdivision of Pleasant City was laid out. Daisy Brunson purchased her land in 1897 and built the first home at Nineteenth Street and Spruce Avenue, when Northwood was not accessible.

In 1903, the railroad extension, the construction of the Royal Poinciana Hotel, and Flagler's mansion were completed.

Wealthy landowners soon began to realize the value of the land rented to blacks and that relocating Styx residents to the west side of Lake Worth was profitable. A fire in 1906 forced some residents to relocate. Unsanitary conditions were the cause of the final exodus, when property owners petitioned the State Board of Health to install a sanitary system or eliminate the community. The Styx was legislated out of existence.

In 1912, George Curry developed a 10-block parcel of land bordered on the north by Twenty-third Street, on the south by Seventeenth Street, on the east by Dixie Highway, and on the west by the Florida East Coast Railroad. In a *Tropical Sun* ad of 1913, Pleasant City was listed as a high-class colored subdivision north of town. Lots sold for $150 and up. Streets were named Beautiful, Cheerful, Merry, Contentment, Comfort, etc., because George Curry felt that blacks, innately happy people, would like them. Single-family homes were built on 50-by-100-foot lots, which had several fruit trees, including mangoes, guavas, mulberries, oranges, lemons, coconuts, and papayas. There were hedges of wild cherries and hibiscus flowers. The Hurricane of 1928 did much damage to Pleasant City homes because they were mostly wooden structures with a few stucco homes.

After the exodus from the Styx to Pleasant City, residents continued to work in the hotels and beautiful mansions owned by the rich, the famous, and royalty. The homes were very spacious and required six to eight servants. These servants were treated very well. Some worked only six months but were paid year round. They were often included in the family will and assisted in educating their children. These wealthy employers supported the community churches and businesses. Spruce Avenue from Fifth Street to Twenty-third Street, and Twentieth Street from Dixie Highway to the railroad was the hub of black business enterprises, many of which started in the Styx. The churches were spiritual pillars of the community, social centers where youth received their basic foundations.

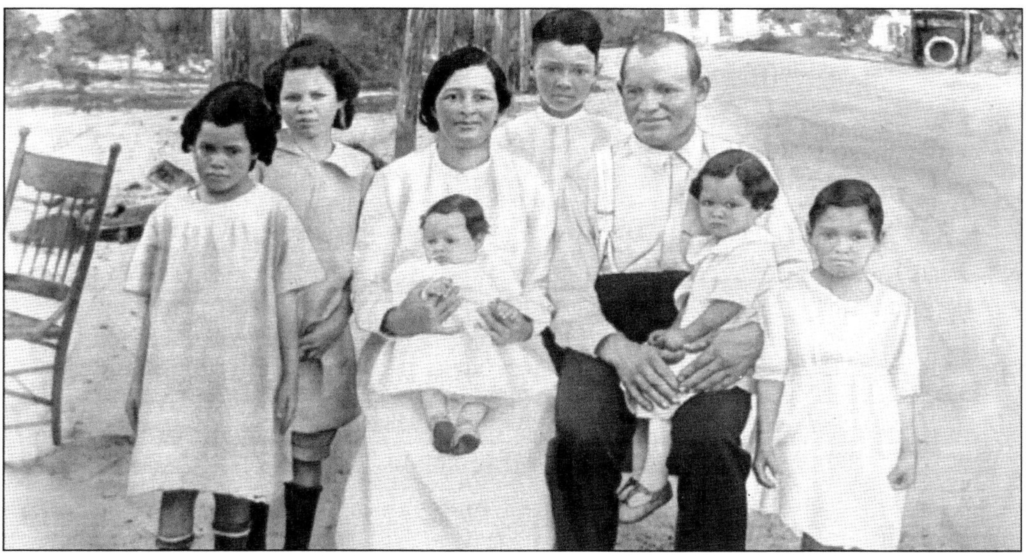

The Fisher family were, from left to right, Rose Ann, Margie, Queen Victoria holding Floyd, Bernard, William Howard holding Edith Mae, and Hazel. William Howard Fisher and Queen Victoria Gibson, parents of Edith Bradberry, came to Pleasant City from Rabon Gap, Georgia, in 1921. They settled at Contentment Avenue and 20th Street. All of the children attended Pleasant City Elementary School.

One

PIONEERS

The exodus of African-American workers from the Styx and Palm Beach was completed in 1912. Many of these workers settled along Poinsettia Avenue between Eighteenth and Twenty-third Streets, in the West Palm Beach area known as Pleasant City. Some moved further toward the Florida East Coast Railway between Seventeenth and Twenty-third Streets. Poinsettia Avenue later became Dixie Highway or U.S. Highway 1.

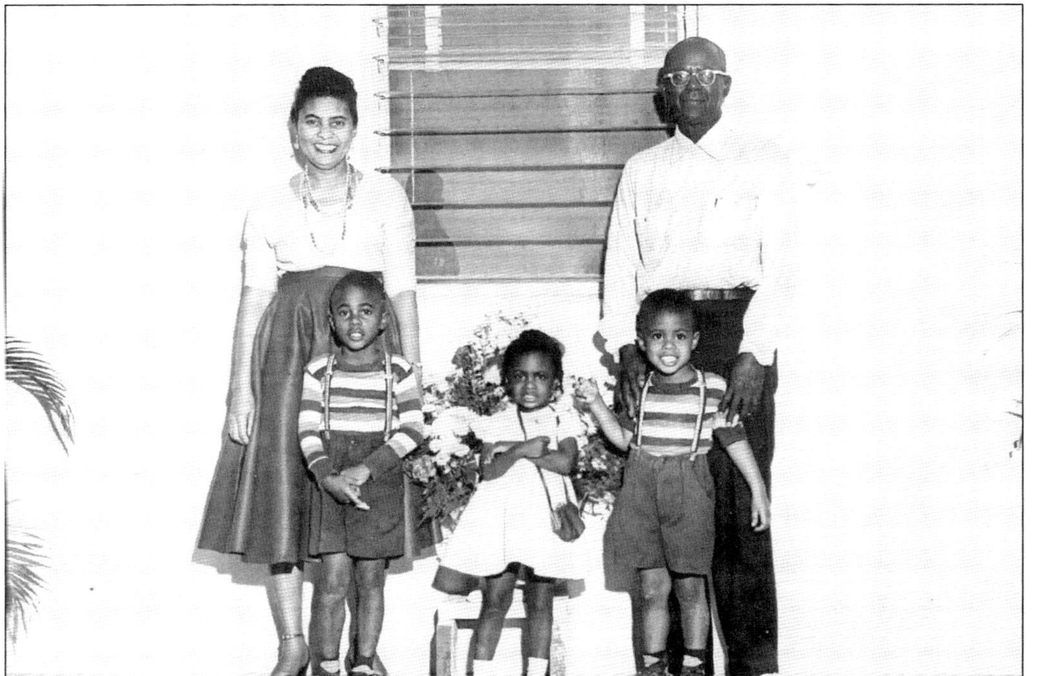

Shown here are, from left to right, Mrs. Lurleen Dyett, J. Russell Dyett Jr., Cheryl Ann, Marvin, and Dr. J. Russell Dyett Sr. Dr. Dyett was a leading doctor in the community.

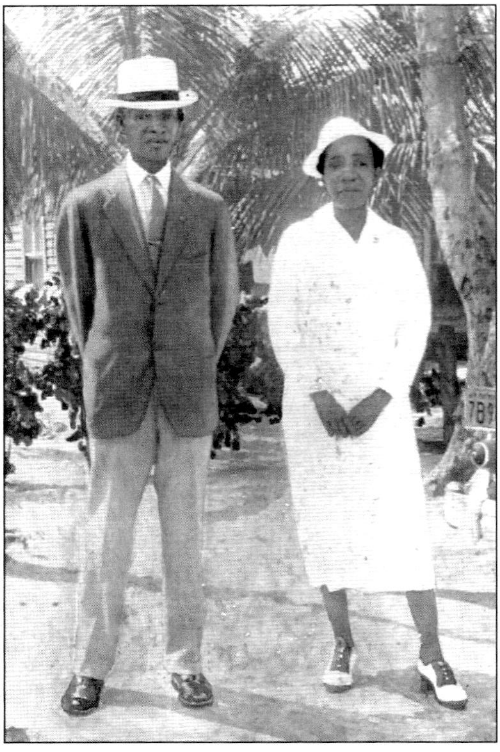

Thomas and Patsy Pryor came from Enterprise, Florida, to the Styx in time for their first child, Louise, to be born in 1905. Eight other children followed, and when the family moved to Nineteenth Street in West Palm Beach, they attended Pleasant City Elementary School. Eddie, Lafayette, Anthony, Mildred, Thomas, Rena, George, and Leroy formed the Pryor Family Choir. Mildred, goddaughter of Rev. W.H.A. Pickett of St. Paul A.M.E. Church, married Oliver W. Burroughs in 1937. Burroughs was ordained and became pastor of St. Paul A.M.E. Church.

below left: "The Fashionable Ladies of 1920," seen at right, are Bertha Williams and Ethel Anderson. Hats were a very important part of their Sunday dress.
below right: An entrepreneur and citrus contractor, Mose Elkins was well-respected in civic and social affairs.

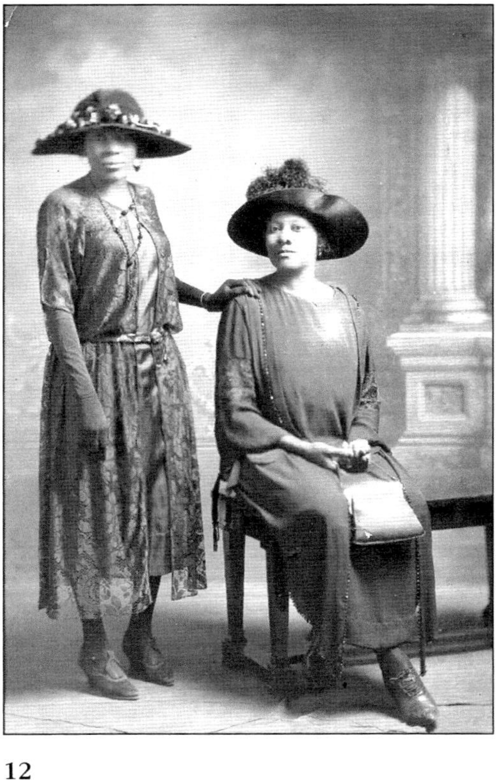

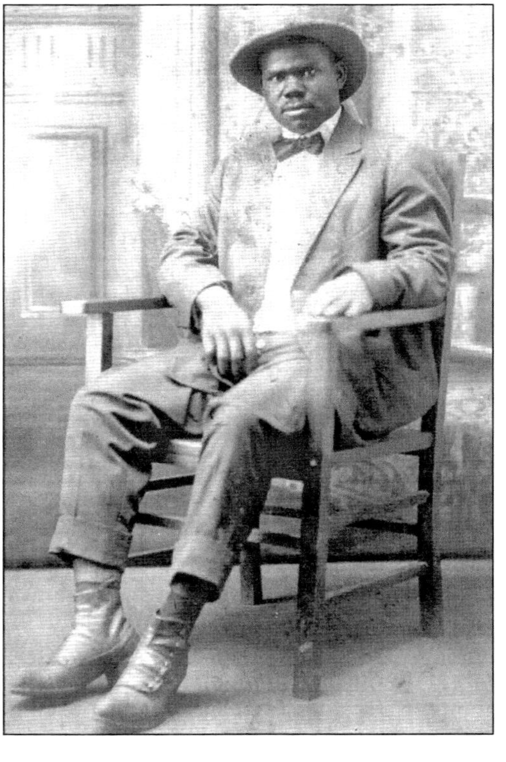

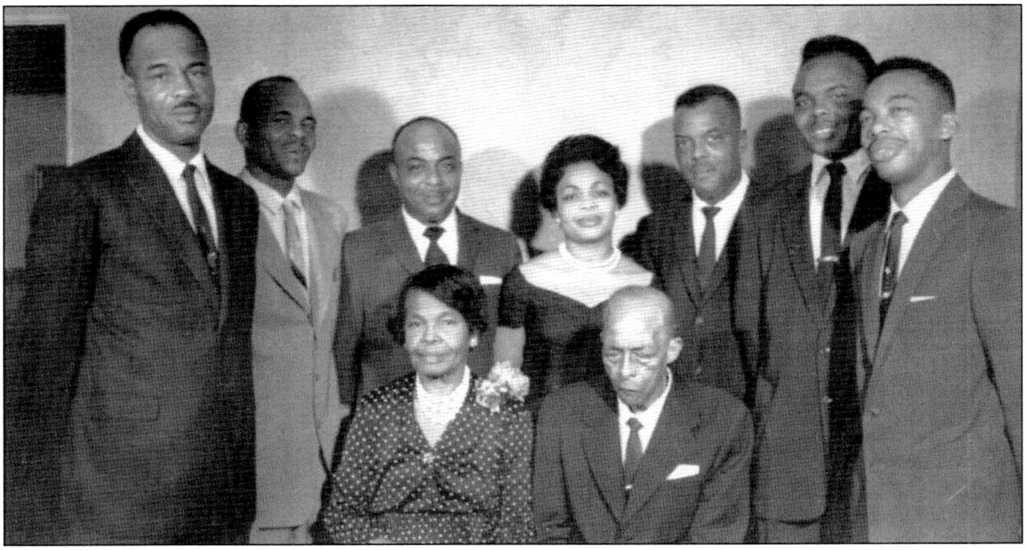

William Jimerson was born to Samuel Jimerson and Elisha Blackshear at Miccosukee, Florida, in 1880. In 1894, the family moved to the Styx, where they lived and worked for 20 years. In 1917, William married Cynthia Darthula Davis, daughter of Patsy Givens and William Penn Davis. William built a home for his bride at 509 Twentieth Street in Pleasant City. Their children, from left to right, are Jesse Lee (May 1, 1918), Emmanuel Well (September 14, 1921), Rufus Osten (August 31, 1923), Everee (July 6, 1926), Andrew (October 28, 1927), Herman (March 6, 1932), and Simeion Warren (March 23, 1934). In 1930, William was ordained an itinerant elder in the A.M.E. Church. He was the pastor of churches in Belle Glade, Hobe Sound, Jupiter, and others in the circuit. He was also an associate minister at St. Paul A.M.E. Church in Pleasant City. Cynthia, aside from being a great mother and homemaker, was a direct salesperson for Watkins and Lucky Heart Personal Care Products.

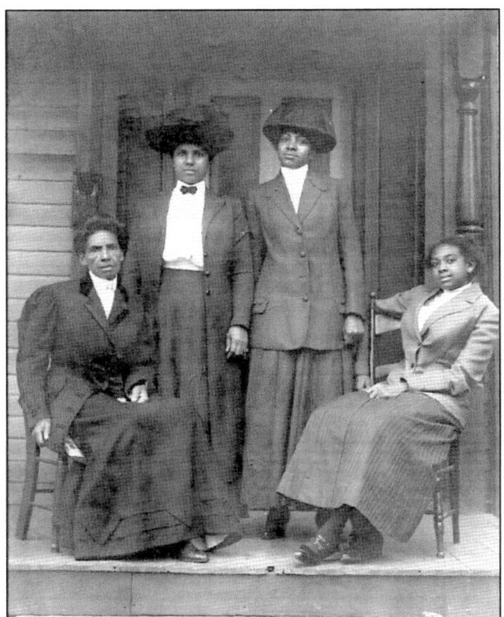

While these elegant ladies on the porch after Sunday service are not identified, they represent the poise, style, and grace of the ladies of the late 1890s.

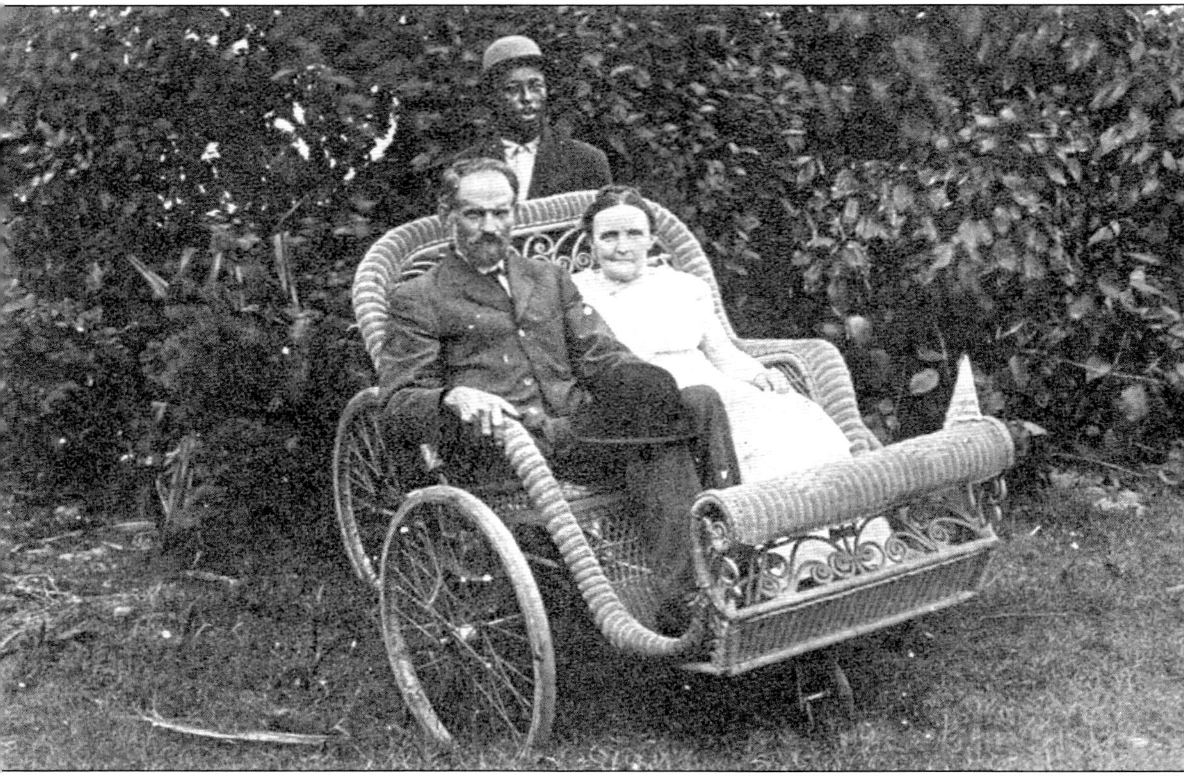

Rev. William Jimerson pushes John Godgrey and Jane Mills Gates around Palm Beach in 1913.

Four generations of the Stevens family are pictured here from left to right: Grandmother Mrs. Ambrister (from the Bahamas), Mrs. Lillian Stevens, her son John Stevens, and his daughter Glenda Stevens. Lillian's sons—Eugene and Roderick, assisted by John, Robert, Leonard, and Arnold—ran the Stevens Brothers Funeral Home.

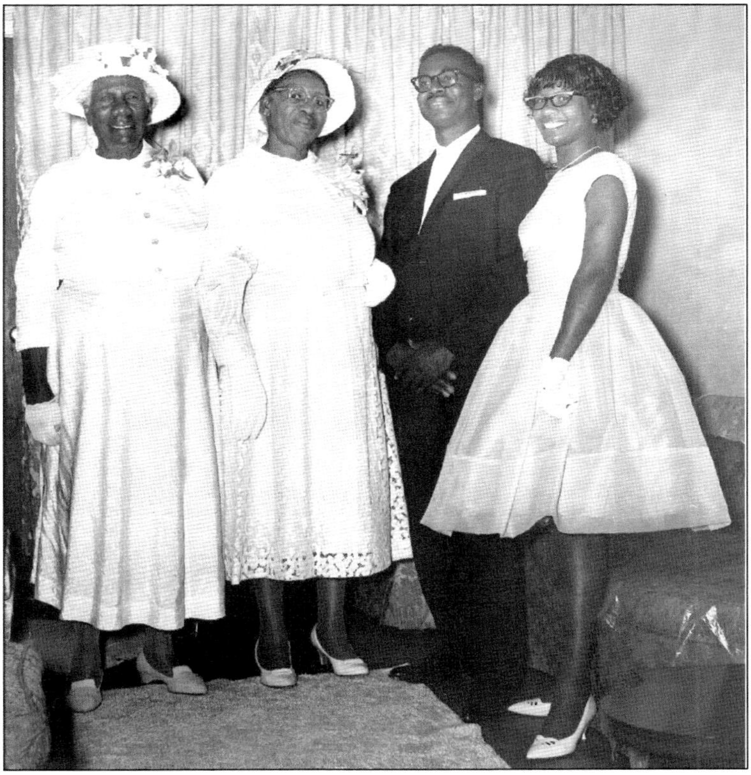

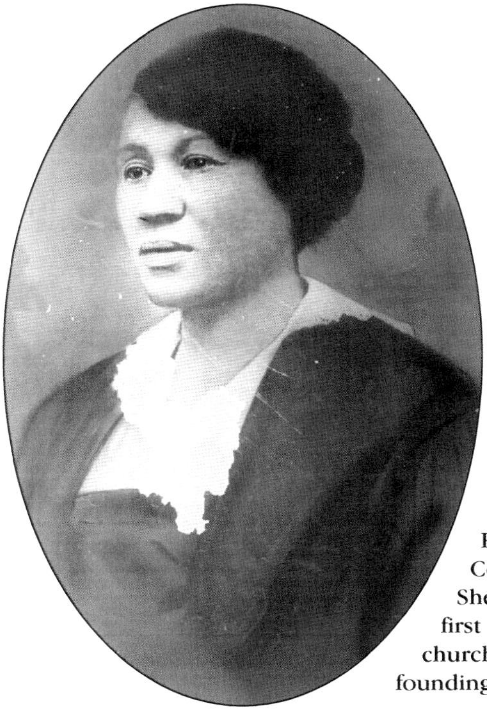

Millie Gildersleeve, 1858–1950, was born in Georgia. A freed slave, she is known as the first African-American pioneer in Palm Beach County, having arrived in 1876. She married M.J. Jake Gildersleeve in 1890 and raised five children. Millie once owned the property site of Perry Oceanographics Riviera Beach, a gift from her mentor, Capt. Elisha Newton Demick. A nurse and midwife by profession, she worked with Richard Potter, the first medical doctor in Palm Beach County, delivering both black and white babies. She and her husband, Jake, resided at 405 Twenty-first Street in Pleasant City. They were active in the church, lodges, and other community activities and were founding members of the Evergreen Cemetery Association.

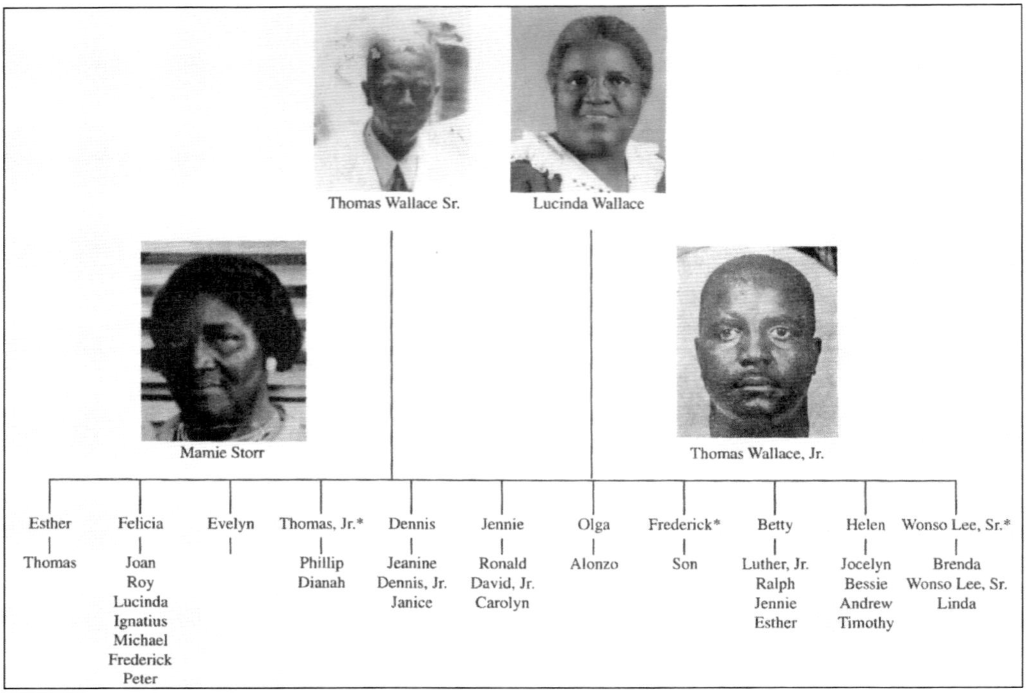

The Wallace family tree shows this pioneer family. Mr. Wallace, born in the Bahamas, was the distributor of the daily newspaper, *The Post*, and the *Pittsburgh Courier*. His wife, Lucinda, and her family lived in the "Styx" prior to moving to Pleasant City.

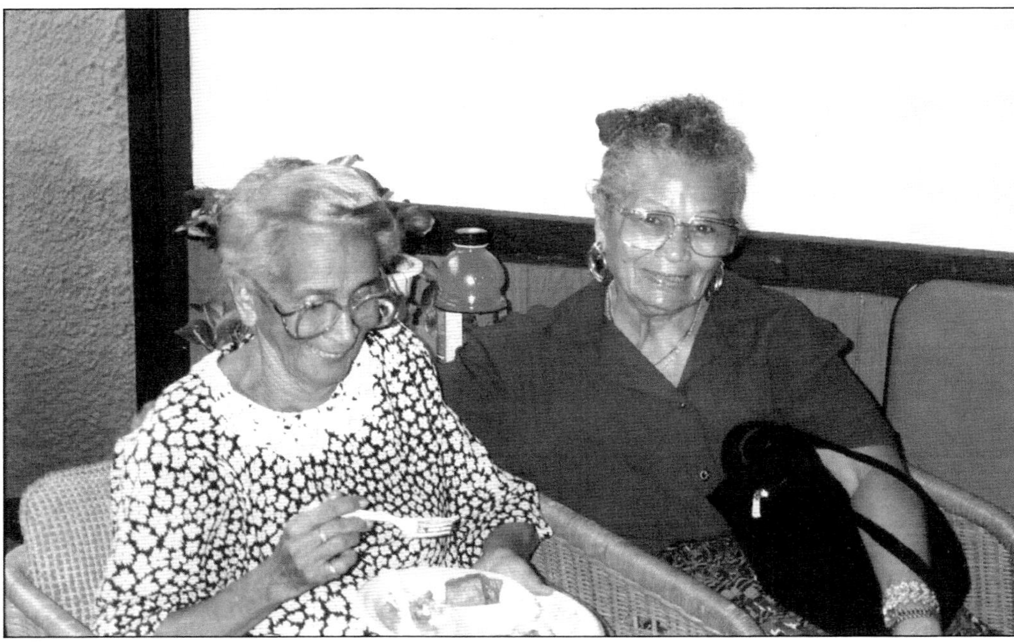

Edith Bradberry (right), 83 years old, celebrates with Dolly Paulk on her 90th birthday. Mrs. Bradberry is Mrs. Paulk's sister-in-law.

Mrs. Adelaide Newbold and her son, Alfred, are pictured here. Thomas and Adelaide Newbold came to this country from the Bahamas in 1892. They lived in the Styx, and they later moved to 437 Eighteenth Street in Pleasant City. Adelaide was a well-known midwife. Siblings included Charlie, Julia, Daisy, Wilhelmena, Eldridge, Joe Leonard, Preston, and Tom.

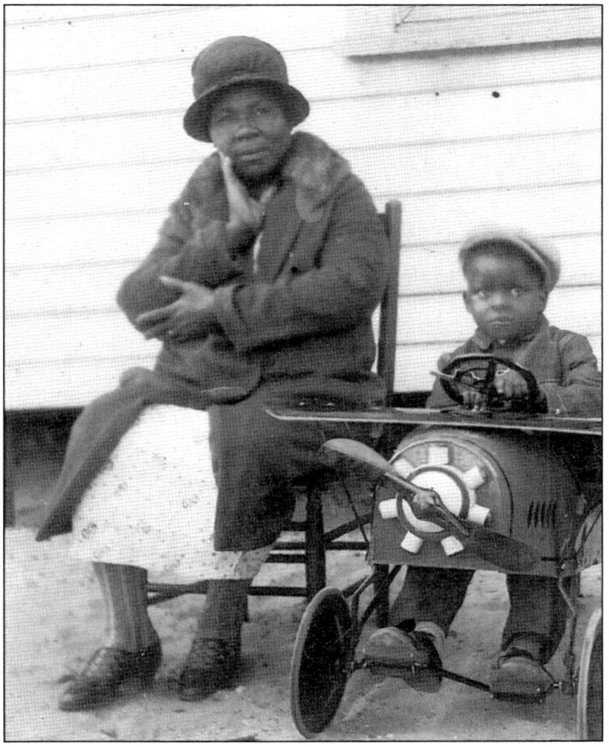

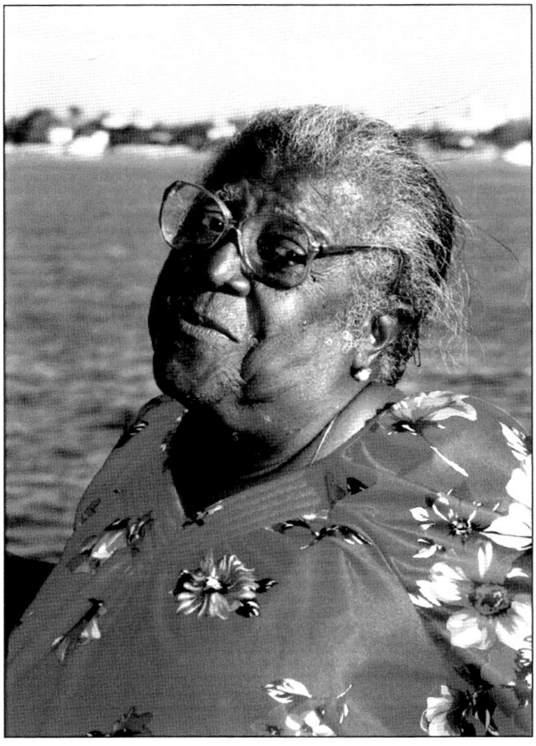

Floretta Mills Ivery was born in Pleasant City on May 22, 1911, at 2218 Contentment Avenue. She was raised by her grandparents, Rosa Mills and Elmore Austin. She and her husband owned a small neighborhood convenience store. She was a survivor of the Hurricane of 1928. Ivery still resides in Pleasant City.

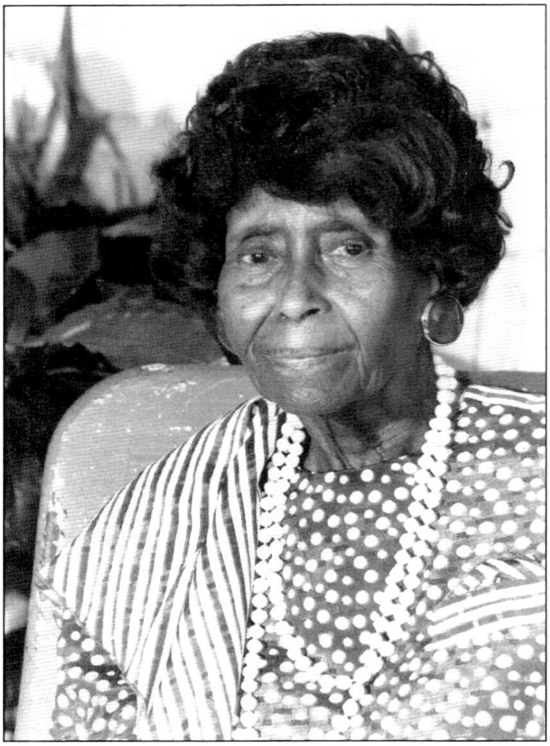

Leona Warren Butler arrived in Pleasant City from Baxley, Georgia, in 1924. She worked for Shelia Demuta, wife of swashbuckling actor Errol Flynn. In 1943, Leona married Sipio Butler, a businessman and Masonic leader. She had two sons and a daughter through a previous marriage. She was a member of Tabernacle Baptist Church for more than 63 years. As a pioneer, she remembers the good old days in Pleasant City when there were no rental apartments but beautiful single-family homes. Many blacks owned and operated businesses on 20th Street between Dixie Highway and the railroad and between 17th and 23rd Streets on Spruce Avenue.

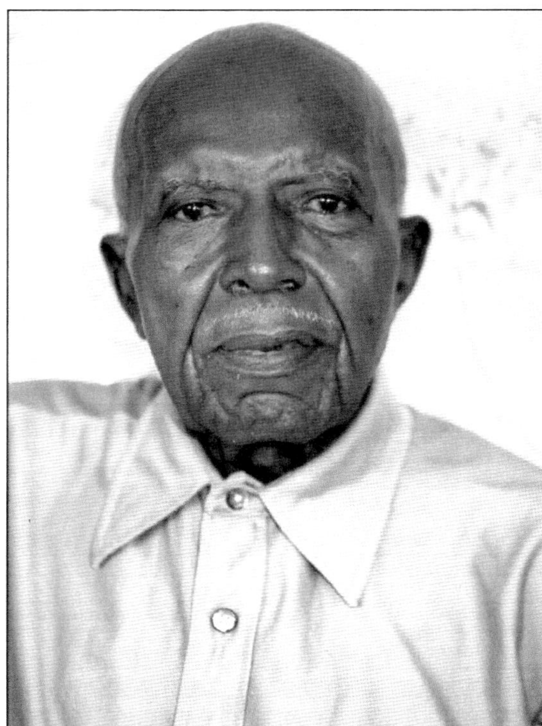

Samuel Denagall came to Pleasant City from Daytona Beach, Florida, in 1922. He was the butler for Ogden Phipps, who had vast holdings in steel, real estate, National Airlines, and racehorse champions, for nearly 60 years. He recalls an undeveloped Pleasant City where men climbed light poles to light gas street lights and early settlers had homes burned by the Klan. Not being able to ride a city bus, he remembers having to walk the Florida East Coast Railway from Fifteenth Street and Sapodilla Avenue through the woods after dark to get to Cheerful Street.

Pioneer Edward J. White Sr. is pictured with his son, Edward J. White Jr. Edward Sr. was a community activist and lay leader in the African Methodist Episcopal Church. Edward Jr. is now retired from the Palm Beach County School System.

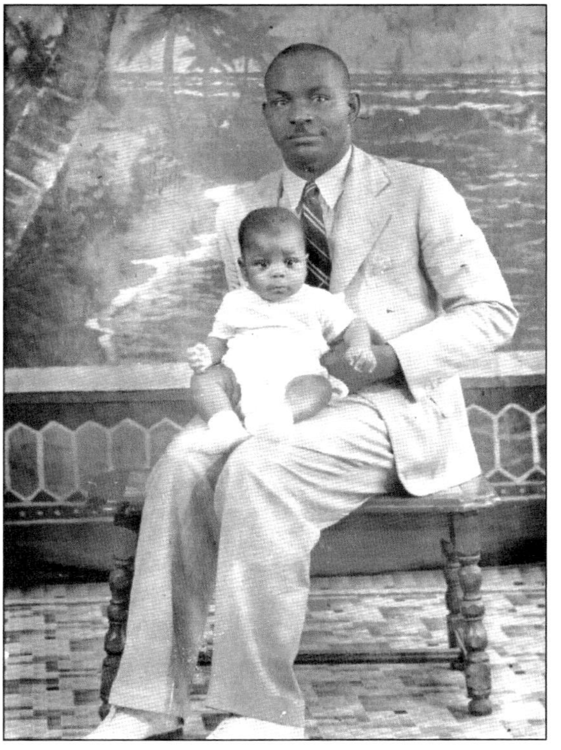

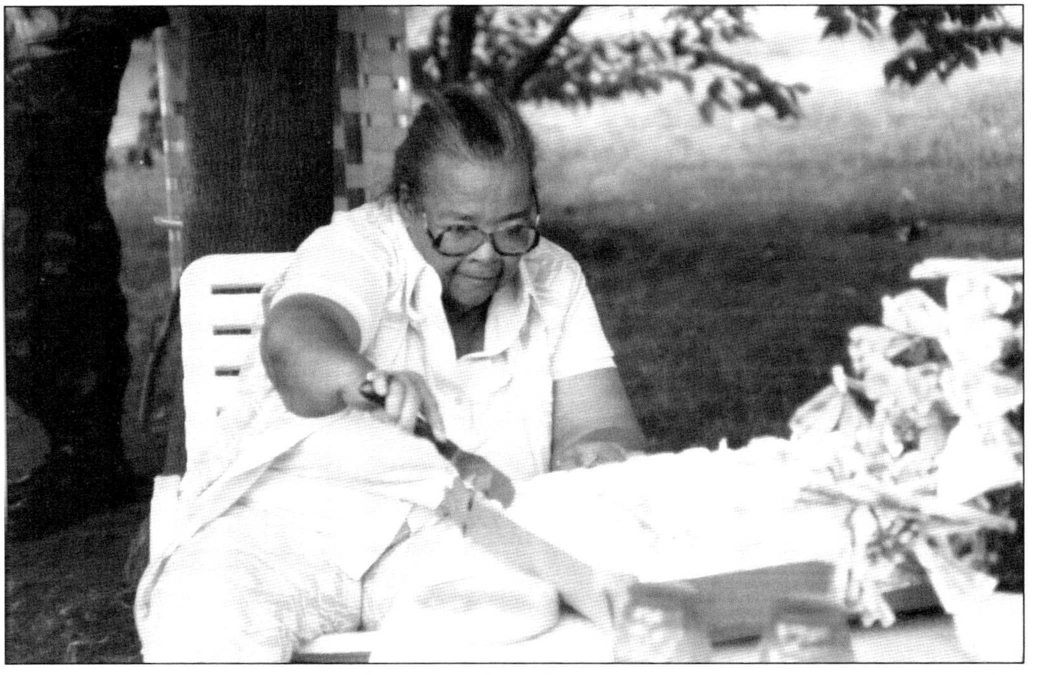

Willie Mae Artson, age 98 in 2004, is the oldest Pleasant City pioneer. She is seen cutting her birthday cake when she turn 80 years old.

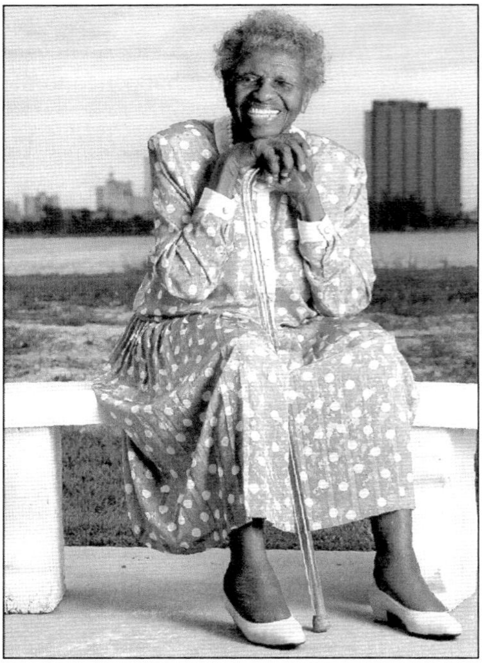

Daughter of pioneers Thomas and Priscilla Peppers, Inez Peppers Lovett spent her early childhood in the Styx. In 1903, her parents enrolled her in Lake Academy. She later attended Spelman Seminary in Atlanta, graduating in 1919. She received a bachelor's degree from Florida A&M University. She taught at Delray Beach Elementary School, Boca Raton, Pleasant City Elementary, and Roosevelt Elementary School, where she retired in 1969. She married Charles Lovett and had one daughter, Charlie Ellington, who is well known in the field of education. Inez was 100 years old when she passed away in 1996.

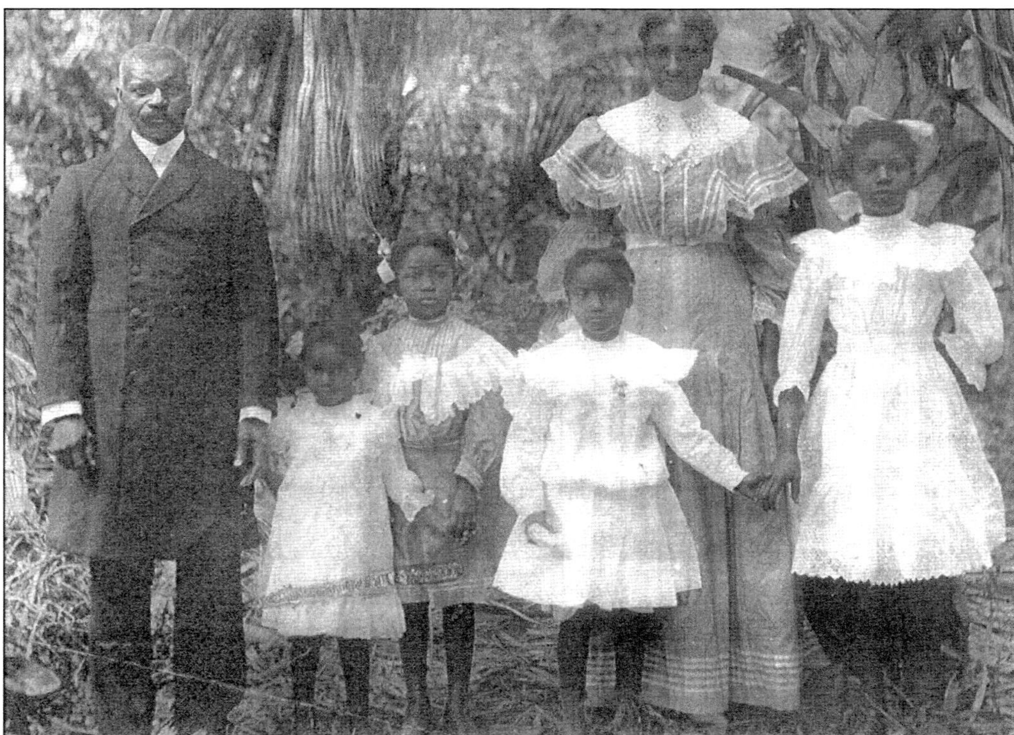

The Peppers family is shown here in the Styx about 1906. From left to right are Thomas Peppers (father), Leaola, Ruth, Olethia, Priscilla (mother), and Inez.

James Isreal Carter, born in Columbus, Georgia, on August 18, 1878. He came to the area to work for Henry Flagler's Royal Poinciana Hotel as a lather and plasterer. In 1910, he brought his wife, Viola, and daughters Louise and Willie Mae to Pleasant City. They resided at 415–417 Twentieth Street. Mr. Carter decided to become self-employed, which required his going to Washington, D.C., to acquire a license. This resulted in his house being set on fire by the Klan. Rev. William Jimerson saved the family.

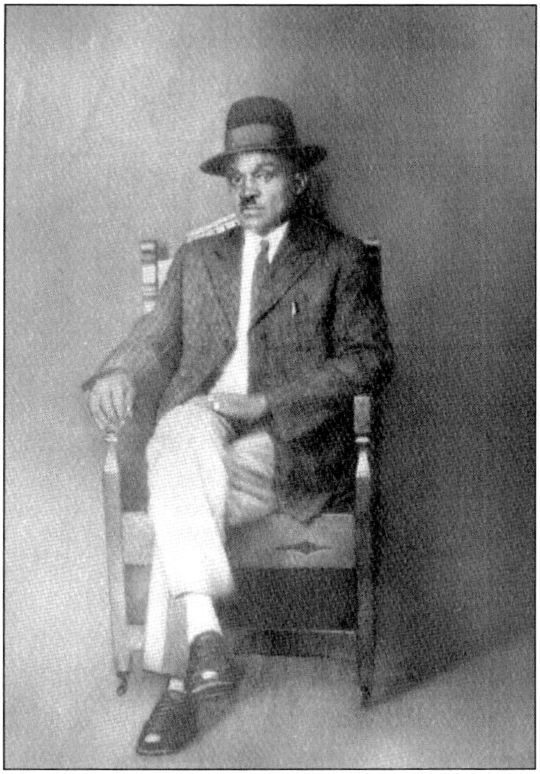

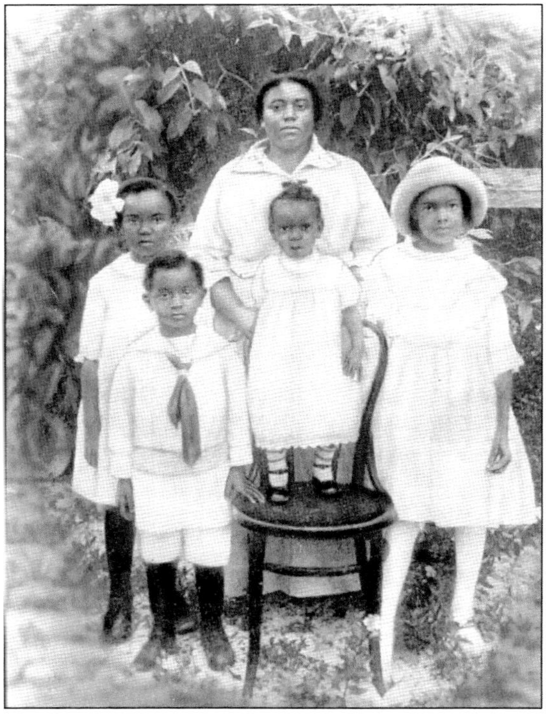

James Carter's family is shown here. They are, from left to right, Louise, Henry, mother Viola, Patsy, and Willie Mae.

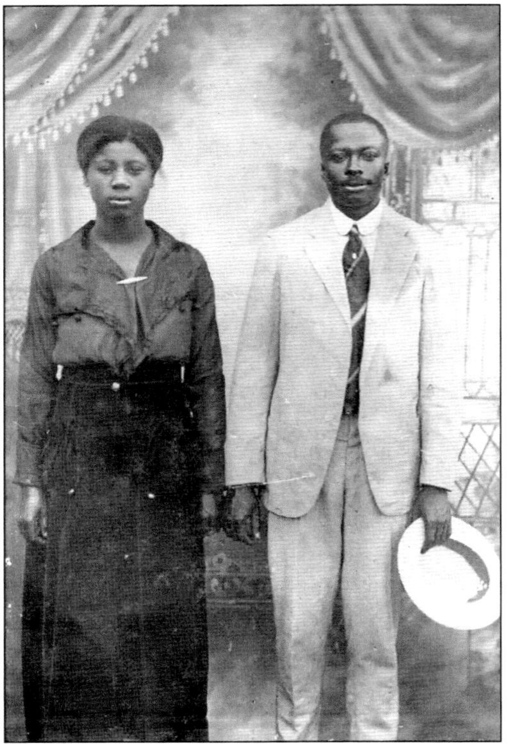

Mr. Lewis Jimerson and Mrs. Martha Jimerson are pictured here. Mr. Jimerson was a watchmaker, and Mrs. Jimerson was a seamstress. They were residents of 511 Twentieth Street. They had two daughters, Carrie and Laura.

William Fernandez (below left), born in Rock Sound, Eleuthera, Bahama Islands, met his wife, Mary (below right), in West Palm Beach. They married and had children Catherine, Herbert, Henry, Banjamin, Geneva, and Lanier. They have two surviving daughters, Geneva Fernandez-Roberts, of East Elmhurst, New York, and Lanier Fernandez Samuels, of Flushing, New York. They were members of St. Patrick Episcopal Church.

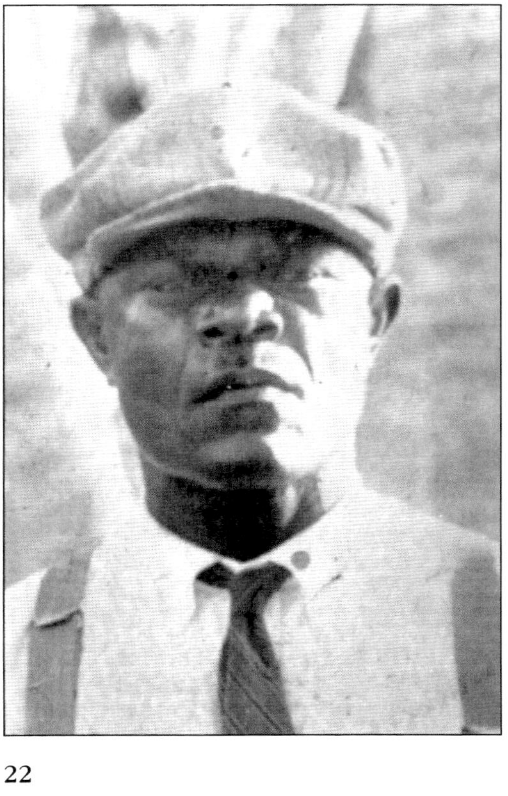

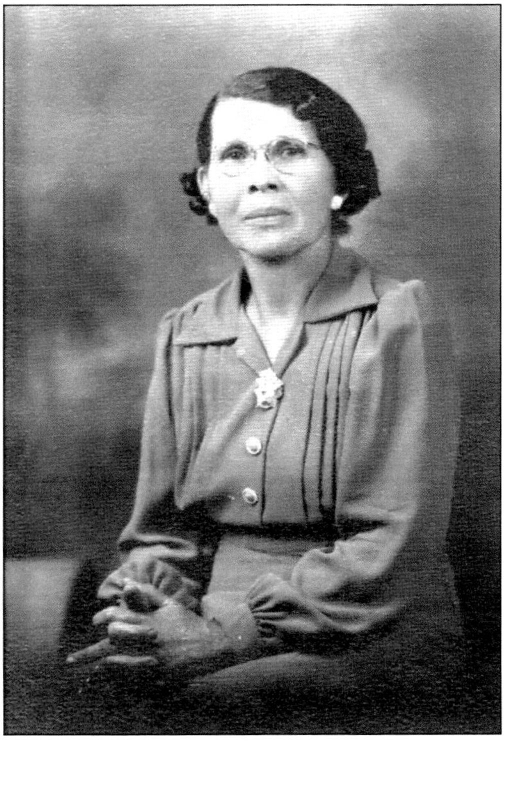

Jesse Lee Jimerson was the son of pioneers Rev. William and Mrs. Cynthia Jimerson. From left to right are Jesse Lee Jimerson holding Larry Jimerson, and Mary Jimerson holding Beverly Jimerson.

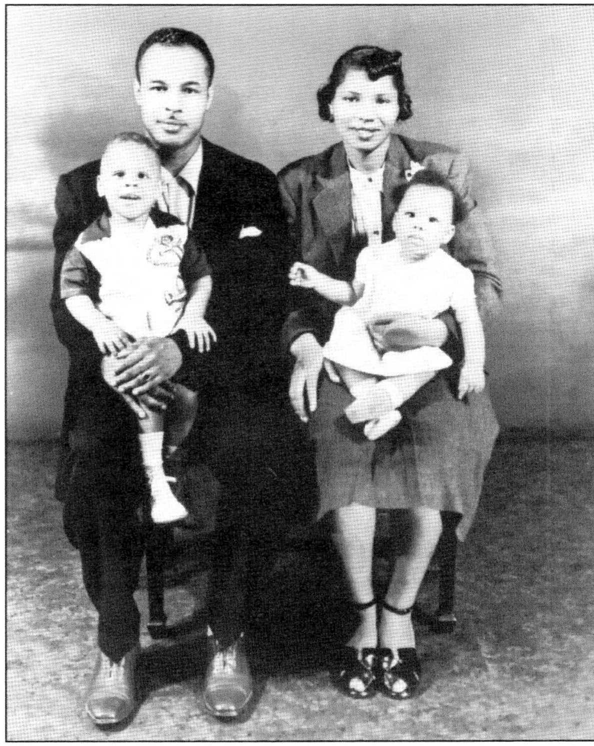

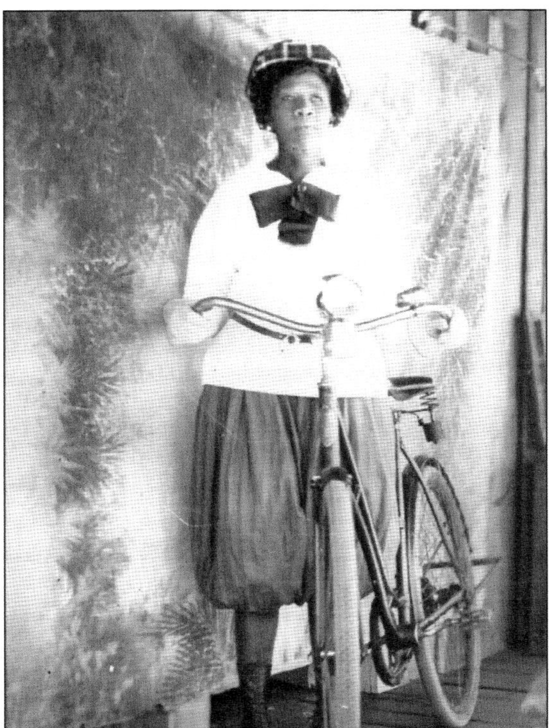

Alma Pryor rode a bicycle to work because that was the only mode of transportation until her father, Mack Pryor, started a bus service. They lived at 428 Nineteenth Street.

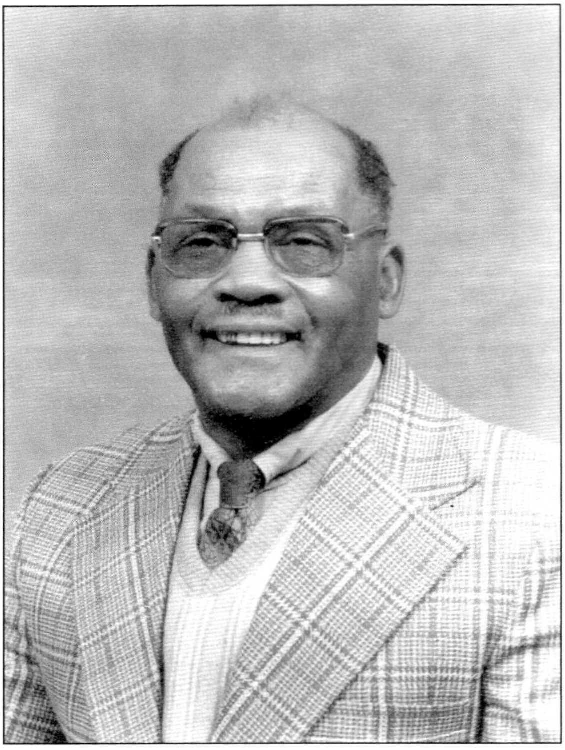

Ulysee Studstill Sr. (1913–1990, born in Jacksonville, Florida) and his wife, Ethel (1912–1997, born in Nicholls, Georgia), came to West Palm Beach from Ocala, Florida, and resided on Twentieth Street near Beautiful Avenue, the site of the Old Blue Goose Tavern, owned by Arthur Stepherson. Mr. Studstill was a janitor for the Palm Beach County School Board. Mrs. Studstill worked at St. Mary's Hospital as a laundress. Their children were Mary Studstill-McFadden, Carolyn Studstill-Lester, Ulysee Studstill Jr. (deceased), Catherine Studstill-Robinson, Oscar Studstill, William Studstill, and Cora Studstill-Perry.

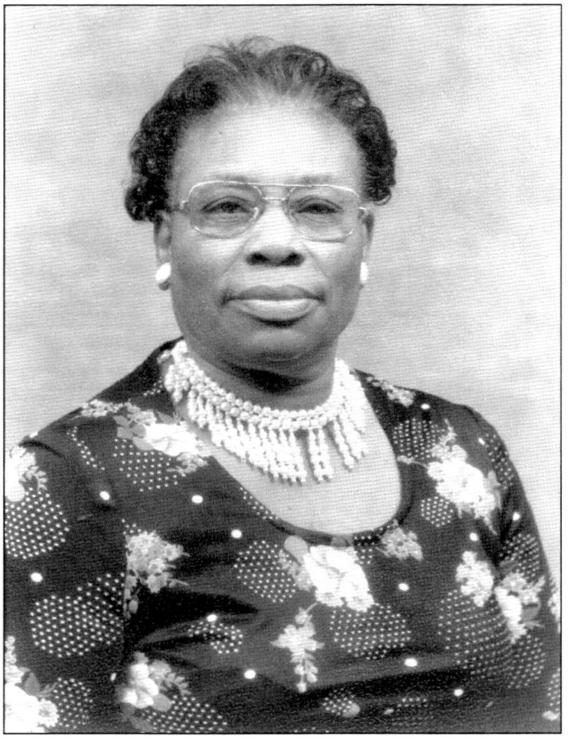

Renee Denise Clarke was born on August 15, 1954, and was laid to rest at Royal Palm Memorial Gardens on August 9, 1972. She was the daughter of Everee Jimerson Clarke and Vospher Lewis Clarke and sister of Frances Yvette Clarke. She was the granddaughter of pioneers Rev. and Mrs. William Jimerson.

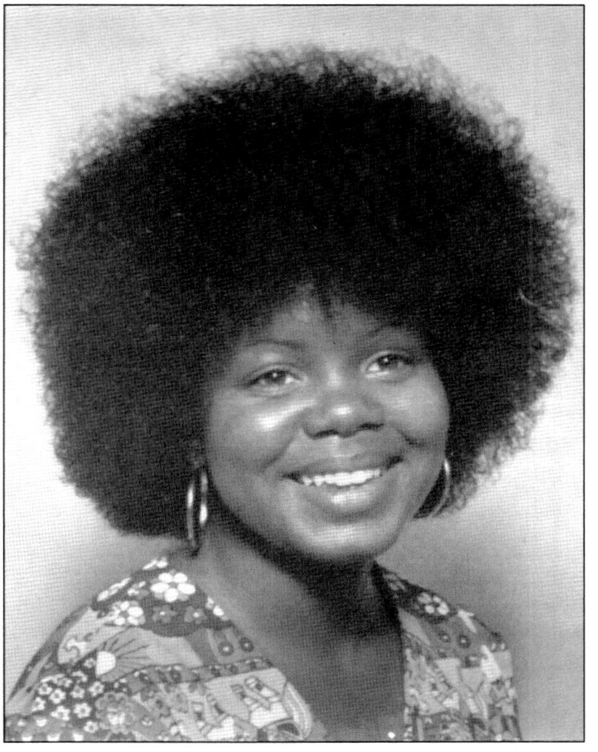

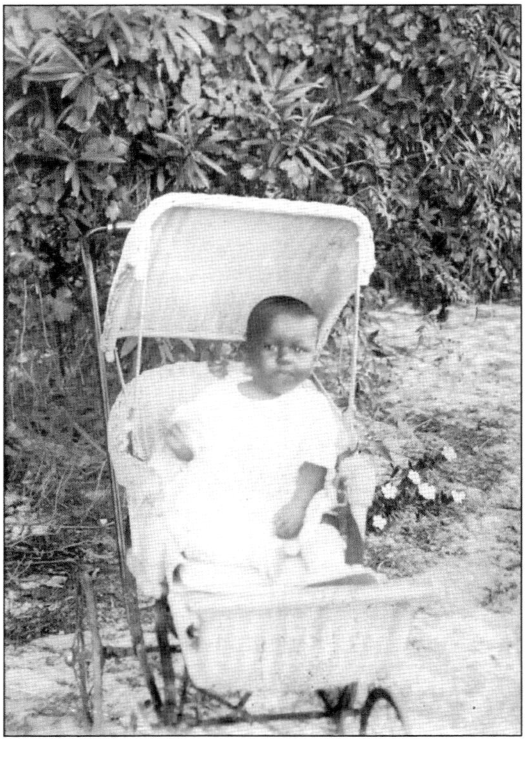

Carrie Jimerson, seen here at 14 months in 1923, was the daughter of Lewis and Martha Jimerson.

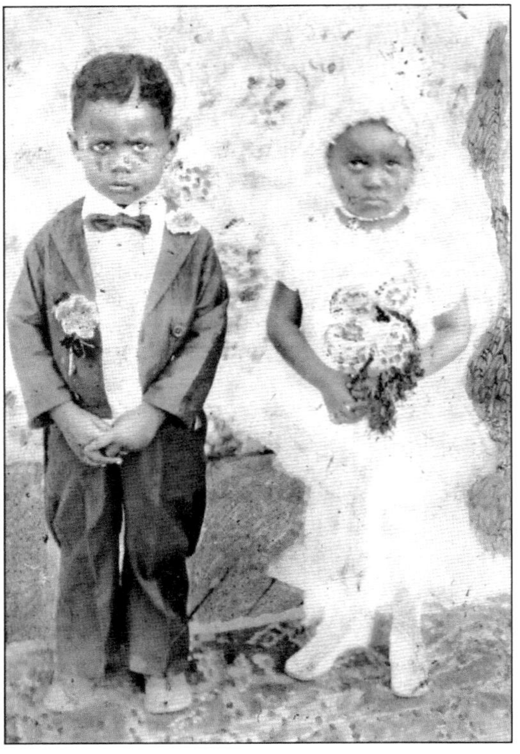

Pictured here is a Tom Thumb wedding at St. Paul A.M.E. Church, at 509 Twenty-first Street. Participants were Warren Hardwick Jr. and Ellen. Warren is the son of Warren Hardwick Sr. and Alma Pryor and the grandson of pioneers Mack and Annie Pryor.

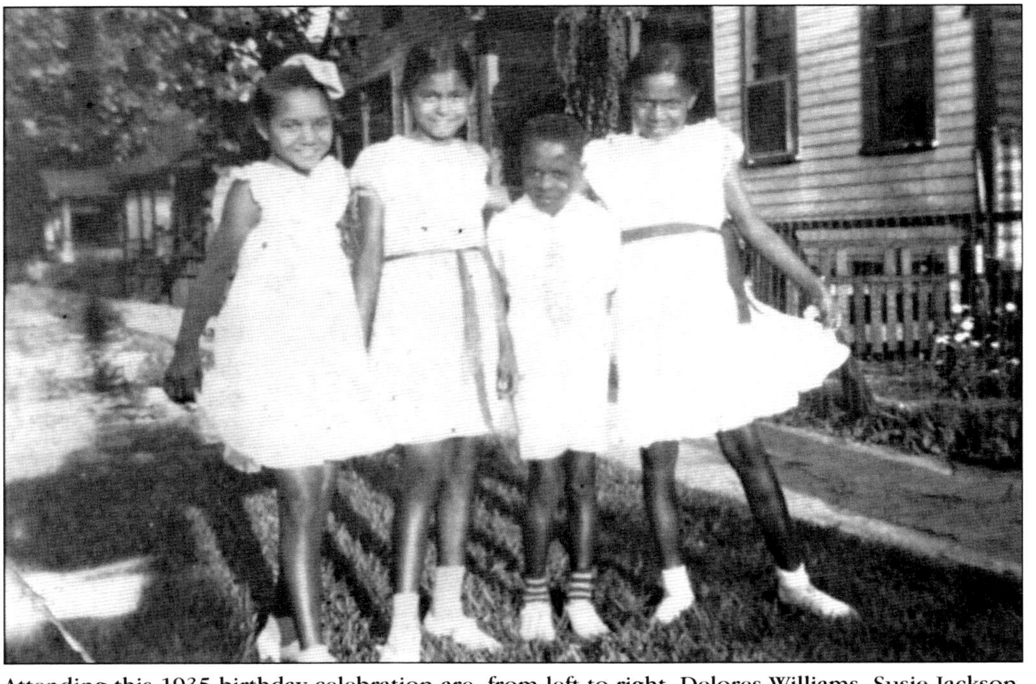

Attending this 1935 birthday celebration are, from left to right, Delores Williams, Susie Jackson, Donnie William, and Marian Nesbitt.

Two

Homes

Most of the homes in Pleasant City were single-family, wood-frame structures with windows in every room and large front porches. There were a few two-story homes to accommodate large families. After the devastating Hurricane of 1928, more homes were of lathe and concrete-block construction with a stucco exterior. Some homes were built from wood salvaged from the Royal Poinciana Hotel after it was razed in the 1930s.

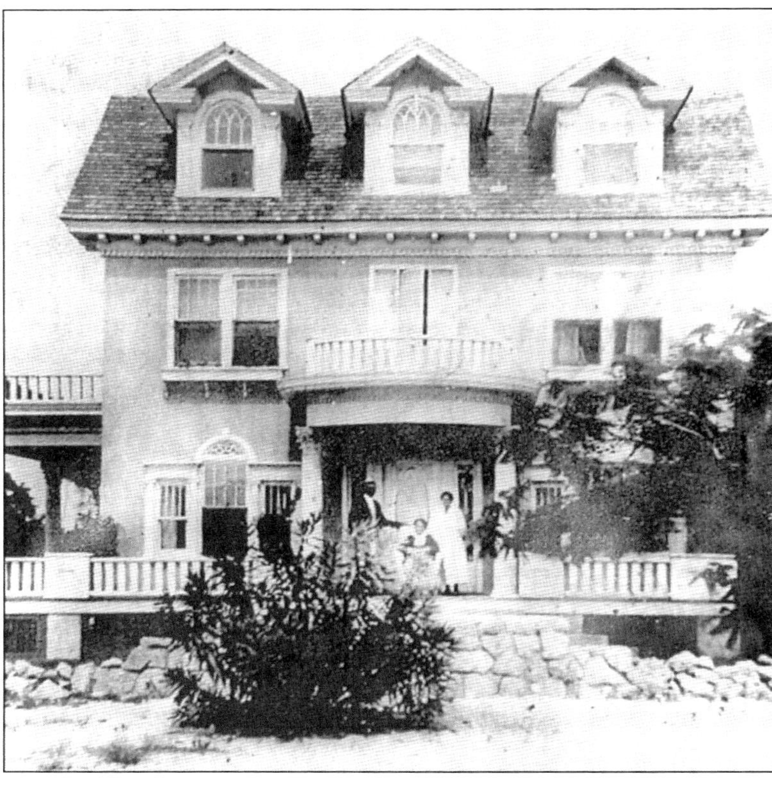

Hazel Agustus was the first African-American architect in Palm Beach County. Agustus and his wife, Mae, lived here at 615 Division Avenue. The home was built in 1917.

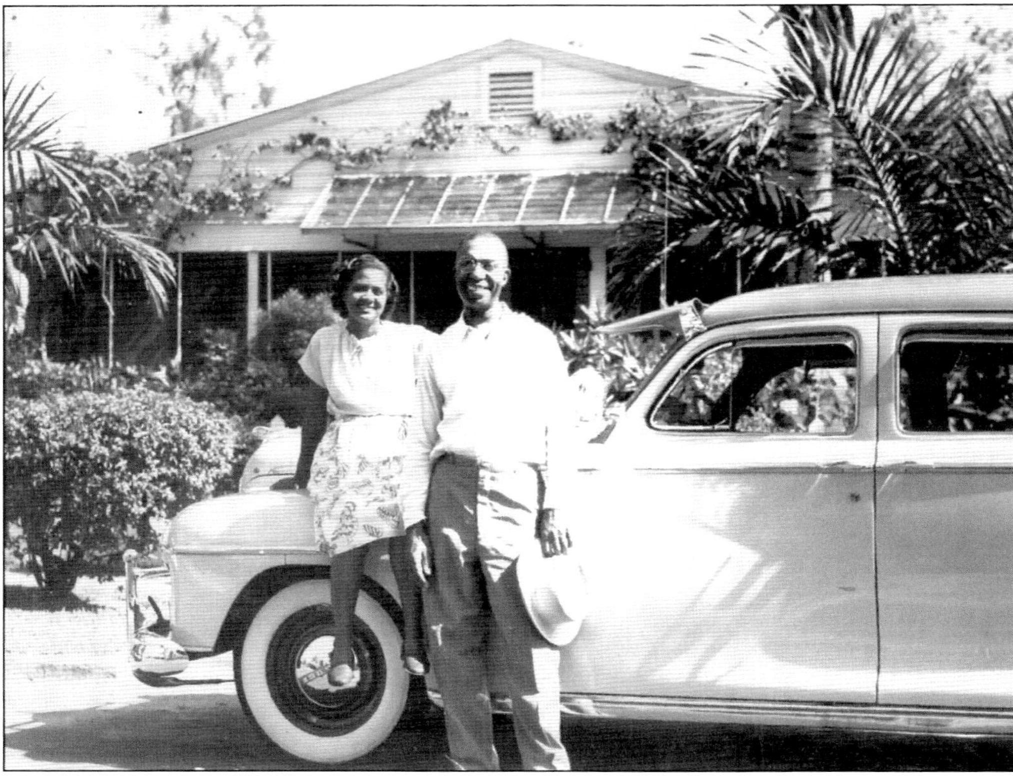

James and Iva Harrell pose in front of their home at 505 Nineteenth Street.

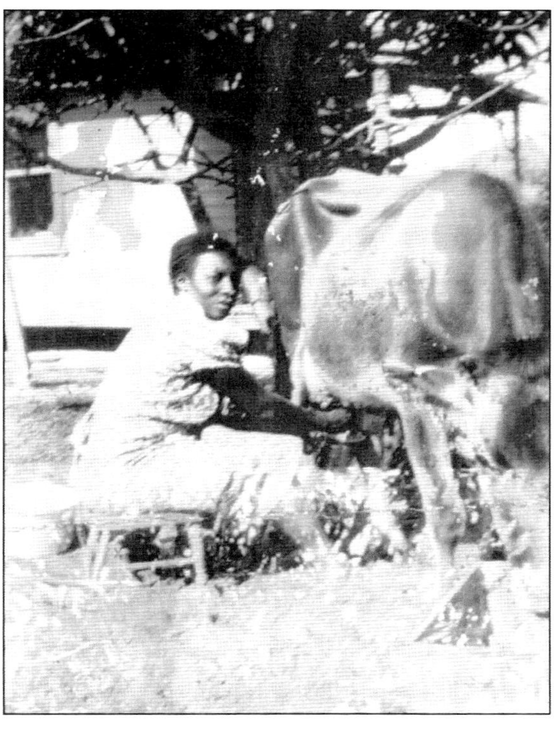

Clara Mills, mother of Floretta Mills Ivery, milks her cow in the yard of their Contentment Avenue home in 1920.

Dunbar Village, established in 1940, was the first public housing project for African Americans in West Palm Beach. Dunbar Village is bound on the north by Grant Street, the south by Fifteenth Street, the east by Division Avenue, and the west by Tamarind Avenue. It is said that the blueprint for Dunbar Village was accidentally switched with the blueprint for a white housing project at the south end of town near Southern Boulevard.

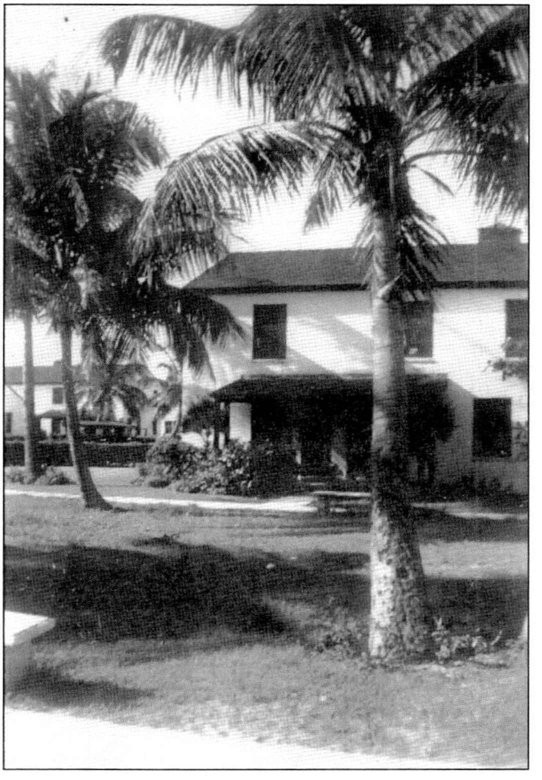

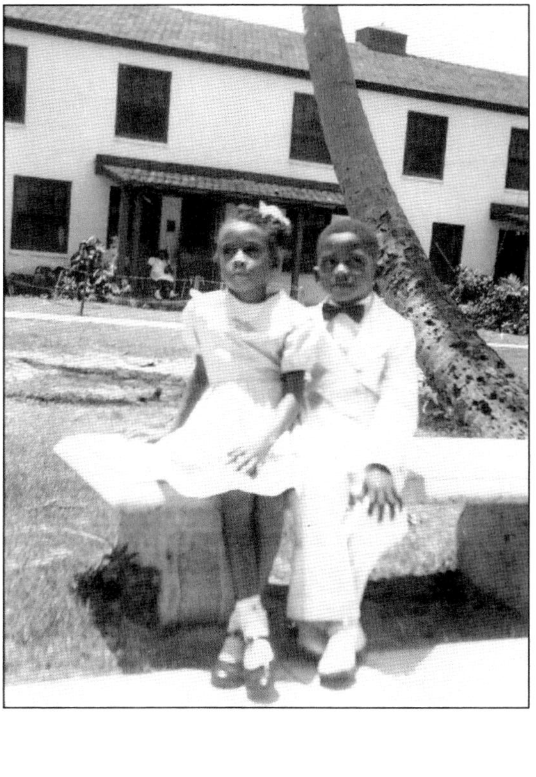

A sunny day in 1942 in Dunbar Village finds Edward Collier and Patricia Robinson seated on a bench.

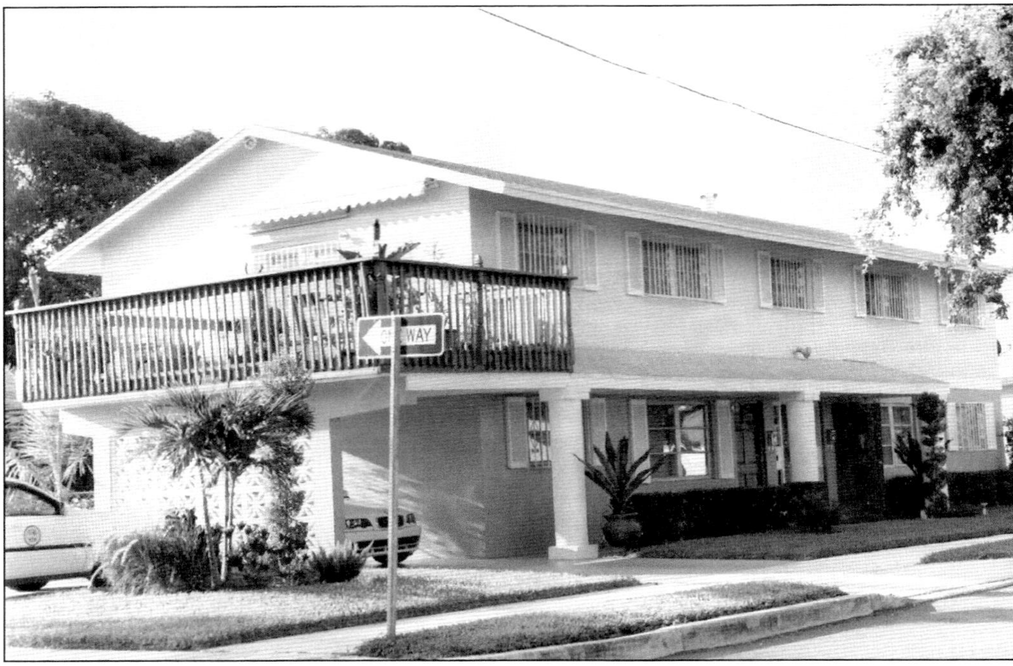

Eva Williams Mack was the first African-American mayor of West Palm Beach. Her home, located at Beautiful Avenue and Cheerful Street, has been renovated and sold.

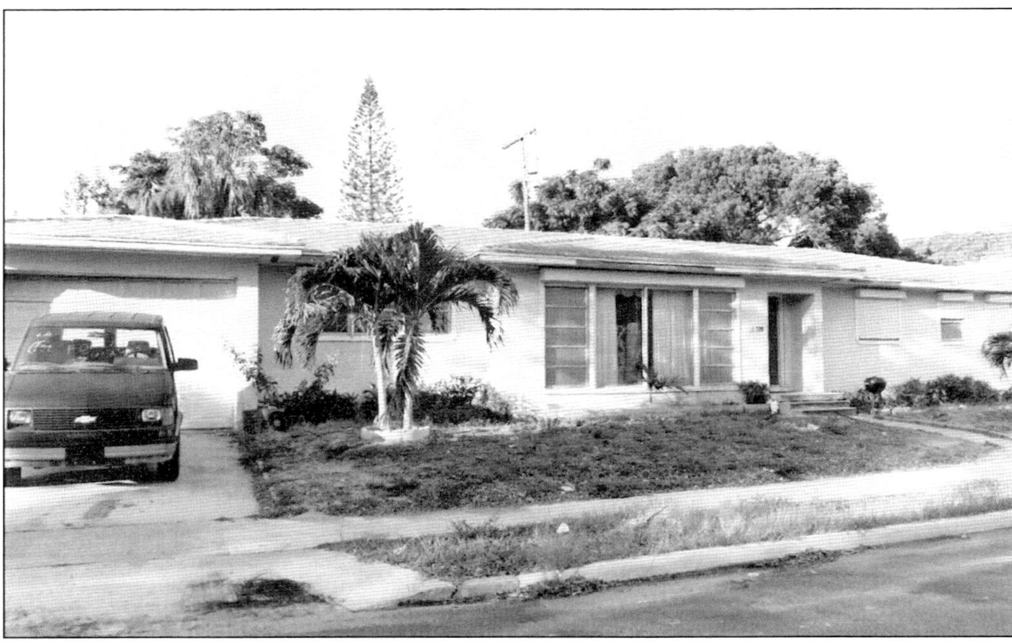

Shown here is the former home of attorney William Holland, who fought to integrate the public schools and other facilities in Palm Beach County. This Seventeenth Street home is still occupied by some family members.

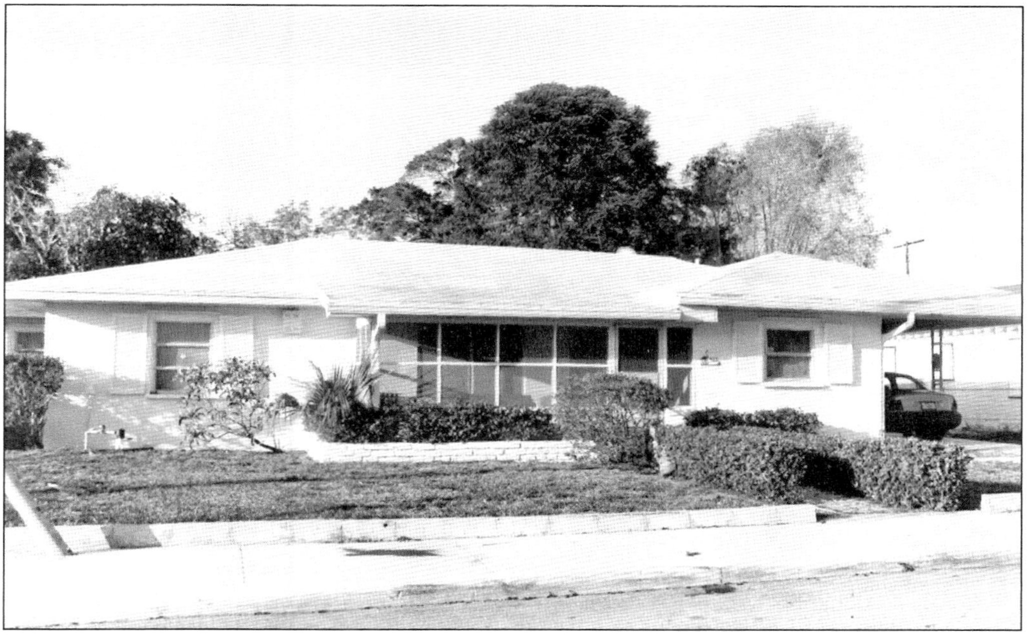

Pictured is the former home of Col. David Brewer, the highest-ranking military officer from Pleasant City.

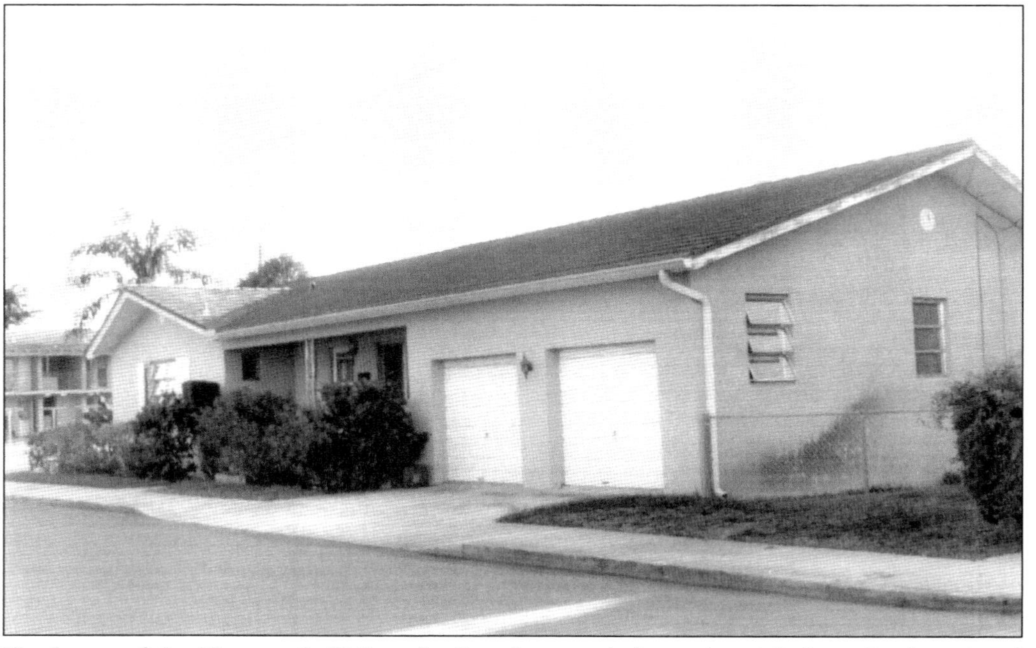

The home of the Thomas C. Wallace family, pioneers, is located at A.E. Isaac Boulevard and Twentieth Street.

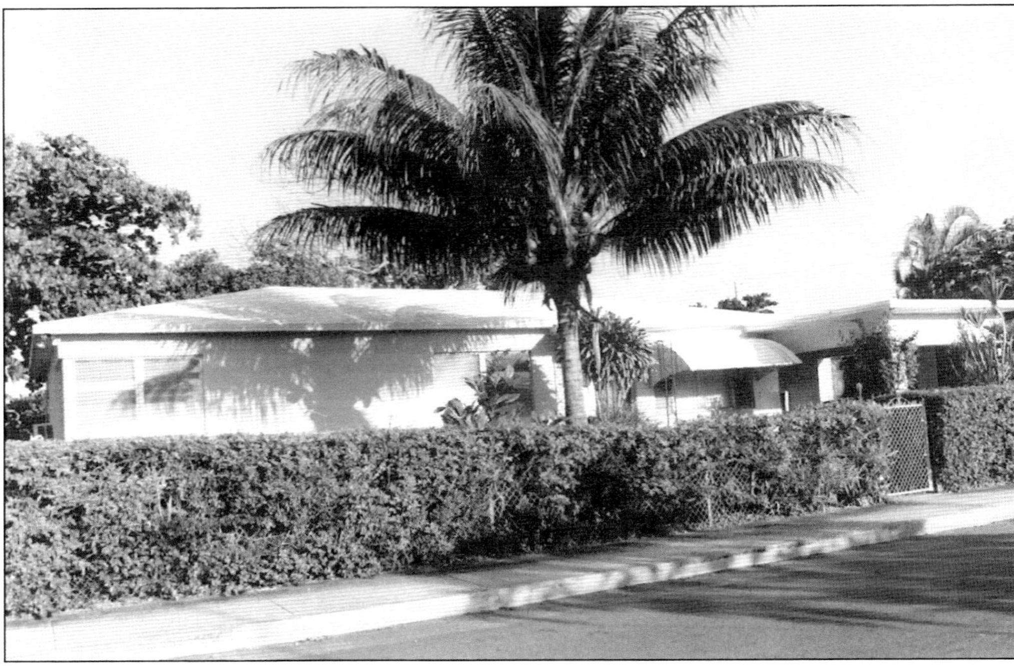

Mr. and Mrs. Cornelius Burns's home is at the corner of A.E. Isaac Avenue and Twenty-first Street.

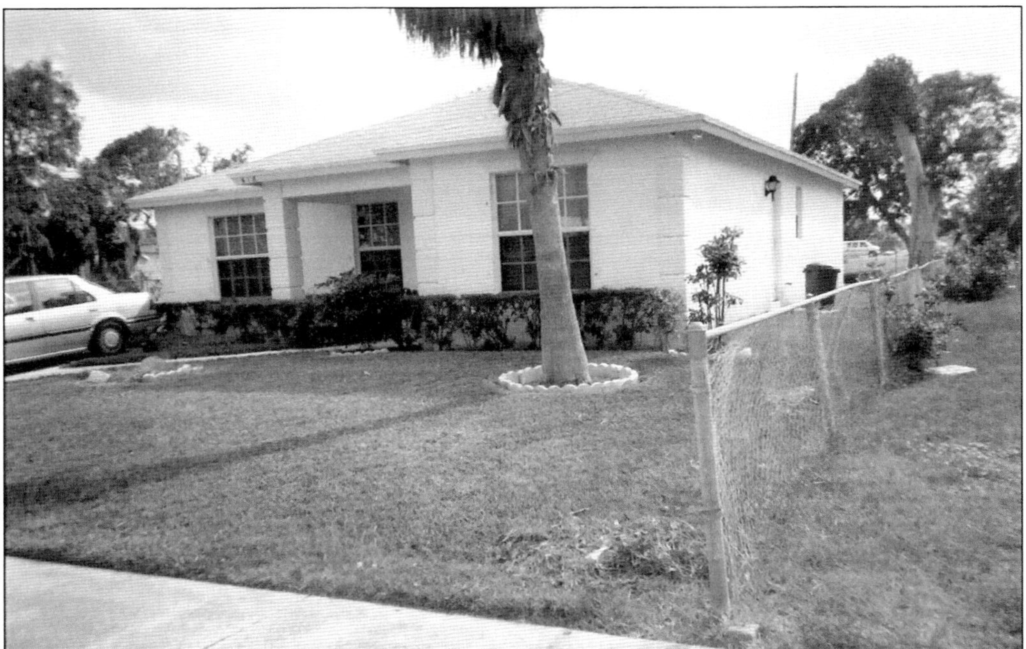

Mike Cleveland, a community activist, lives at 418 Twentieth Street. His home is the former site of the Phillips Open Air School.

Three

EDUCATION

The single element in the success of Pleasant City-ites has been education. Both prior to and since the desegregation of public schools, parents have made sacrifices—often against insurmountable odds—to make education for future generations possible.

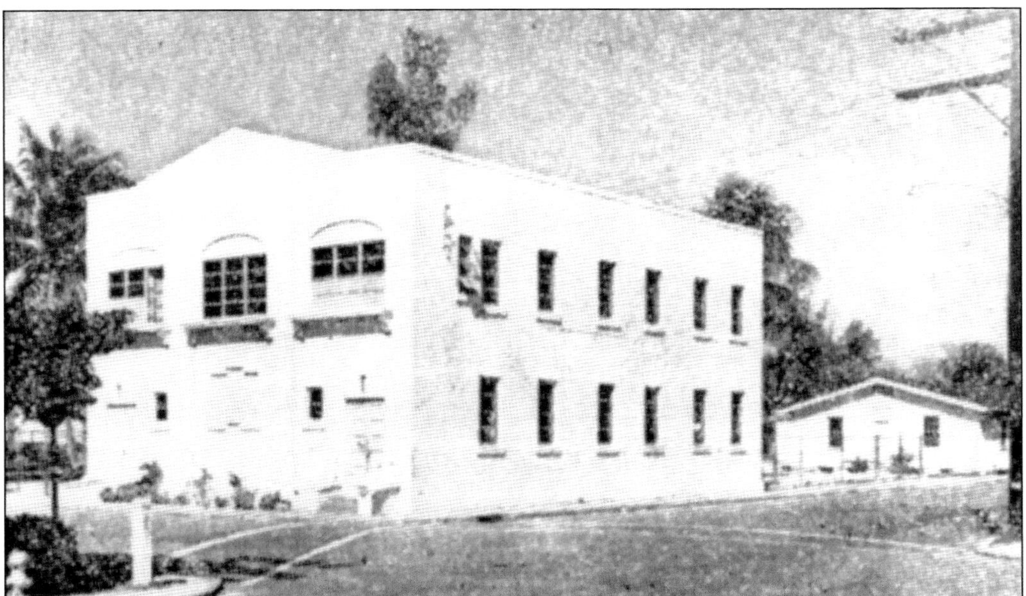

One of two black schools in West Palm Beach, Pleasant City Elementary School was located at 501 Twenty-first Street and began on the first floor of the Mount Parnassis Odd Fellows Hall in 1921. Constructed in 1914, this was the only building in the Pleasant City area designed by Hazel Augustus, the first black architect in Palm Beach County. The school board purchased and renovated the building in 1926. In the early 1960s, the city acquired it from the school board for a recreational center; it was used until 1965, after the new recreation center was opened on Twenty-second Street.

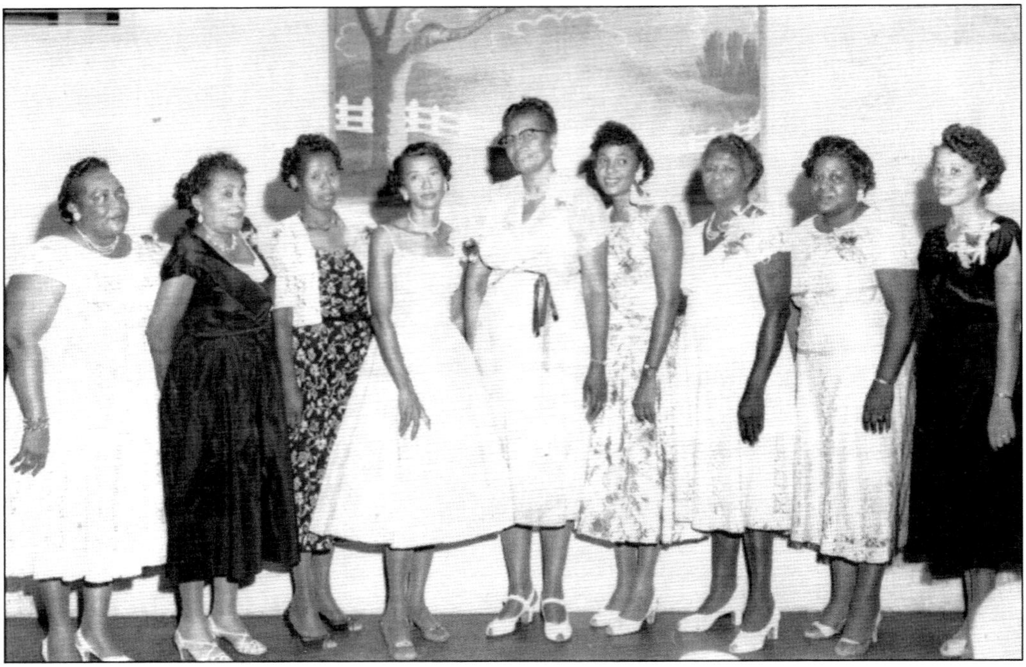

The first teachers of Pleasant City Elementary School in 1959 were, from left to right, Ida Alexander Randolph, Marian Hicks, Trudie Sims Davis, Arlene Kinsey Fretwell, Woodie Dellinger, Evelyn Collier Wildgoose, Inez Peppers Lovett, Sadie Thompson McCray, and Lula Thomas.

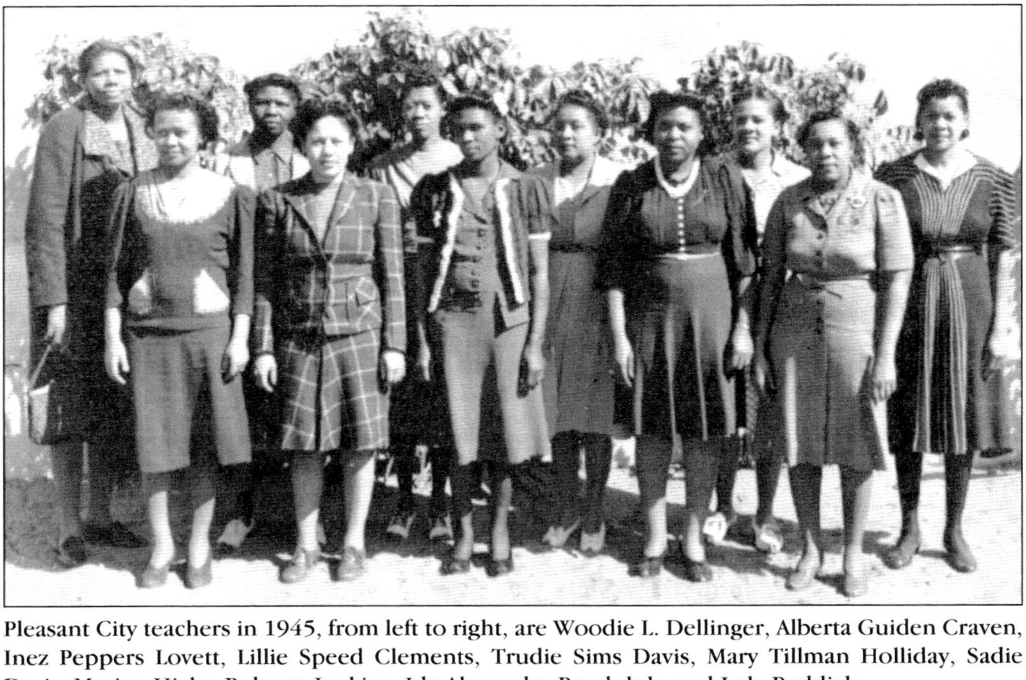

Pleasant City teachers in 1945, from left to right, are Woodie L. Dellinger, Alberta Guiden Craven, Inez Peppers Lovett, Lillie Speed Clements, Trudie Sims Davis, Mary Tillman Holliday, Sadie Davis, Marian Hicks, Roberta Jenkins, Ida Alexander Randolph, and Lula Reddick.

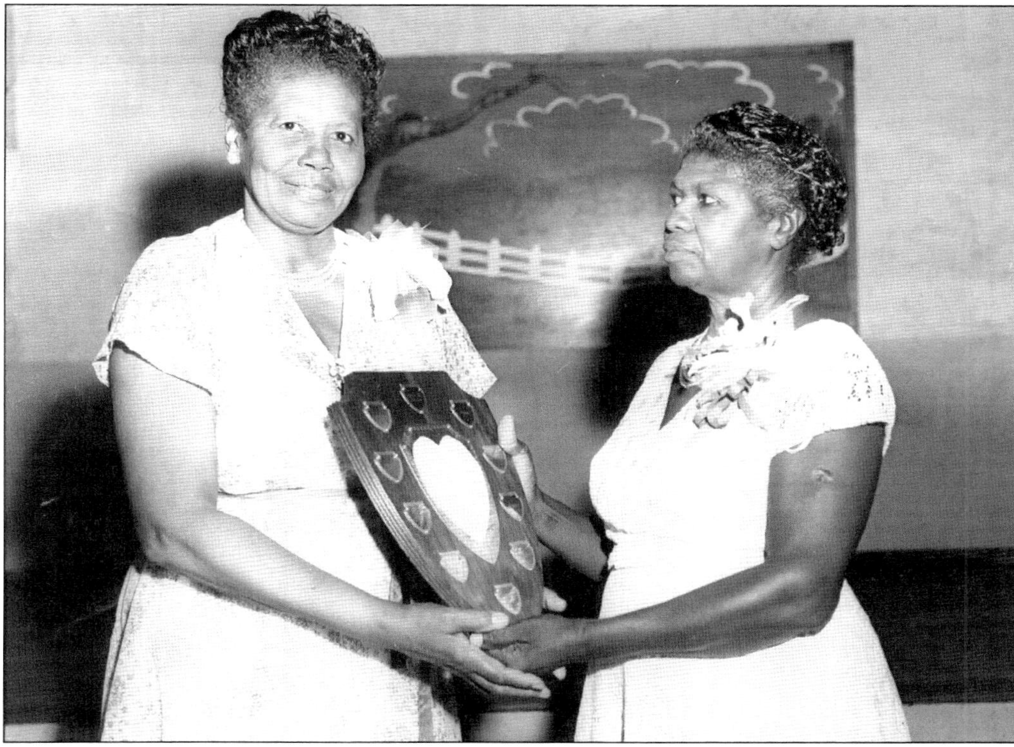

Mrs. Woodie Dellinger (left), principal of Pleasant City Elementary School, makes a presentation to Mrs. Inez Peppers Lovett, instructor, in 1959.

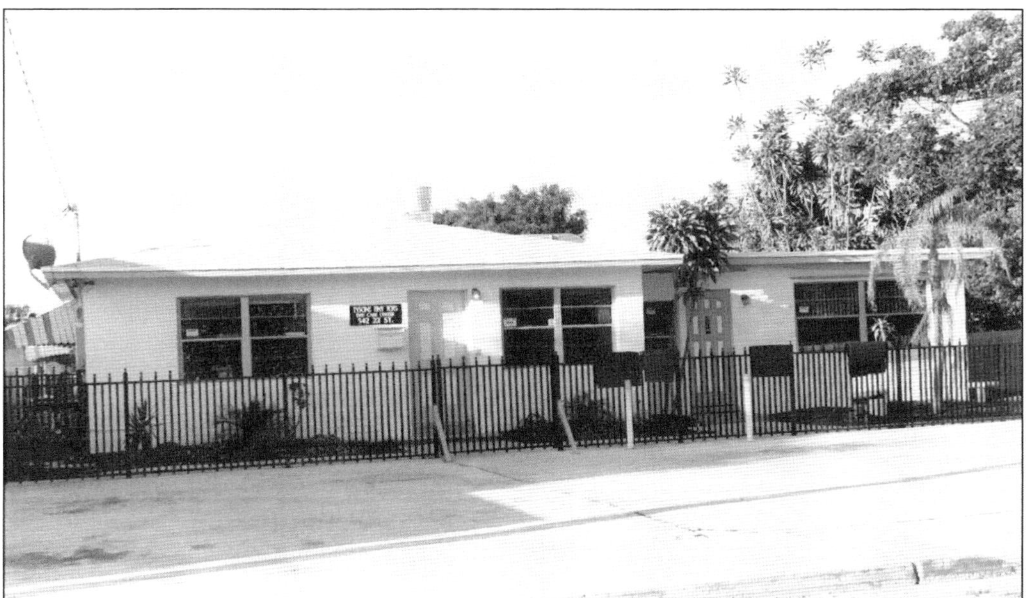

Tyson's Tiny Tots, located on 22nd Street off A.E. Isaacs Avenue, is owned and operated by Malissa Nelson Tyson, daughter of the pioneer Nelson family.

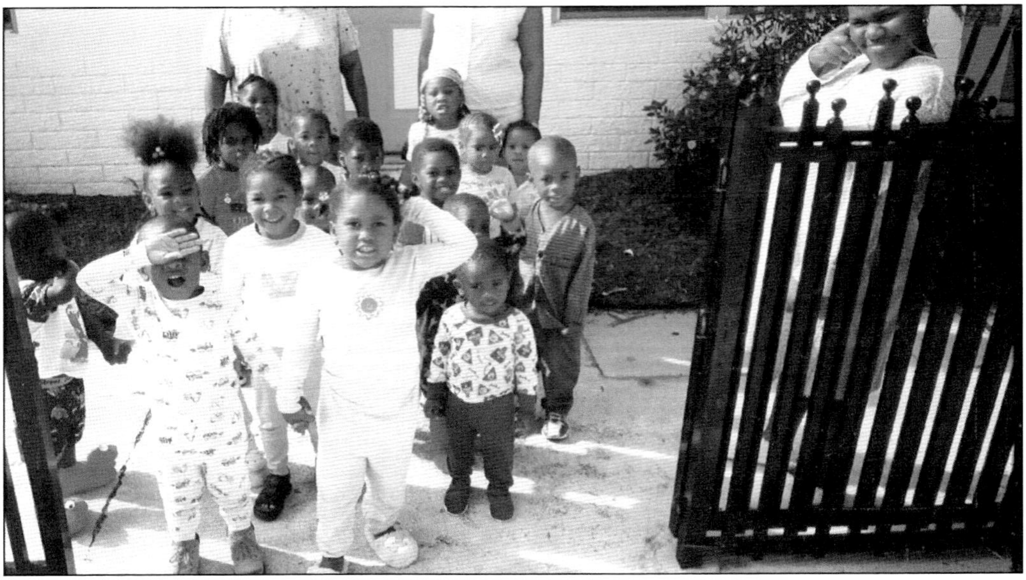

Tyson's Tiny Tots children had a pajama party at the day care center.

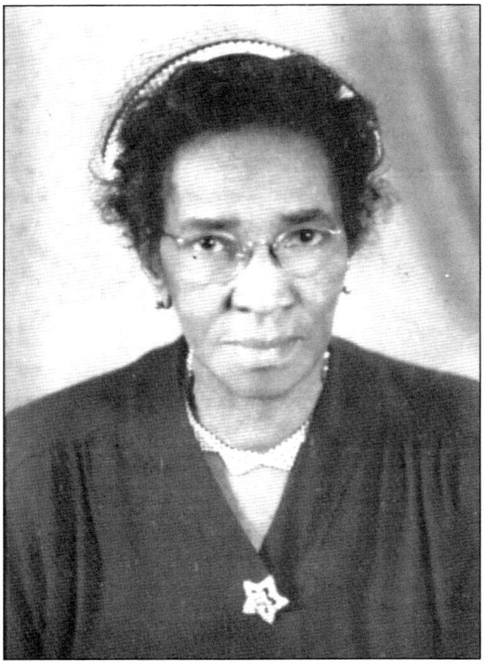

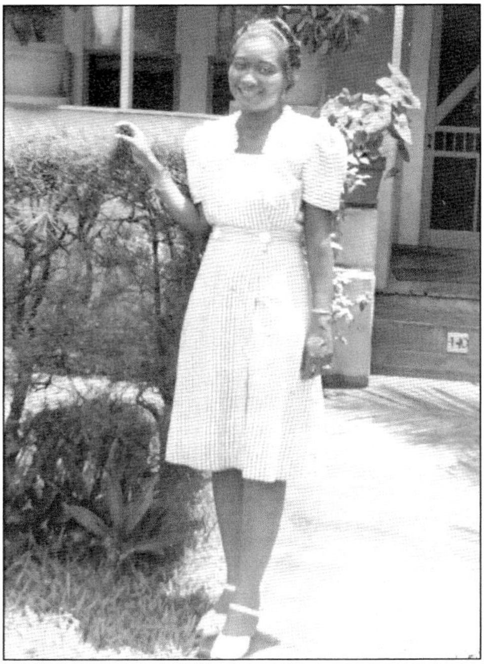

above left: Fanny L. Phillips was the owner-operator of the Phillips Open Air School, located at 418 Twentieth Street in Pleasant City. Any child attending her private school received a solid foundation in reading, writing, and arithmetic. A very strict disciplinarian, she insisted on all students doing their very best.

above right: Gertrude Walker Eutsay was a daughter of pioneers Willie and Louise Walker. She retired from the Palm Beach County School District after many years of service. She was very helpful in helping to compile information on former school teachers.

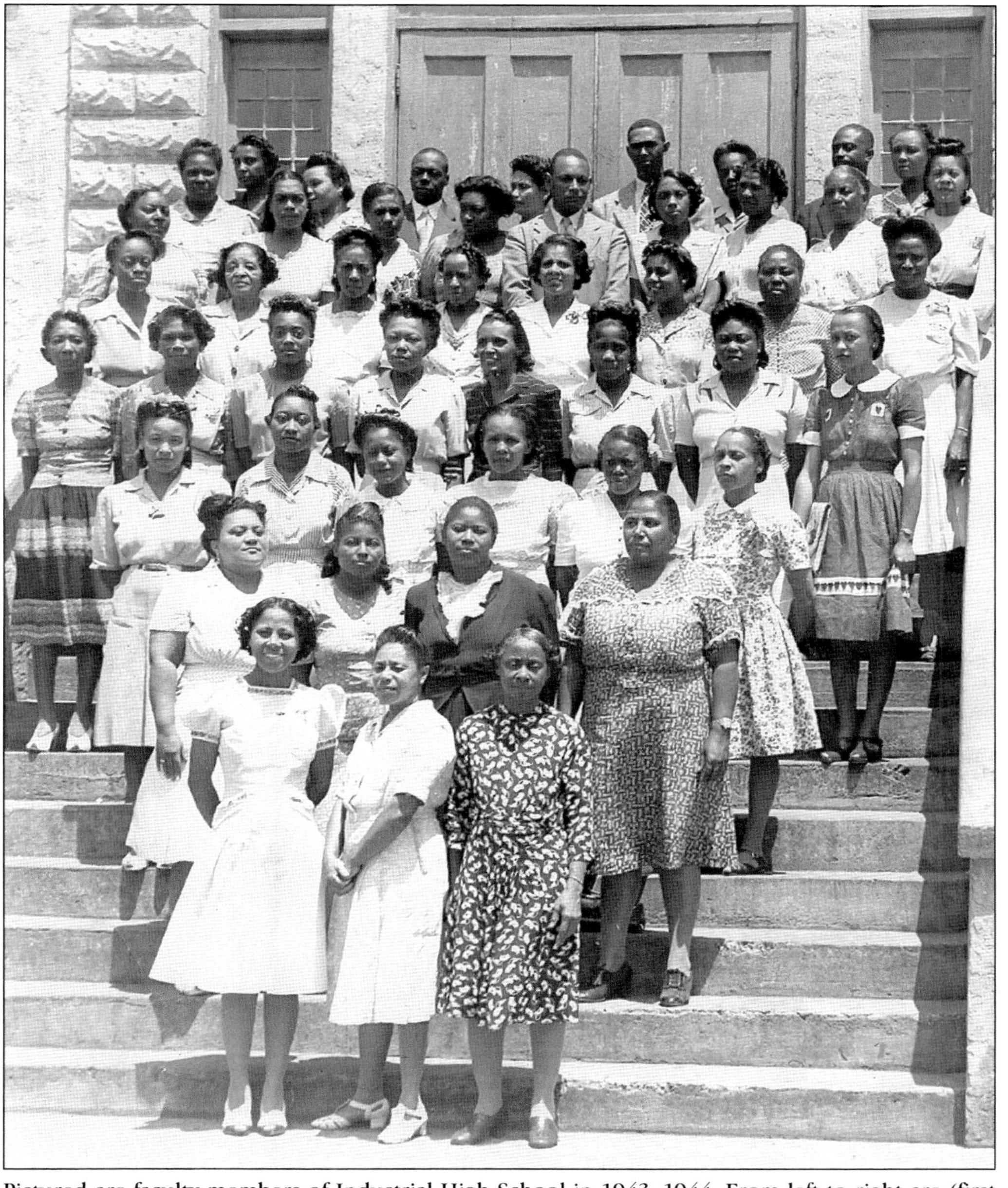

Pictured are faculty members of Industrial High School in 1943–1944. From left to right are (first row) Ella Clayton, Lillie Speed, and Mrs. Lula Weston; (second row) Claudia Johnson, unidentified, Thelma Reynolds, and Thelma Wilkens; (third row) Altamese Jenkins, Gertrude Eutsay, Doris Matthews, Ida Weeks, Victoria Holmes, and Juanita Williams; (fourth row) Ollie G. McCoy, Mary T. Holliday, Essie James, Annie Motley, Ellen DeLancy Keys, Alice Moore, Gertrude Hanford, and Mamie Shannon; (fifth row) M.A.H. Williams, Alice Jordon, Mrs. Edith Fells, Hisetta Dyson, Gladys Peak, Mary Holmes, and Inez Speed; (sixth row) Ruby Greaux, Alvita Lightbourn, Winifred Bates, Mercedes Patrick, William B. Stewart (principal), Bertha Parrish, Merdia Ward, Julia Savage, and Lula Reddick; (seventh row) unidentified, Gladys Bonner, John Hector, Ann Brewer (assistant principal), Ulysses B. Kinsey, Parlie Walker, Dourest Robinson, and Ethel Moore.

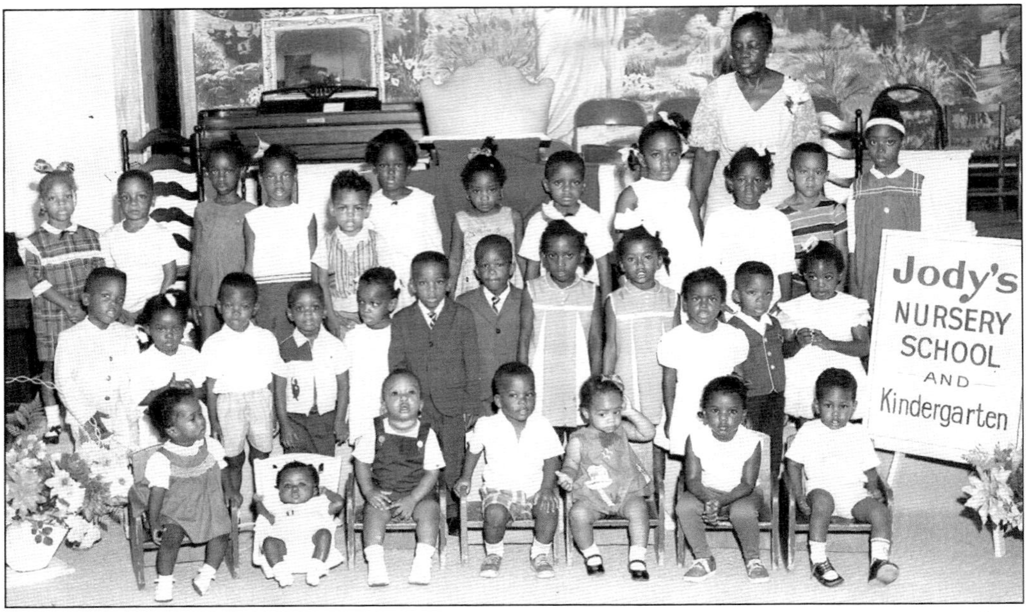

Mrs. Margaret Jordan owned and directed Jody's Nursery School and Kindergarten, located on 19th Street and Spruce Avenue, in 1967.

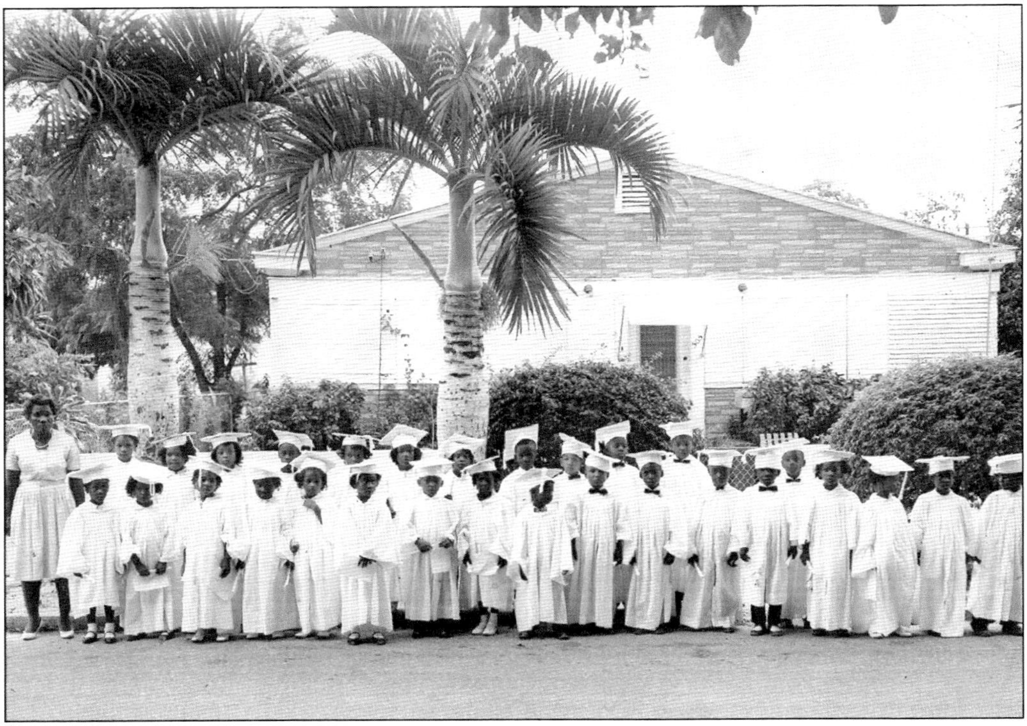

Mrs. Margaret Jordan is pictured with the graduating class of Jody's Nursery School in 1971.

David Preston is a public school instructor and photographer. The son of the late Eugene and Lula Preston, he grew up in Pleasant City and graduated from Roosevelt High School. He earned an associate's degree in elementary education from Palm Beach Junior College and bachelor's and master's degrees from Florida Atlantic University. He has been an instructor in the Palm Beach County School System for 32 years, and he is a trustee at Antioch Missionary Baptist church and treasurer of the Pleasant City Family Reunion Committee. He photographed numerous images in this book.

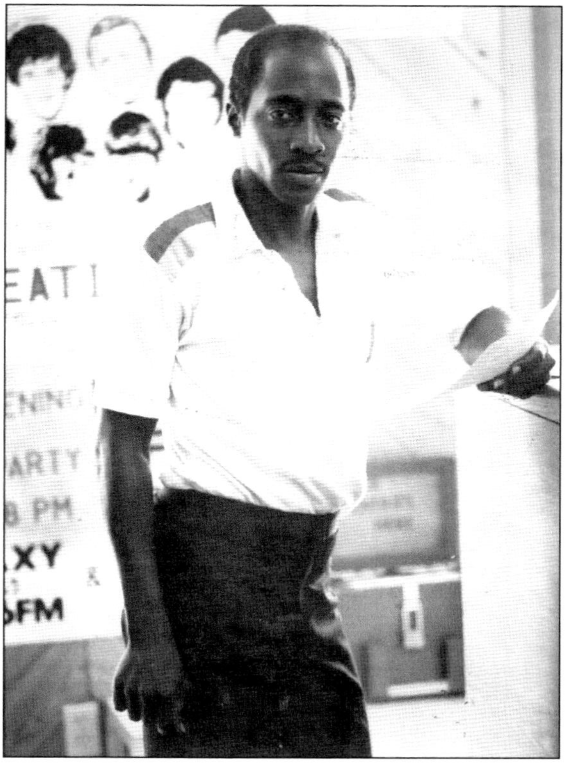

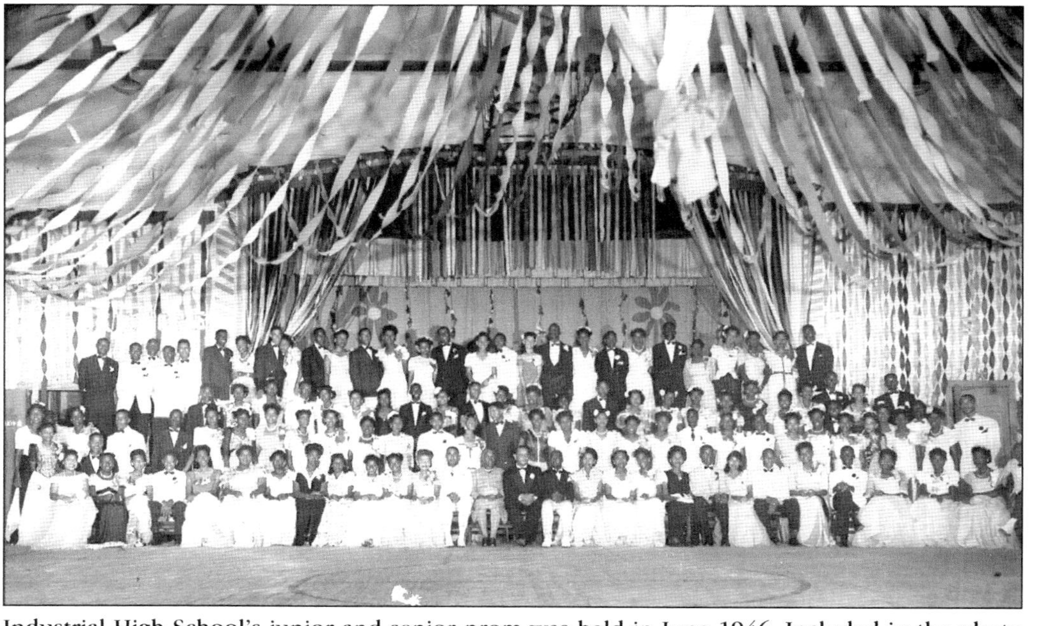

Industrial High School's junior and senior prom was held in June 1946. Included in the photo are Principal W.B. Stewart and chaperones U.B. Kinsey, Mrs. Julia Savage, John Hector, and Bertha Parrish.

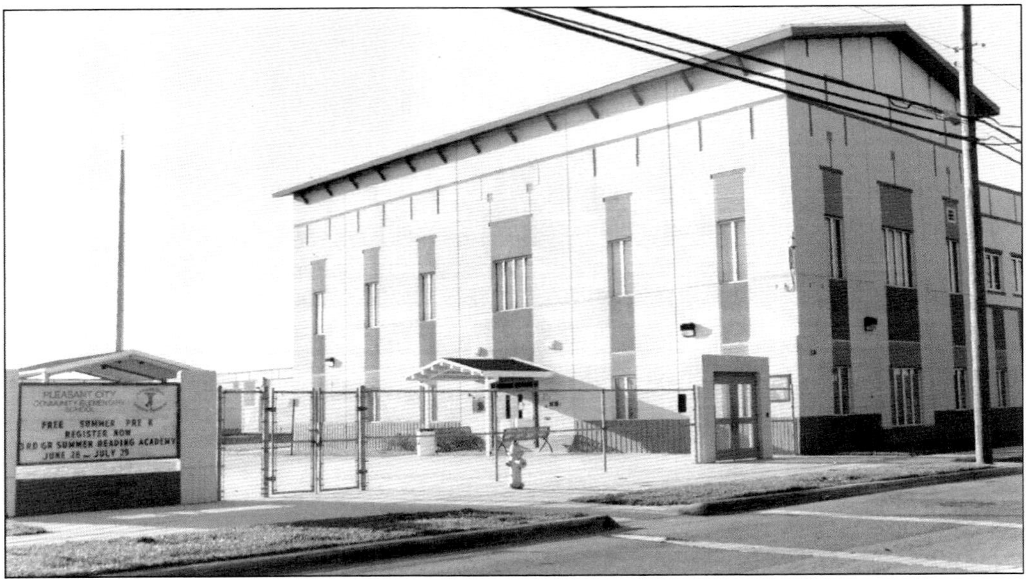

The new Pleasant City Elementary School, located at 21st Street and Spruce Avenue, opened in 2000.

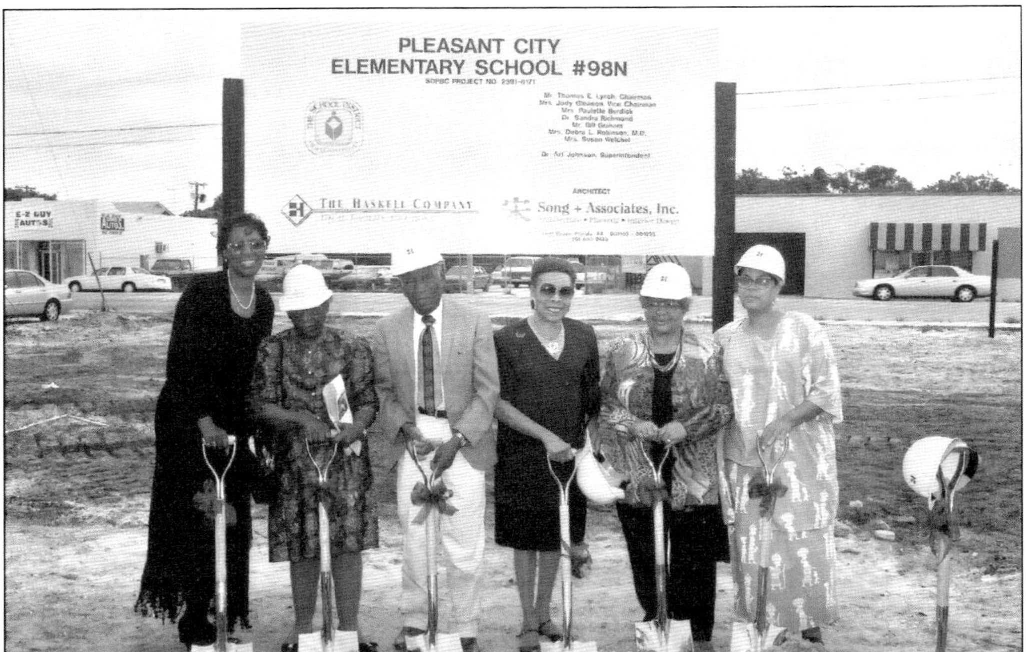

Pictured is the groundbreaking ceremony for the first school to be built in the Pleasant City area in 40 years. From left to right are Mrs. Andrea Peppers, principal; pioneer Mrs. Gladys Crawford; Preston Tiliman, real estate broker; Mrs. Ineria Hudnell, historian; Everee Jimerson Clarke, The Family Reunion Committee founder; and Dr. Debra Robinson, Palm Beach County School Board member.

Four

Religion

Early churches were the spiritual, educational, and social centers in the community. They assisted African-American businesses that could not obtain financing from local banks, regardless of credentials or experience. They also helped to provide educational scholarships for youth.

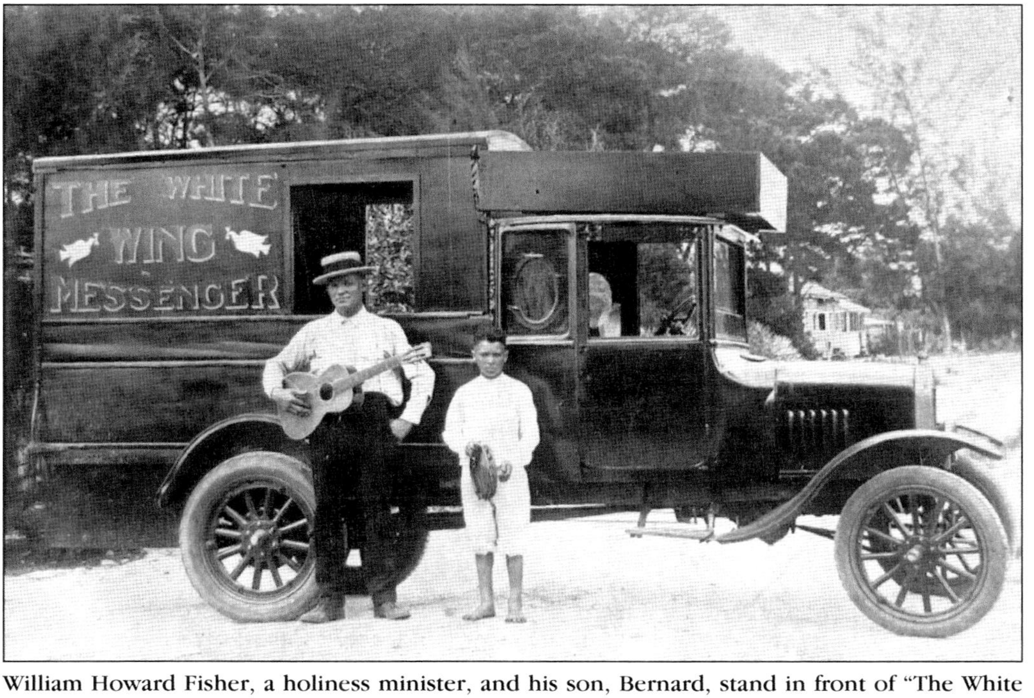

William Howard Fisher, a holiness minister, and his son, Bernard, stand in front of "The White Wing Messenger" truck, used in William's ministry. He was also an inventor and mechanic. In 1932, he built a tractor-trailer from an old Model T Ford. He took his invention to Inkster, Michigan, with hopes of selling the idea there.

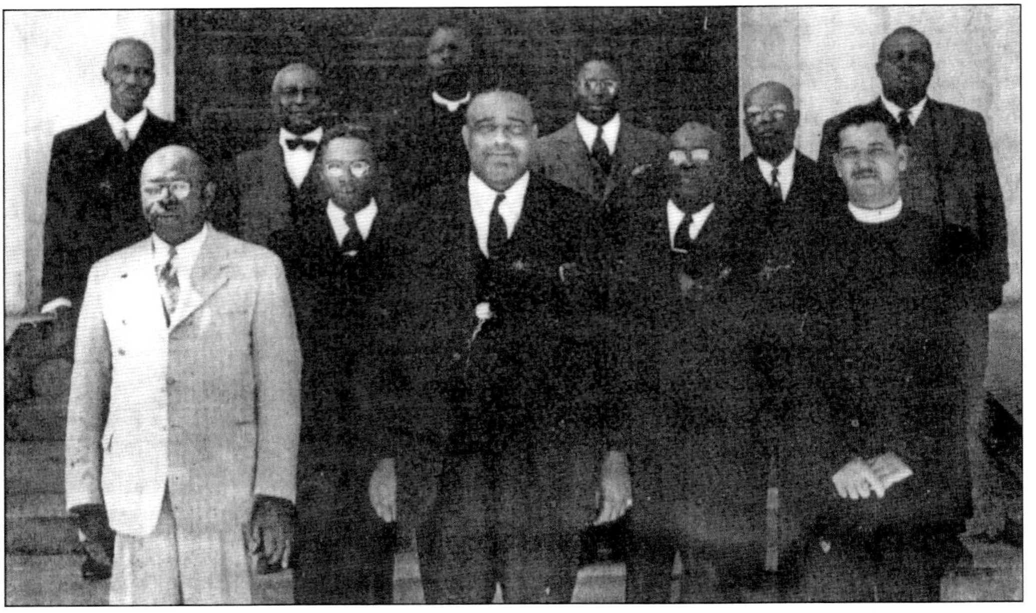

West Palm Beach Ministerial Alliance was, from left to right, Reverends Collier, Hall, Jake Parson, Mapson, Cousin, King, Smith, R.D. Powell, D.N. Conner, and Dolphus.

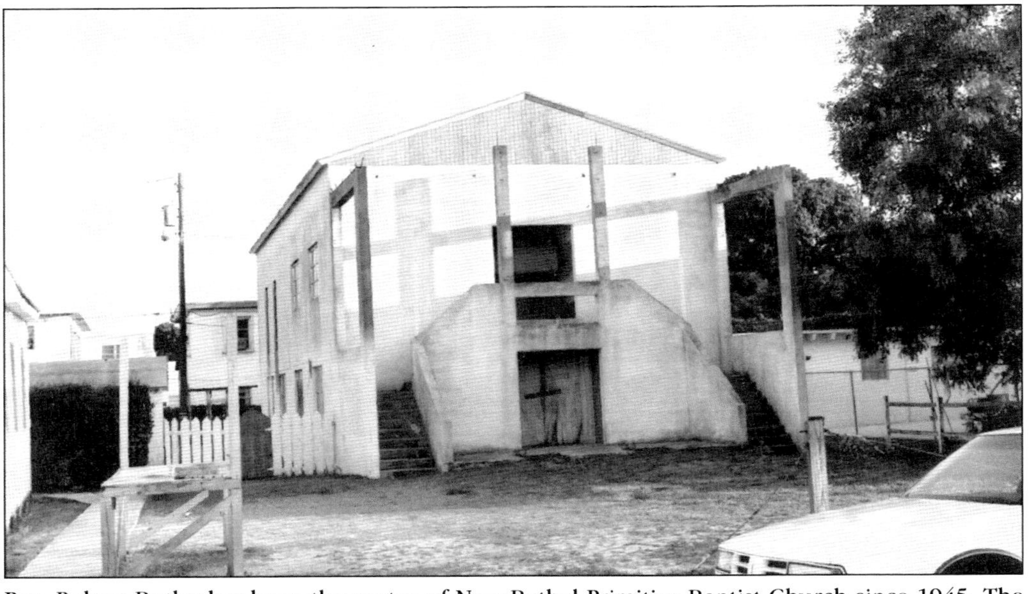

Rev. Robert Butler has been the pastor of New Bethel Primitive Baptist Church since 1945. The church organized in 1929 and moved to the present site at 504 19th Street in 1942. Members purchased the land and converted an old house into a church. In 1950, Reverend Butler and his congregation decided to build a larger church on the west side of the existing one. They chose to start the project the old-fashioned way, without a loan from the bank or donations from the East Coast Primitive Baptist Association. Things have changed tremendously over the years, but Reverend Butler has been working on the building the entire time. For 53 years, at the age of 90, he still dreams of completing the church.

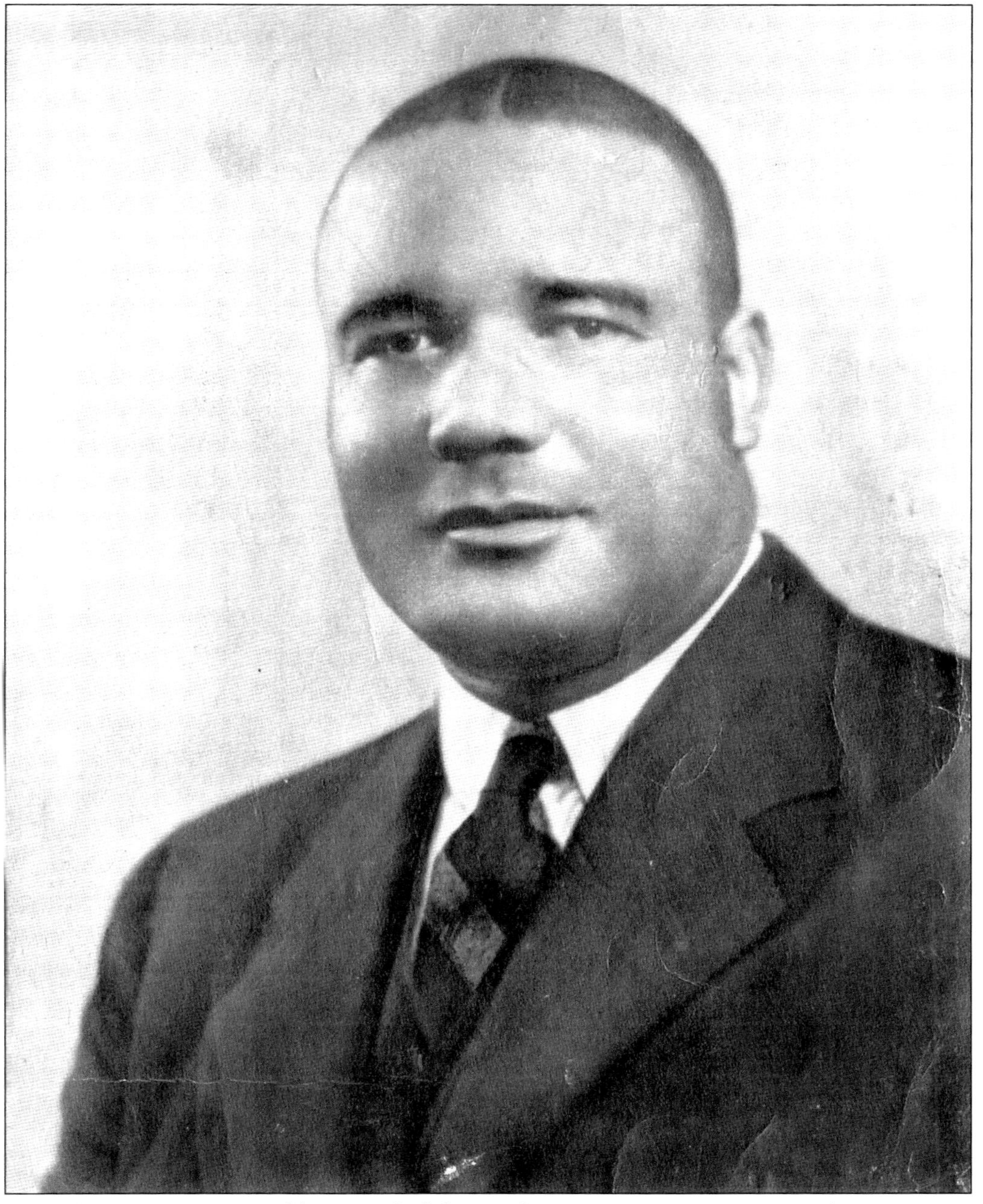

Rev. Jake Parson (1902–1964) was called from Tifton, Georgia, to pastor St. John Missionary Baptist Church in Pleasant City in 1932. He served as pastor for three years. In 1935, he organized Antioch Baptist Church and was pastor until his death in 1964. He became a real estate investor and developer who purchased 165 acres of land in Riviera Beach, making it possible for African Americans to own their own homes. In 1955, Reverend Parson incorporated acreage of 110 CBS (concrete block and steel) homes that bear his name—Parson Heights—in Riviera Beach.

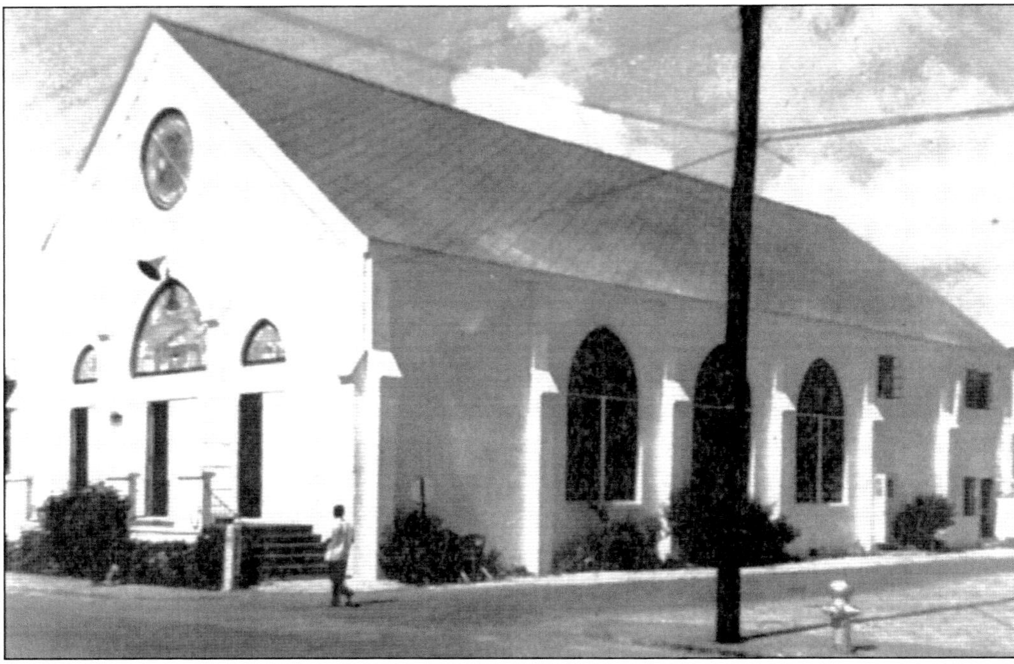

Greater Antioch Missionary Baptist Church was organized in 1935 at First Mount Olive Baptist Church in West Palm Beach with Rev. J.M. Coleman serving as moderator. Rev. Jake Parson was called to be the first pastor, and he served for 29 years. Little Antioch was built in 1939, and the present edifice was built in 1948. A daycare center was founded in 1952. Rev. Bing Crosby Thomas served as pastor from September 1967 through April 1989. Rev. Larry Isaac Frank Scott was called to pastor in December 1989. The late Rev. Frank Jefferson was the last pastor.

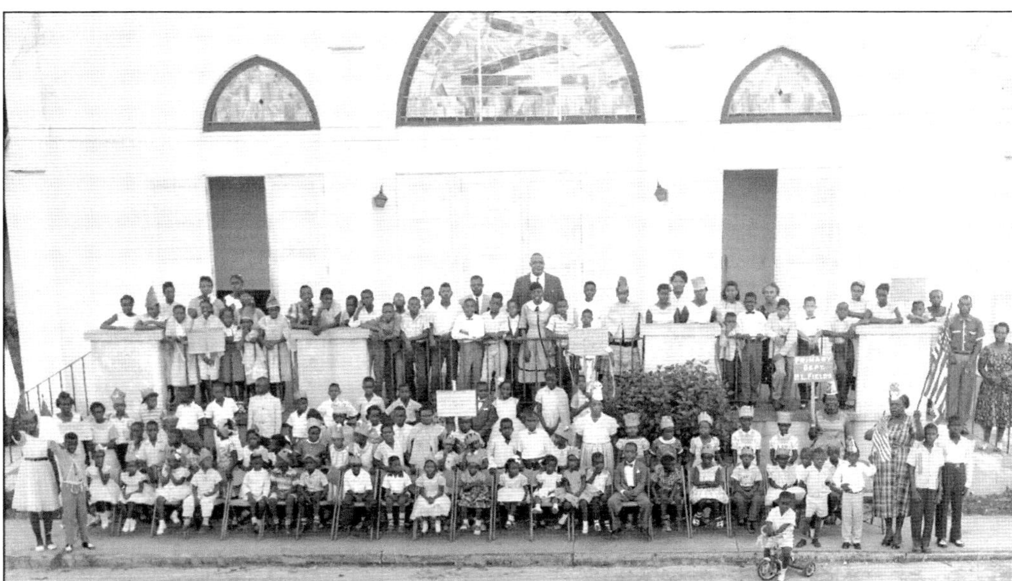

Jake Parson is pictured with Vacation Bible School attendees at Antioch Baptist Church in 1957.

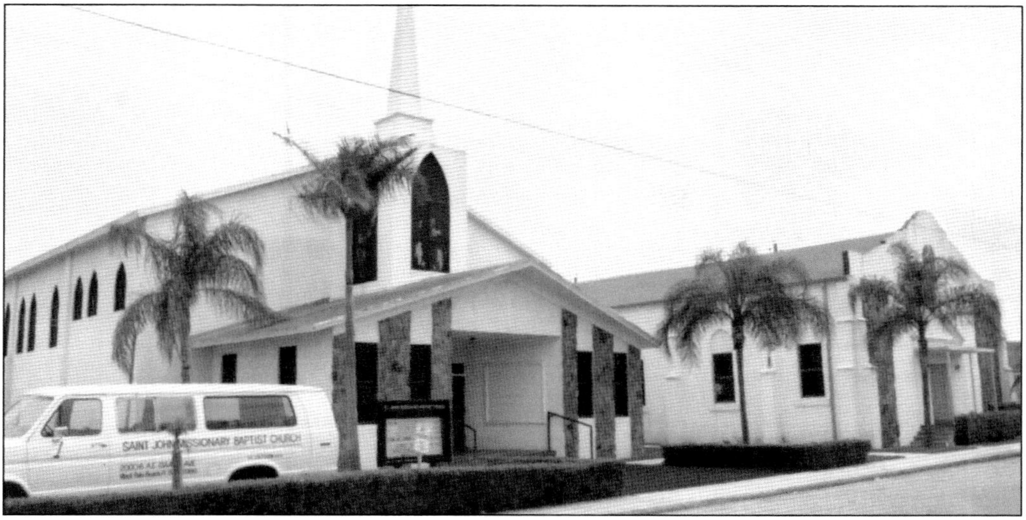

Rev. J.B. Ealy founded St. John Missionary Baptist Church in 1903. The church relocated to Twenty-second Street between Contentment and Spruce Avenues in 1922. The first floor was used for worship and the first school for children of Pleasant City. The second floor was used as an Odd Fellow's Hall. The church was completely demolished by the 1928 storm. St. John Missionary Baptist Church has been located at Nineteenth Street and Contentment Avenue (A.E. Isaac Avenue) since 1929. Rev. Joseph B. Tyson has been the pastor since 1984.

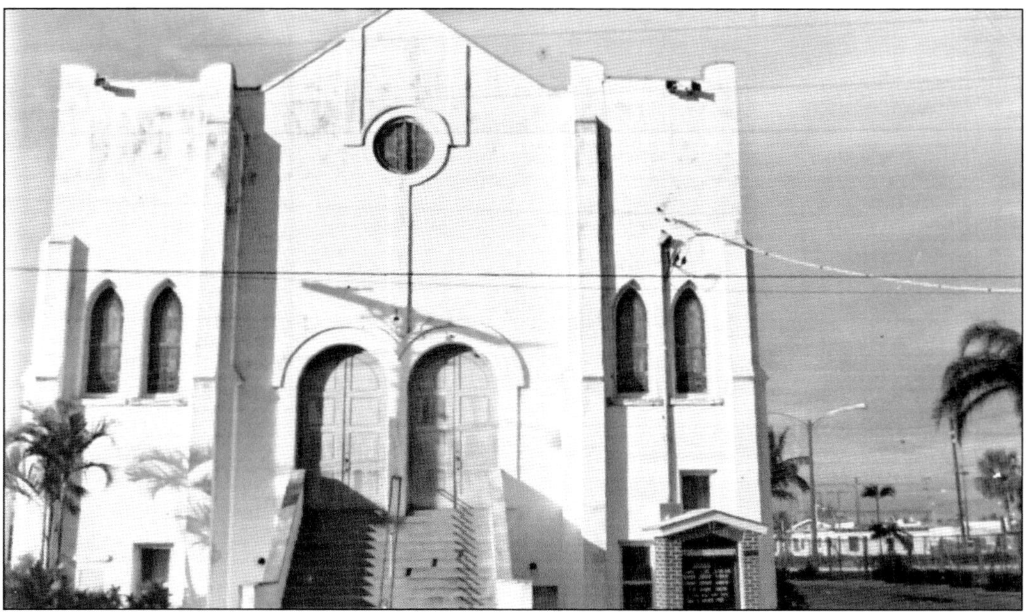

St. Paul A.M.E. Church, the oldest church in Pleasant City, was organized by Rev. Charles Sumner Long Sr. in 1900. As the membership grew, they built a small church and named it Gethsemane. During the pastorate of Rev. S.A. Harris, all of the African-American families were forced to move from Palm Beach. Many settled in Pleasant City, where they built another church and named it St. Paul. Currently, the church is located at 3345 North Haverhill Road, West Palm Beach, and Rev. James H. Russell Sr. is the pastor.

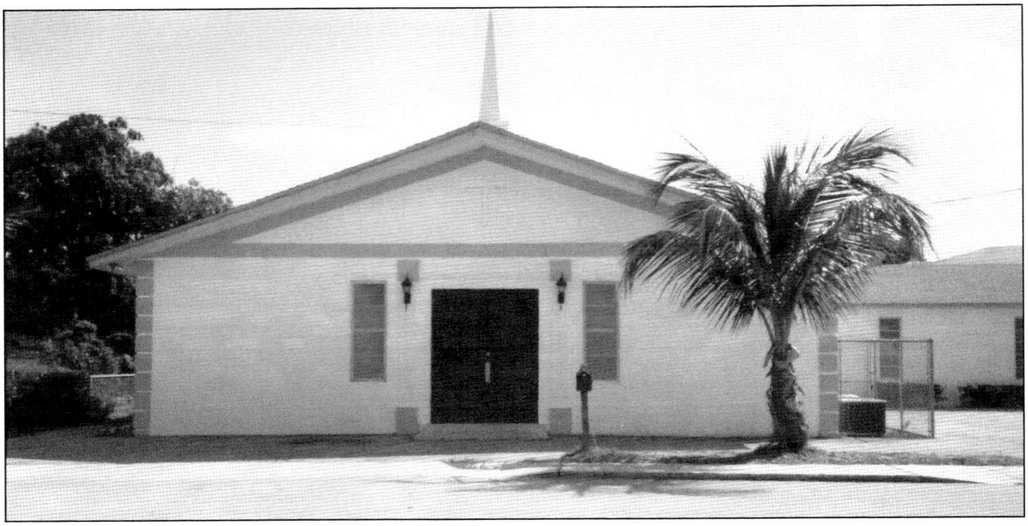

The Pentecostal Church of God in Christ, USA (COGIC) was established in 1967 at 540 Cheerful Street under the leadership of Elder Arthur Lee Hightower. The congregation marched into the new church on August 1, 1975. Elder Arthur Lee Hightower became a senior bishop of the COGIC in July 1981. Bishop Hightower passed away on December 20, 1991, and the Executive Board of the Pentecostal COGIC appointed his son, Elder Randy Hightower, as pastor.

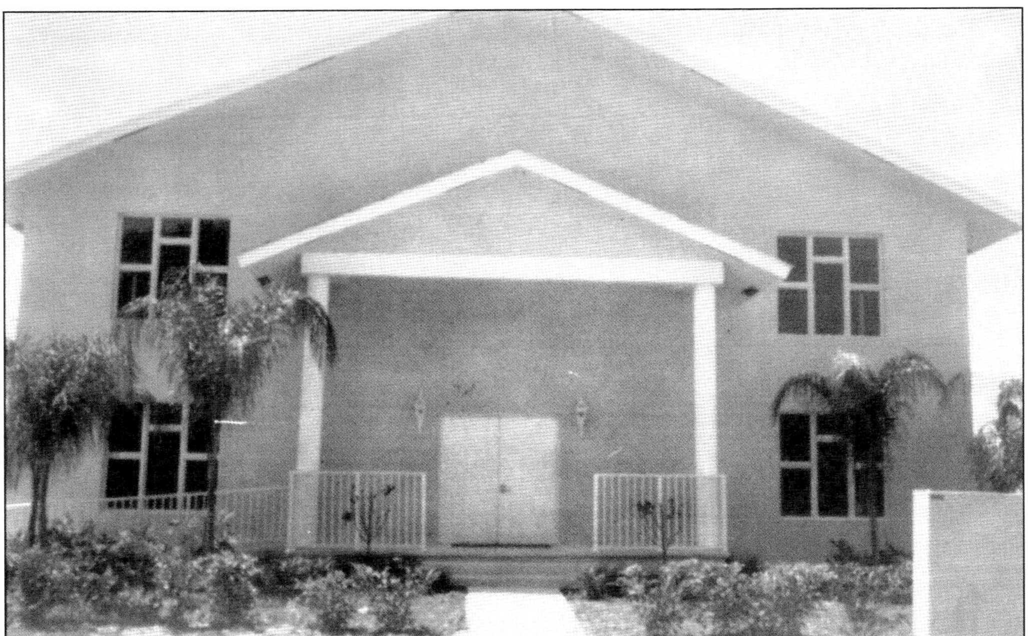

On April 12, 1989, Bing Crosby Thomas and 20 Christian followers, along with Rev. J.H.H. Thomas Jr., Rev. R. Sears, and Rev. B.W. Williams, met at 609 Nineteenth Street in Pleasant City and organized the Bibleway Missionary Baptist Church. Rev. B.W. Williams served as assistant pastor to Rev. B.C. Thomas. Rev. James Bentley was called to be the new pastor on March 25, 1990. Under his leadership, the membership grew, and a new church was built at 506 Fifteenth Street.

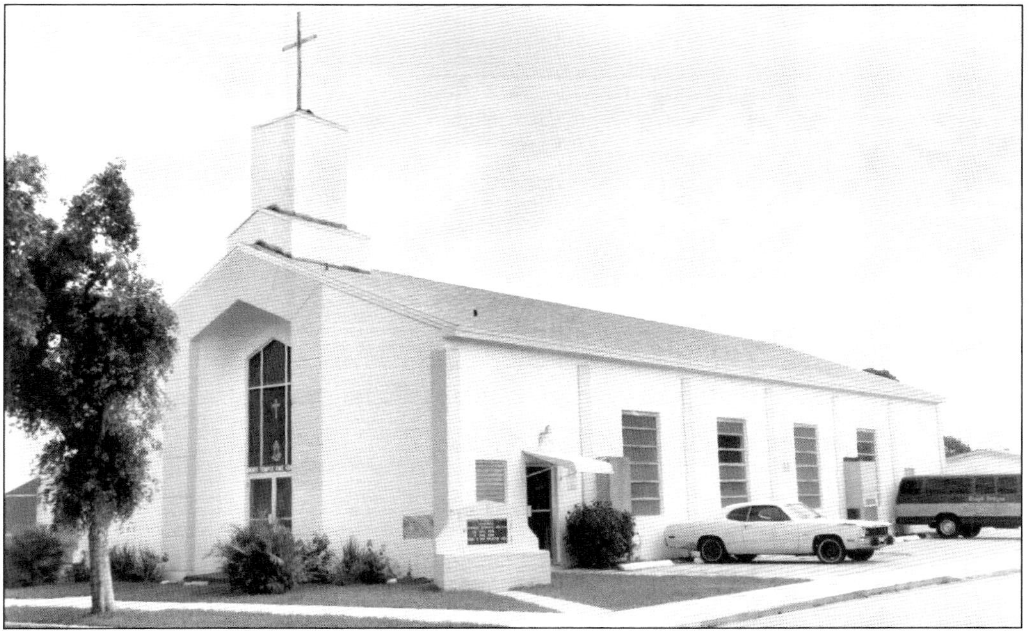

Rev. and Mrs. H.H. Gray, ardent members of the Colored Methodist Episcopal Church in Gray, Georgia, moved to West Palm Beach in 1902. The Grays purchased property and donated a lot for the first C.M.E. church in West Palm Beach at Eighteenth Street and Beautiful Avenue. Charter members were Herbert and Florence Rolle, William Young, Edward Smith, and Mr. and Mrs. Ford. Rev. Dr. Lionel Walker is the pastor.

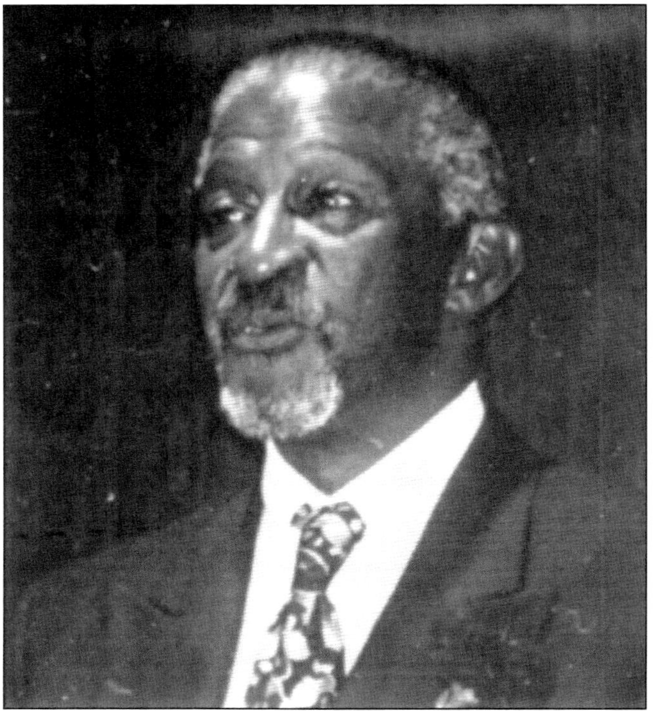

In 1969, J.B. Fields "heard the Voice" and went into the ministry as God's servant in the pulpit. He married Geneva Galloway in 1950 and brought her to the community he called home. They raised eight children and remained happily married. Reverend Fields was an associate minister at Gray's Temple Christian Methodist Episcopal Church, second vice president of the P.E.A.C.E. (People Engaged in Active Community Efforts) Organization, and a very strong advocate for the residents of Pleasant City.

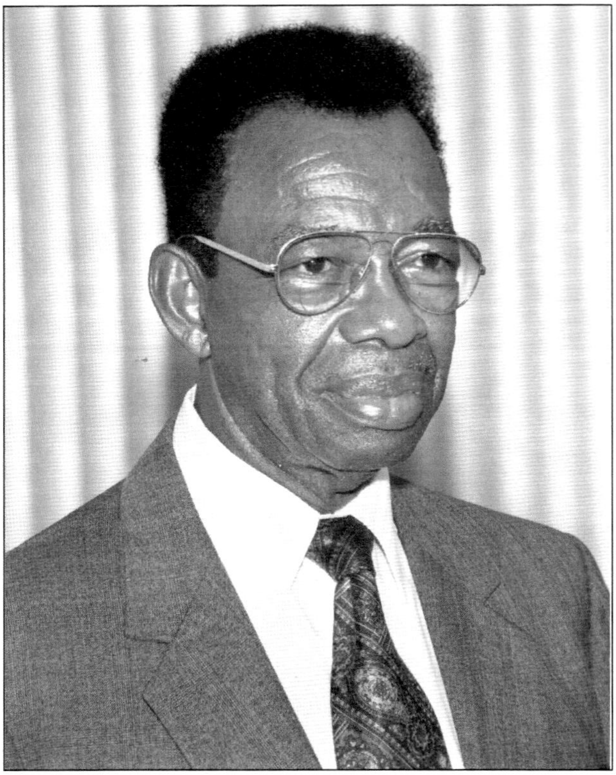

Elder Simeon Jimerson is the youngest son of pioneers Rev. William and Mrs. Cynthia Darthula Jimerson. He is a member of the First Church of God in Christ, located at Fourteenth Street and Henrietta Avenue. He has served as pastor for more than 20 years. A barber by trade, he owns a barbershop and other business enterprises in Riviera Beach.

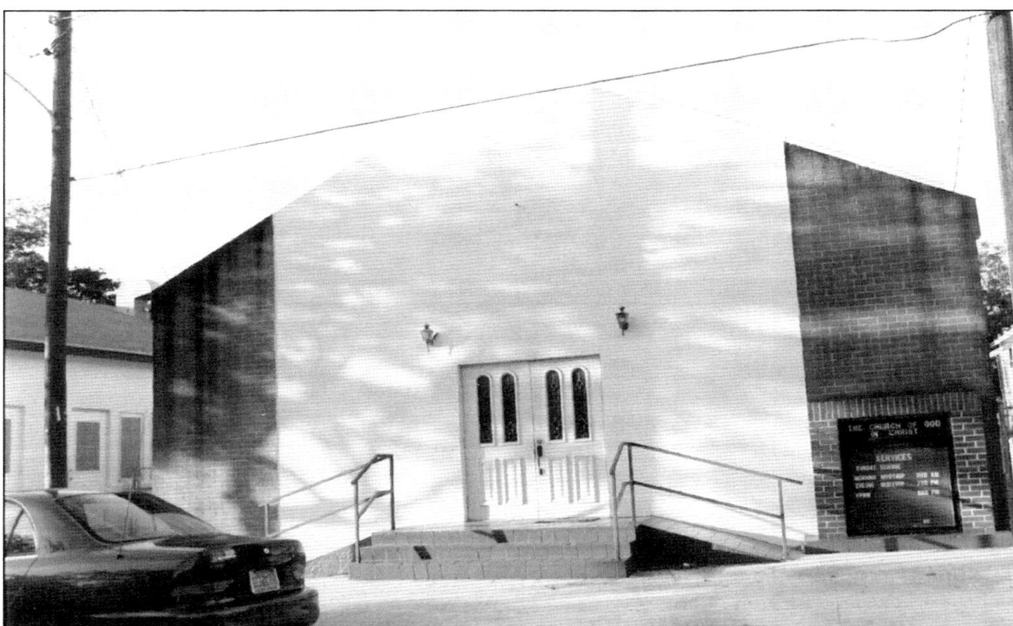

The First Church of God and Christ, located at Fourteenth Street and Henrietta Avenue, celebrated its 80th anniversary in 2004.

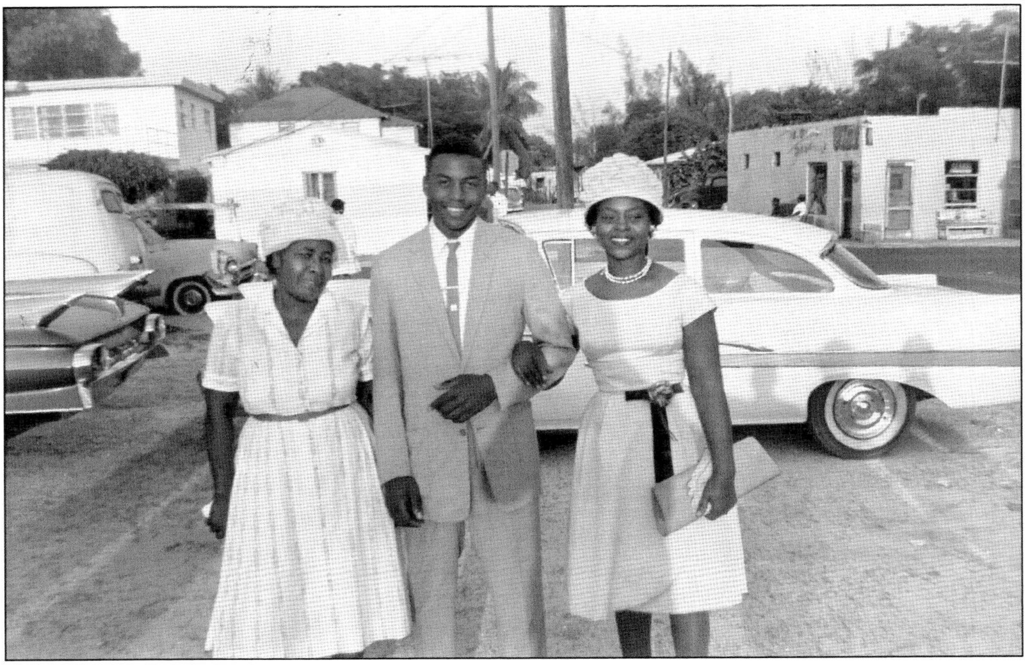

From left to right are Mary Lowery, Ulysee Studstill, and Carolyn Lester.

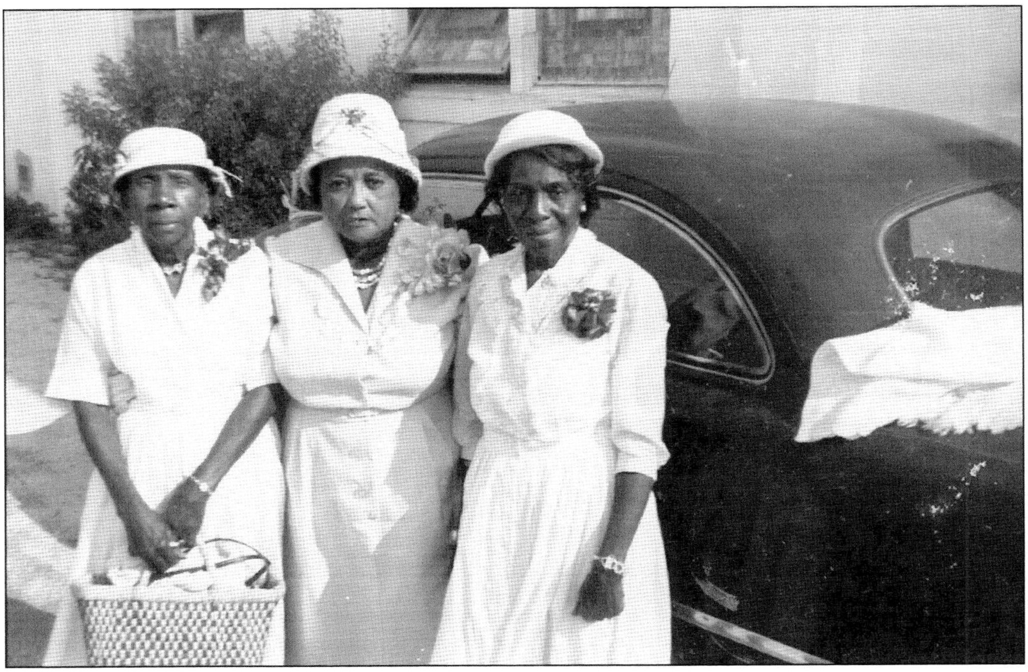

Members of the Antioch Baptist Church family include, from left to right, Laura Horne, Aletha Parson, and Cora Robinson.

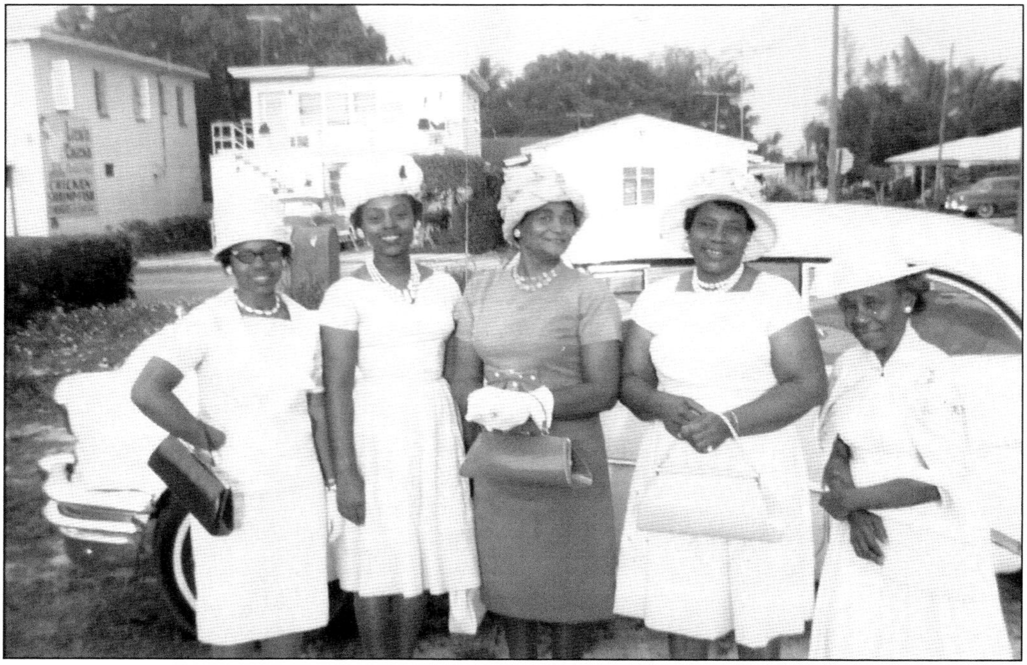

From left to right are Catherine Robinson, Carolyn Lester, Linda Smith, Ethel Studstill, and Elizabeth Cooper.

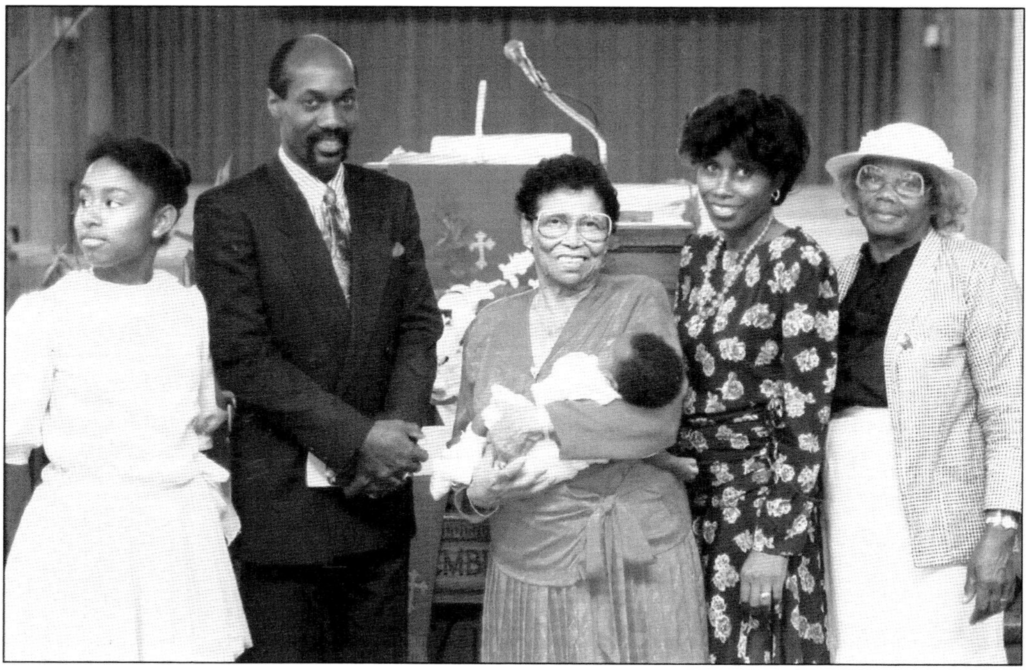

Shown is the baptism of Tommie and Evon Simmons' grandson. From left to right are granddaughter Ava, son Terry, godmother Evelyn Turner, mother Hodola Redding, and Mrs. Fisher.

Ladies ready for the annual spring tea at St. Paul A.M.E. Church in 1975 are, from left to right, Lois Evans, Mary Feacher, and Jessie Holloway.

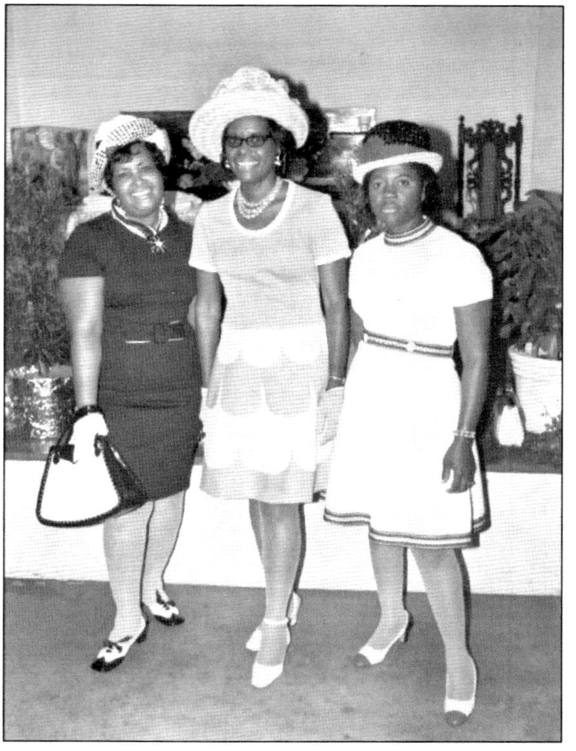

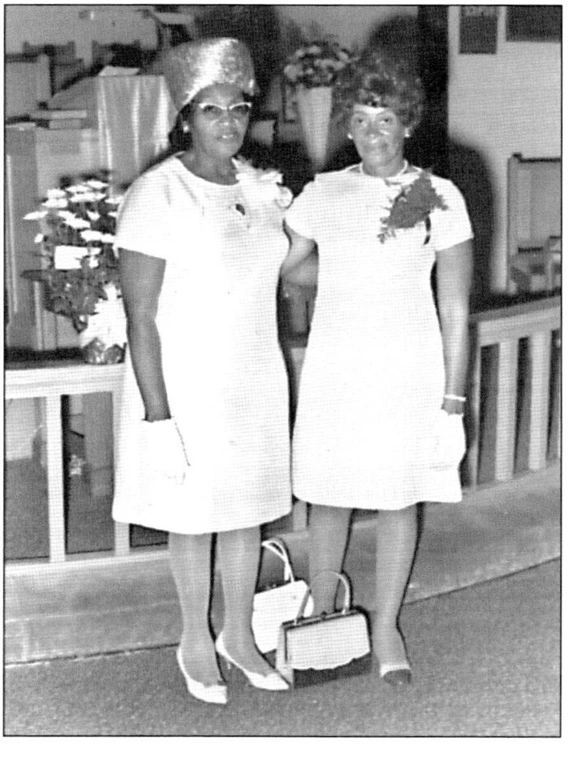

Lula Mae Thomas and mother Annie Mae Thomas are seen here at St. Paul A.M.E. Church. Lula Thomas is the only surviving teacher of the old Pleasant City Elementary School.

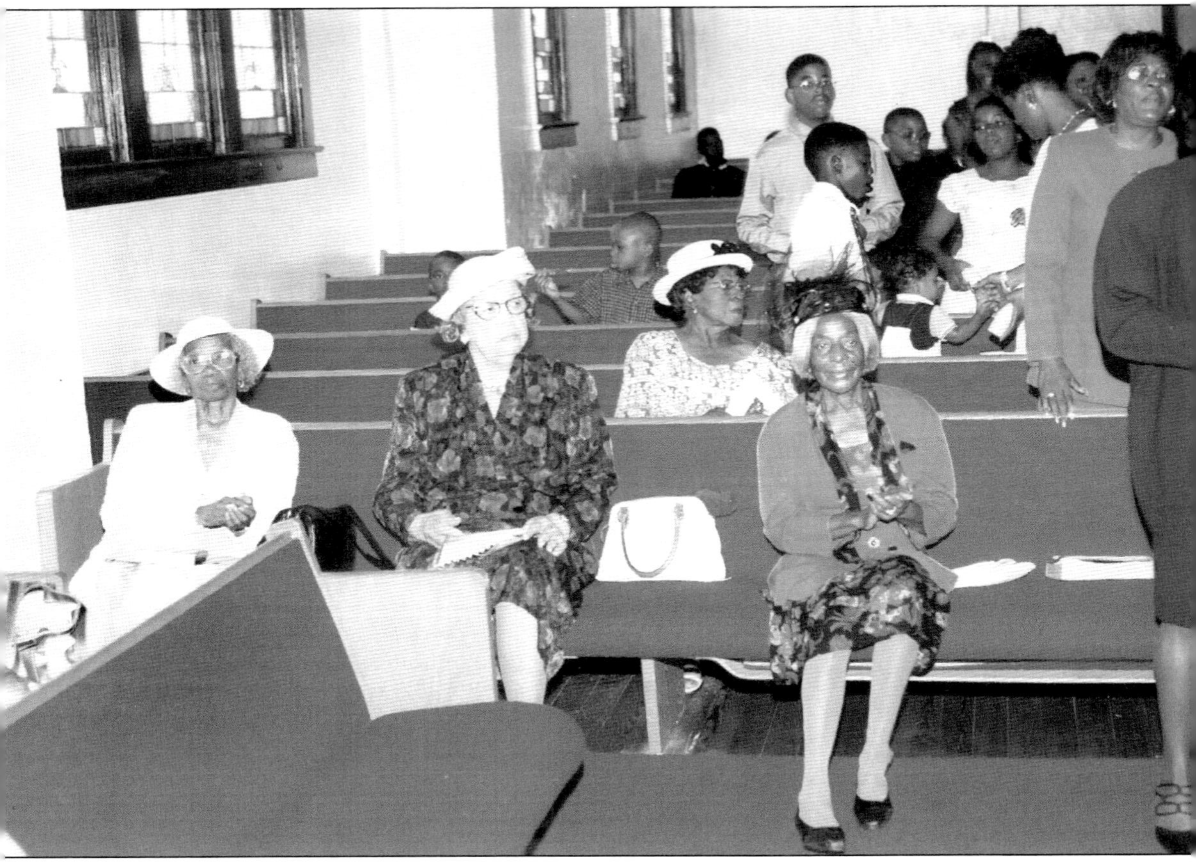

Shown here at the Pleasant City Community Reunion religious service at St. Paul A.M.E. Church are, from left to right, (first pew) Rena Pryor Gaskin, Ora Lee Felder, and Johnnie Mae Alexander; (second pew) Annie Mae Wilson.

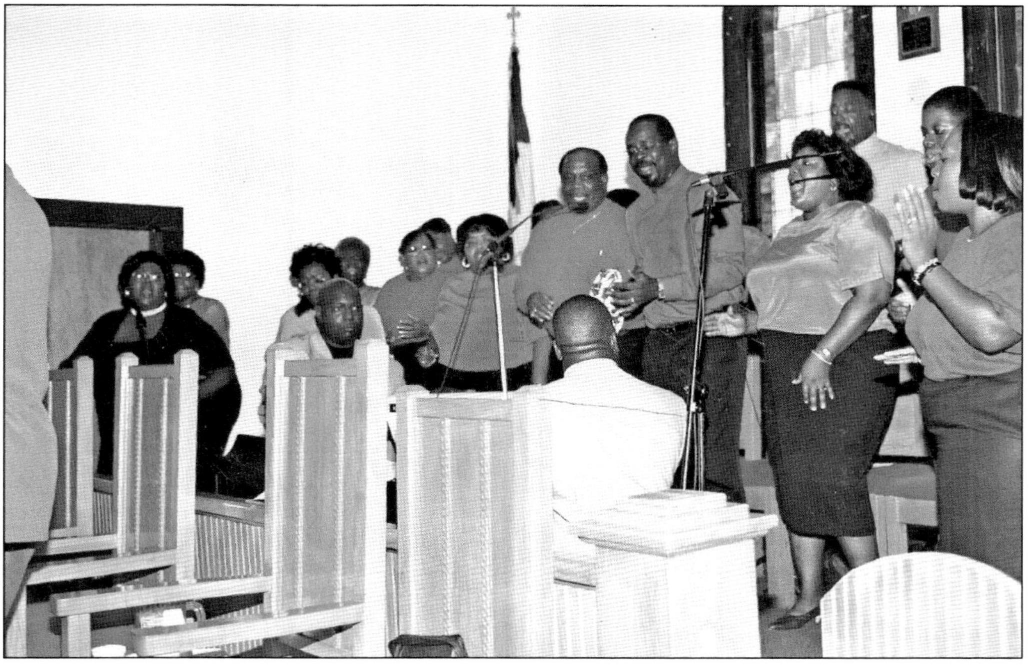
The J.R. Russell Praise Team, led by Timothy Kitchen, sings God's praises during the Pleasant City reunion church service in 1996.

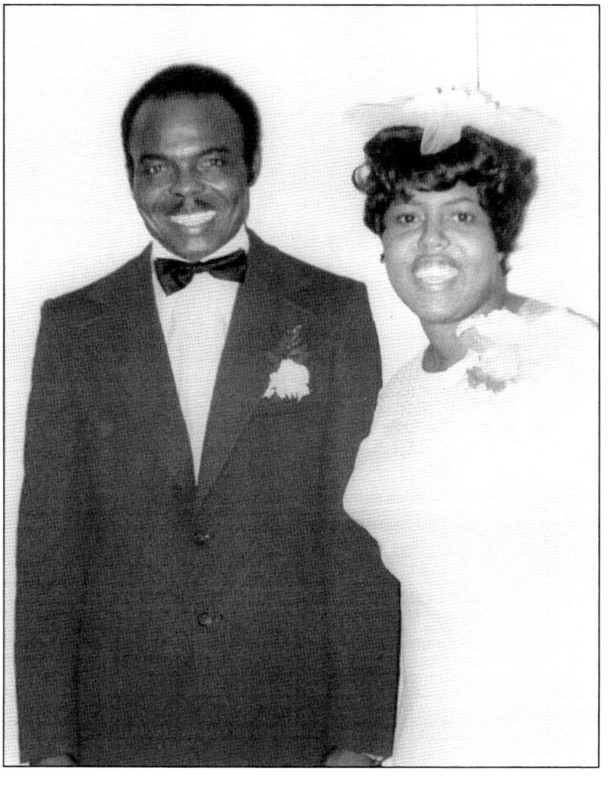
Herman Jimerson married Karen Frances Toombs in West Palm Beach on July 1, 1973. The bride is the daughter of the late Louis and Isadora Toombs of Gainesville, Florida. The Jimersons were married at the First Church of God in Christ, where they are very active and dedicated members.

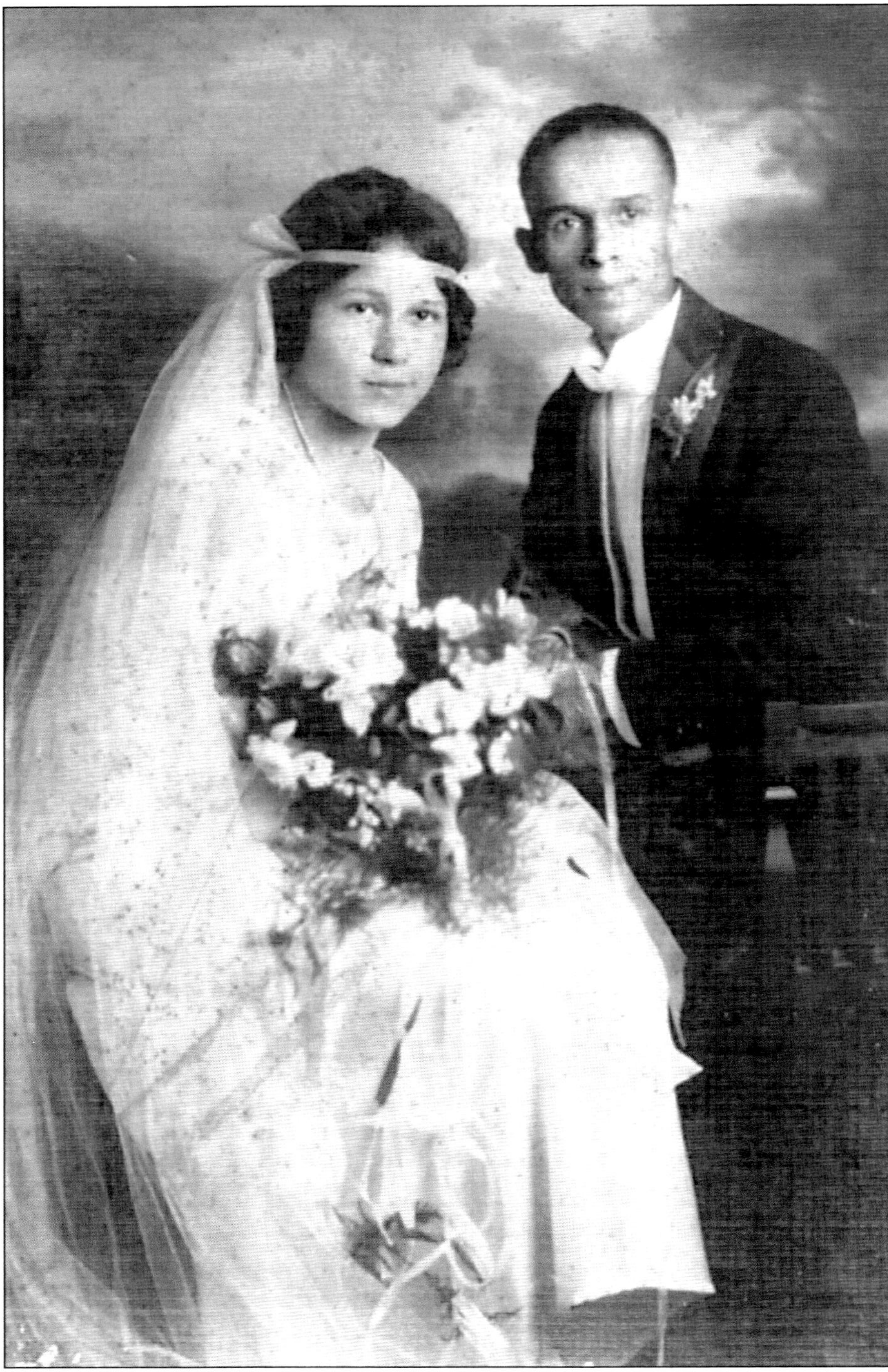

This photograph was found in the estate of Lula Williams and may show her on her wedding day or perhaps her parents on their wedding day. Mrs. Williams was an outstanding resident who contributed greatly to community and religious affairs.

Five

Business

Many of the businesses that began in the Styx relocated to Spruce and Poinsettia Avenue—now Dixie Highway—between Eighteenth and Twenty-third Streets. Twentieth Street between Dixie Highway and Contentment Avenue was the hub of black business enterprise in 1916. These business owners were the leadership of the community, an inspiration and role model for youths.

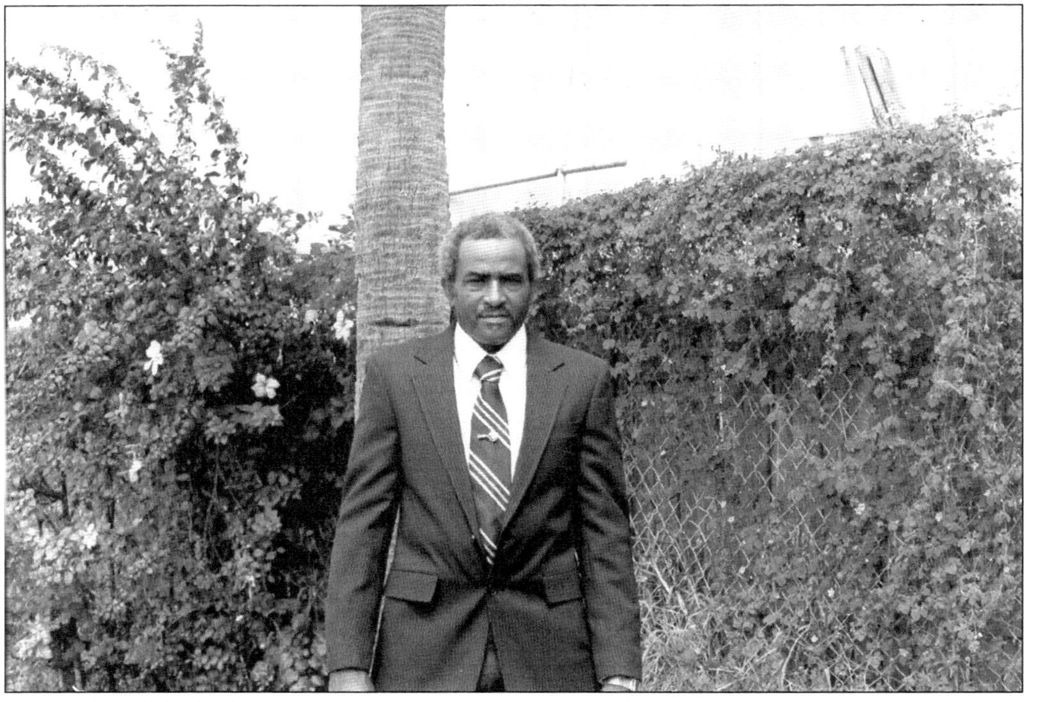

James Edward Littles has owned James Auto Service since the 1960s.

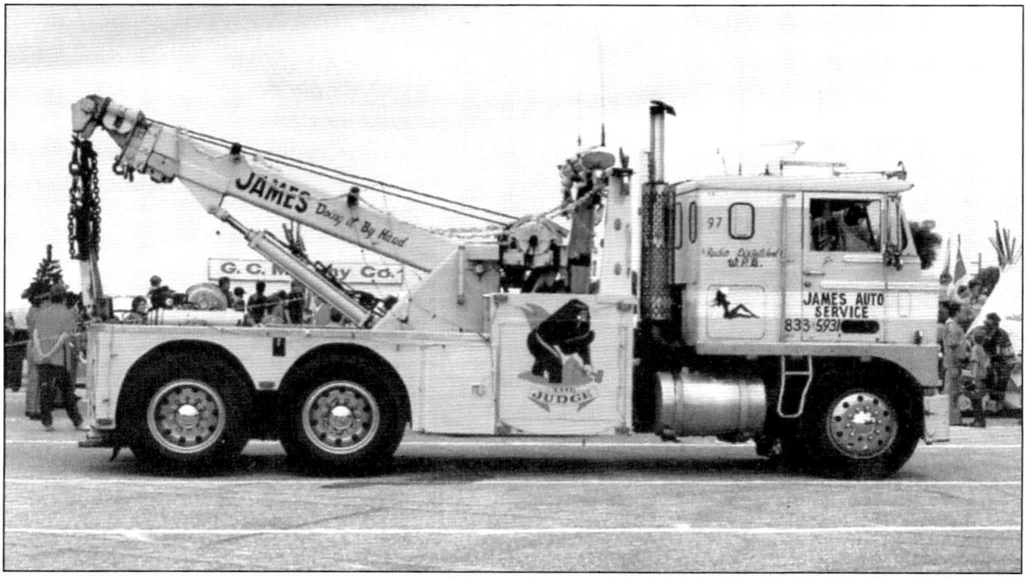

This vehicle was built by James Little. He was the first African American to have a large contract with the City of West Palm Beach to do auto towing.

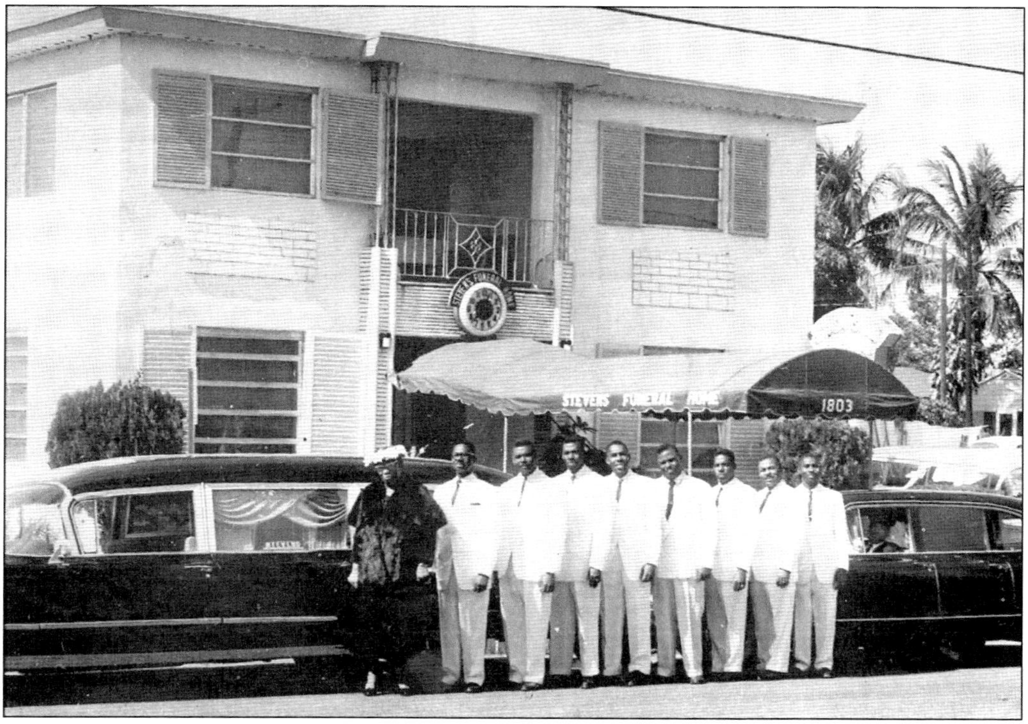

The original facility for Stevens Funeral Home, established in 1954, was at 1803 N. Tamarind Avenue in West Palm Beach. From left to right are mother Lillian Stevens and her eight sons John, Arnold, Vincent, Robert, Leonard, Howard, Eugene, and Roderick Stevens. Seated in the car is their father, William Stevens.

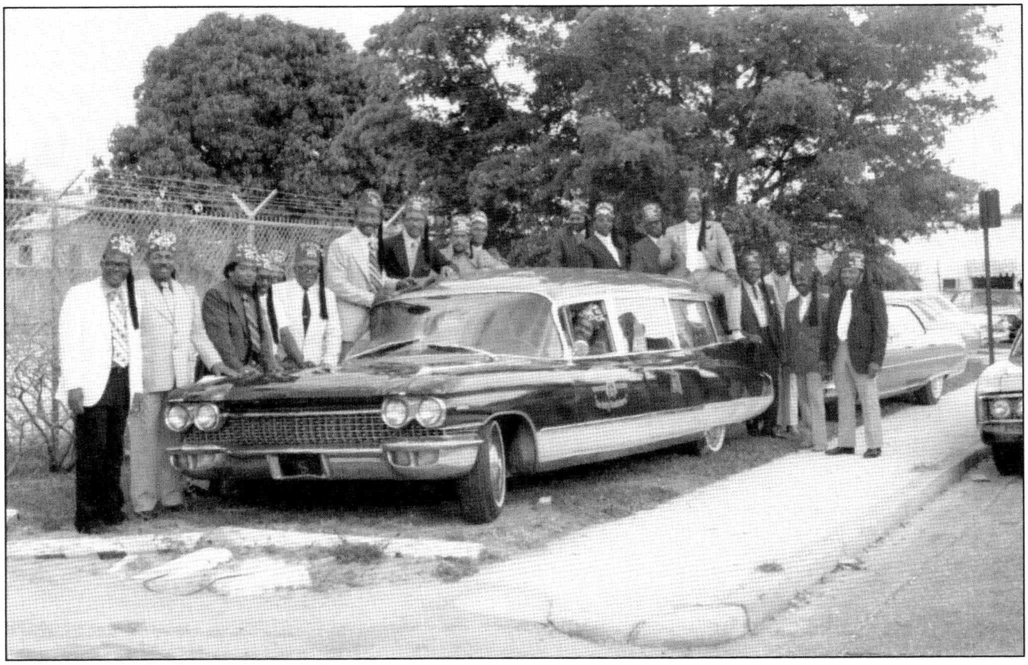

Stevens Brothers Funeral Home donates an old hearse to the Shriners for their parades.

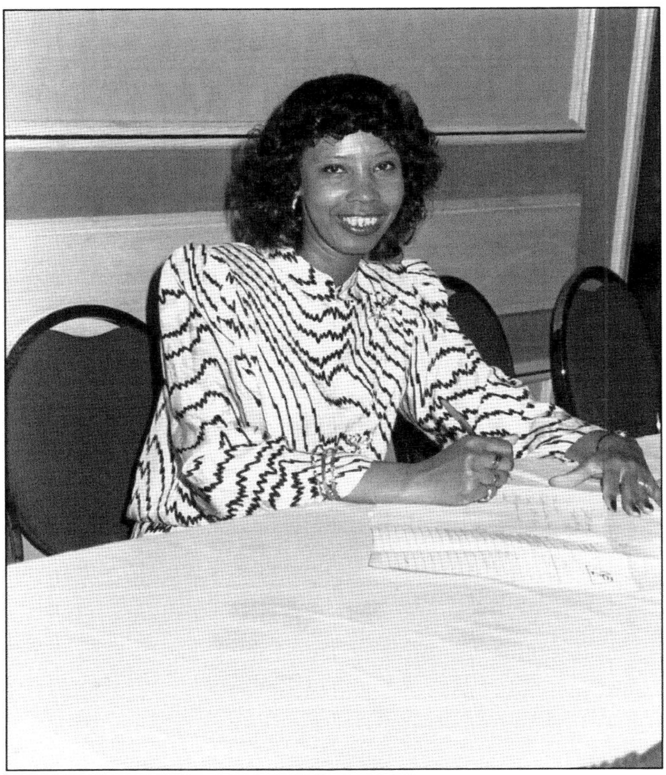

Josie Studstill co-owned Port Printing in Riviera Beach and was a member of the Tri-County Chapter of the National Business League.

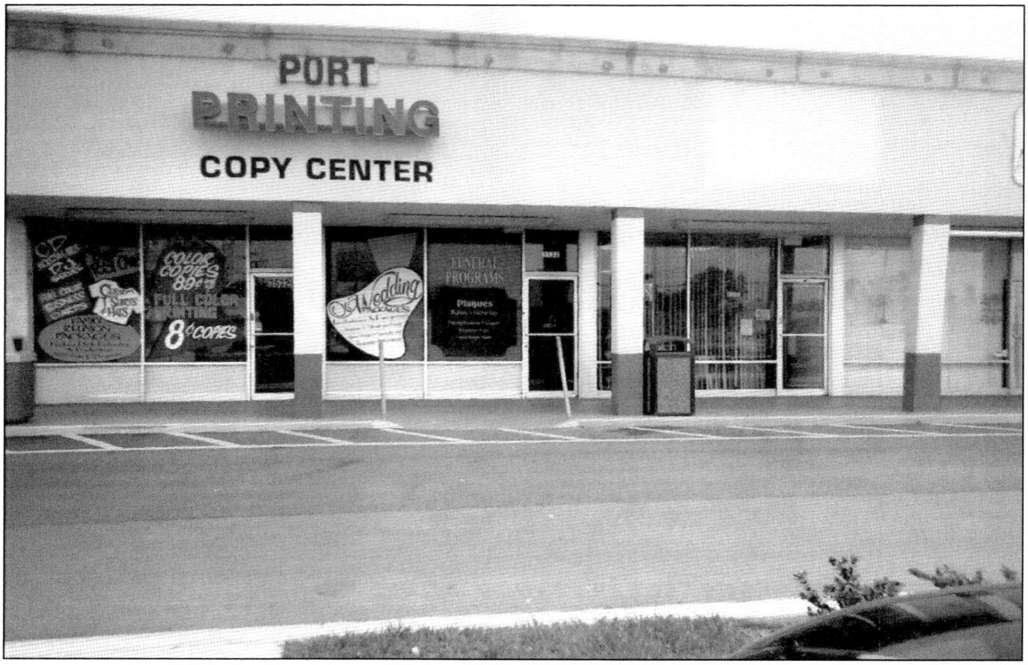

Port Printing in Riviera Beach, co-owned by Josie Studstill, is pictured here.

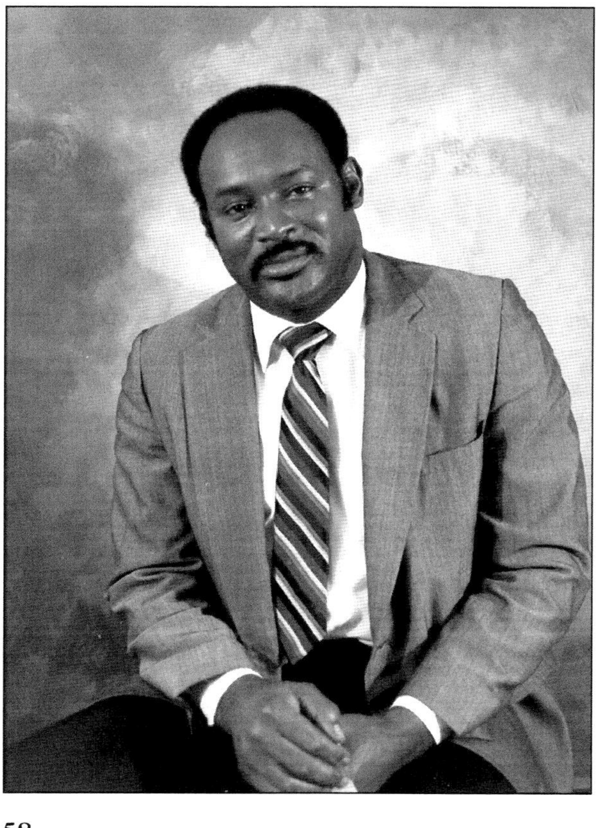

Warcecer Jakes owned State Farm Insurance Agency in West Palm Beach and was a member of the Tri-County Chapter of the National Business League.

Blue Front Bar-b-que Sauce, owned by Norris Nelson, is sold in all major supermarkets. Standing in front of the building after a 1972 Tri-County Chapter of the National Business League (NBL) meeting are, from left to right, Betty Smith; president Everee Clarke; Richmond Scruggs, owner of an upholstery business; secretary Gertrude Burney; and treasurer Virginia Merritt.

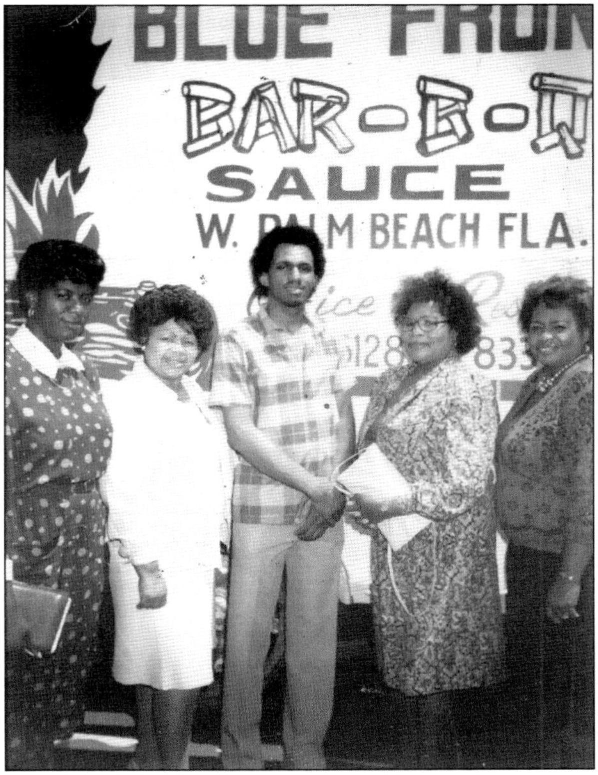

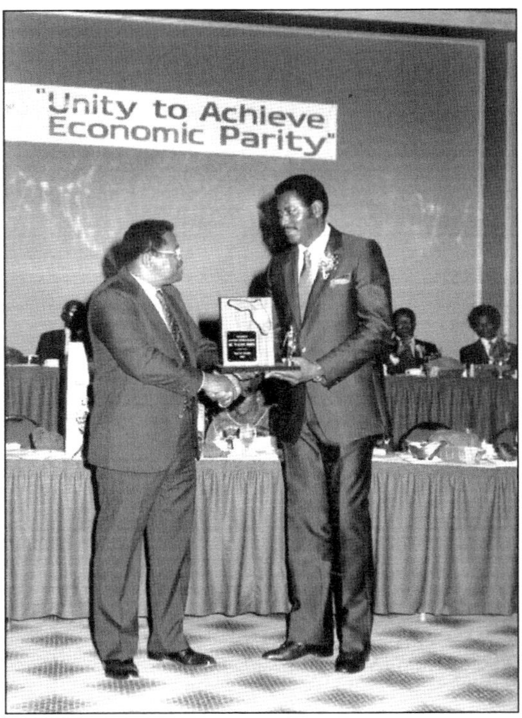

Frank Saulsby, NBL board chairman, presents an award to Walter Embry, the Top Ten Award winner in 1975. The NBL Tri County Chapter was organized in 1969 to assist minority businesses through seminars and workshops, which were conducted by the SBA, HUD, and other agencies, to improve the quality of businesses.

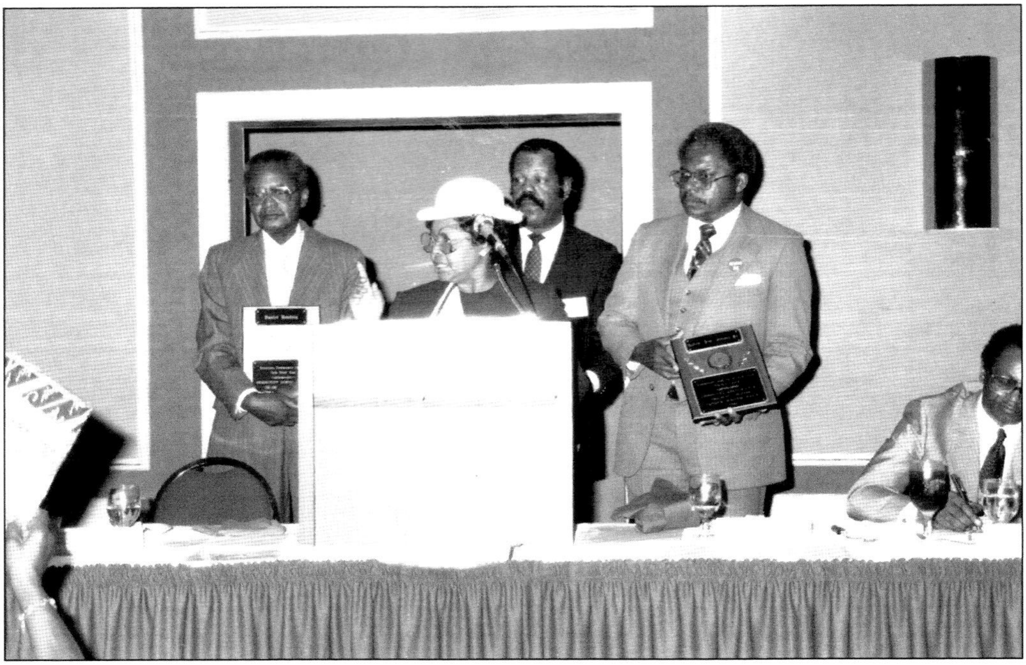

From left to right are Daniel Hendrix, NBL president; Everee Clarke; Edward White; and Bob Mitchell. The Tri-County Chapter honors Daniel Hendrix, the first African American elected to the school board in 1970 and the first elected to any countywide office in Palm Beach County. He was one of six Roosevelt Junior College staff members placed at Palm Beach Junior College after the merger in 1965.

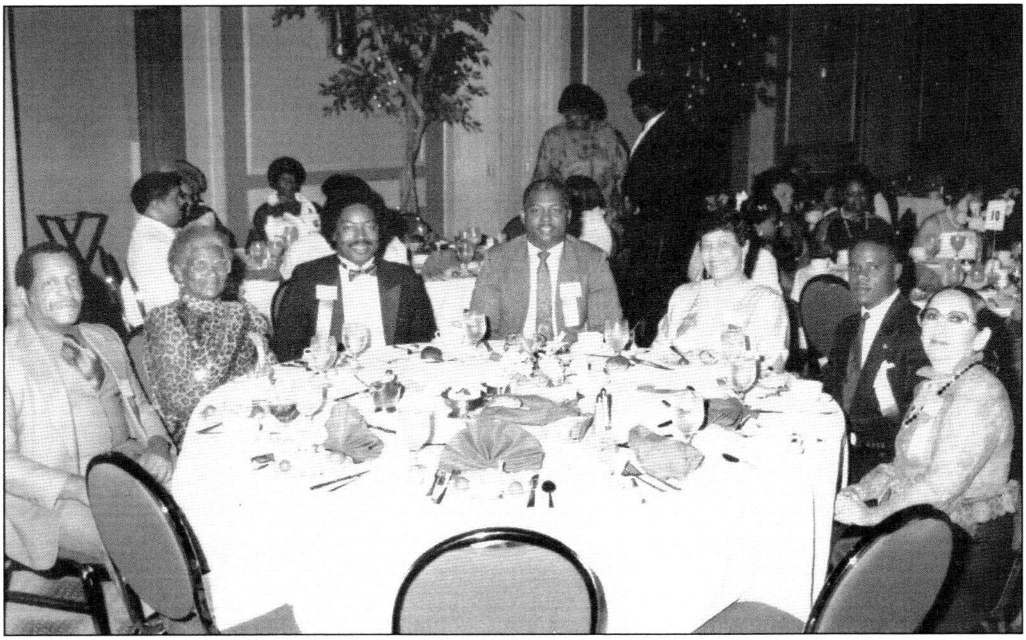

The Tri-County Chapter of the National Business League honors Daniel Hendrix.

Pioneer businessman and resident of Cheerful Street, Cisro Dillard was active in religious and community affairs. Dillard was a jitney driver in the community for a number of years. He passed away in 2004.

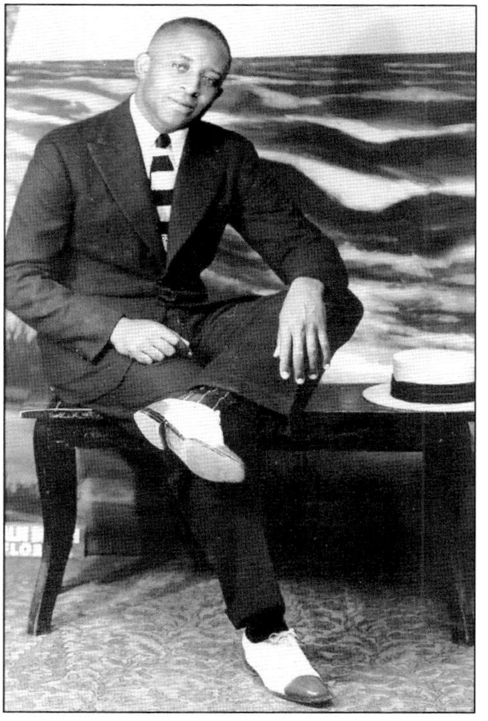

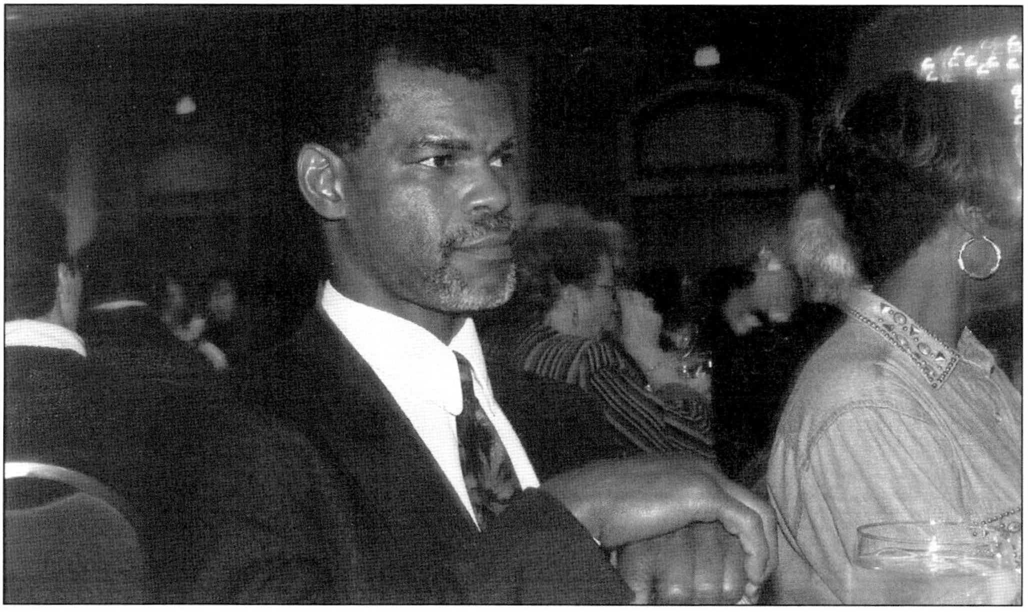

Michael Cleveland is a community activist and president of the Pleasant City Neighborhood Association. He is a graduate of Roosevelt High School and a decorated Marine Corp veteran who served in Vietnam and the Mediterranean. He is the president and CEO of IMPACT and a member of the board of the West Palm Beach CRA. His grandparents were pioneers Thomas and Lucinda Wallace.

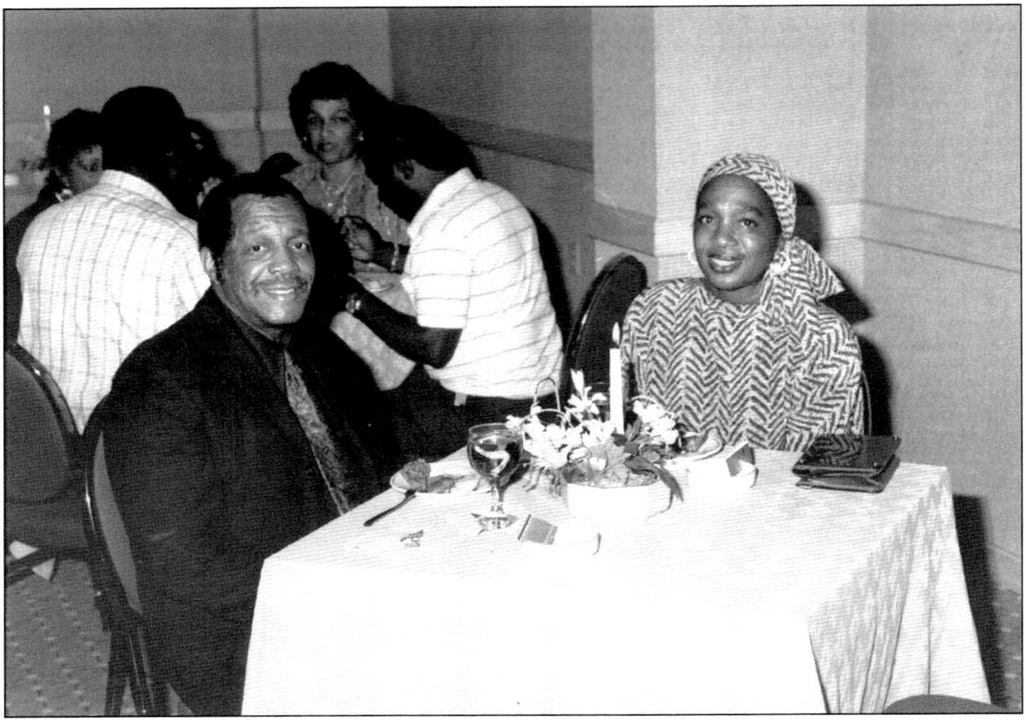

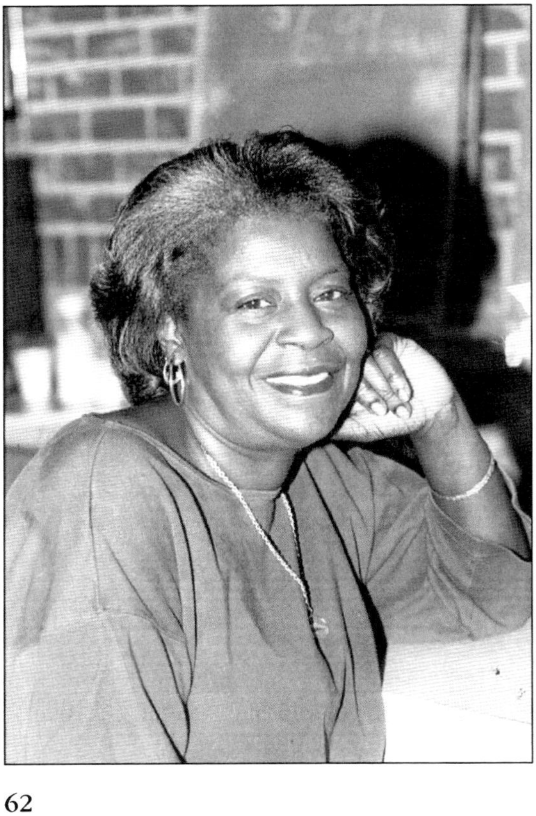

Wilbert Ellis Watson, son of Wilbert Sr. and Mrs. Sally Watson, was born on September 20, 1928, just a short time after the devastating 1928 storm. He attended Brooklyn College and Julliard School of Music in New York. He studied dance along with the famous Hines brothers. The family operated a grocery store at the corner of Twenty-second Street and Tamarind Avenue. He and his parents are deceased. His widow, Willye Watson, is president and CEO of Housing Services of Palm Beach County, with an office in Riviera Beach.

Yvonne Peterman is the owner and manager of the World Famous Restaurant. Yvonne had been the manager of Kenwood Nursing Home for 21 years when she decided to enter the restaurant business. She and her three daughters opened the restaurant at 701 Twenty-third Street, near the railroad, on January 12, 1992. The restaurant, now located at 415 Northwood Road, houses a stage, dance floor, and bar. Aside from catering and the regular food service, "Jazz in the Hood," Blue Monday, and holiday dinners are special events.

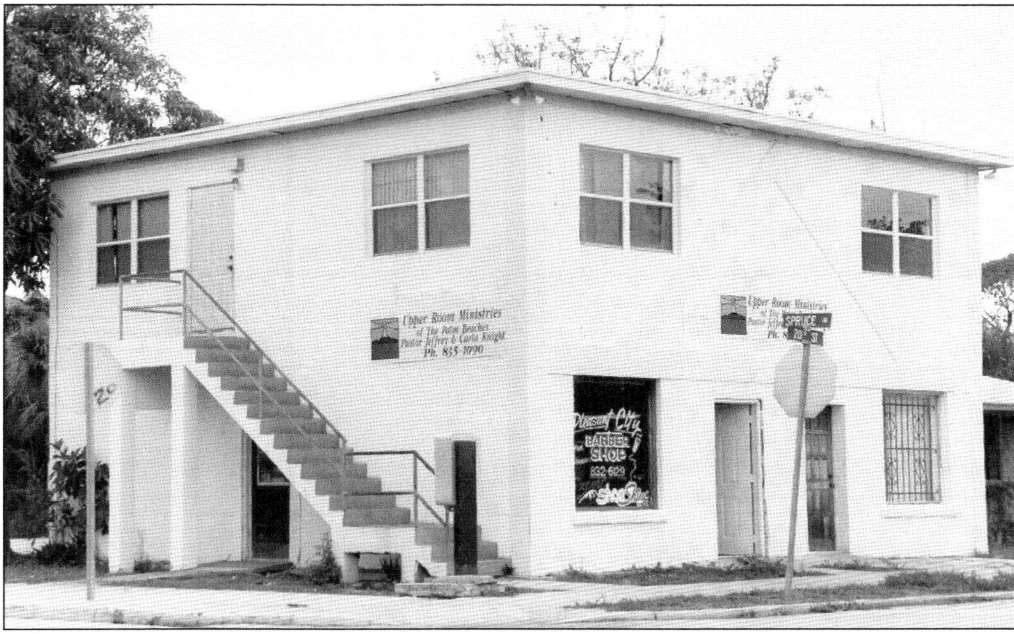

Adolphus Montgomery established the Pleasant City Barber Shop at Twentieth Street and Spruce Avenue in the late 1950s.

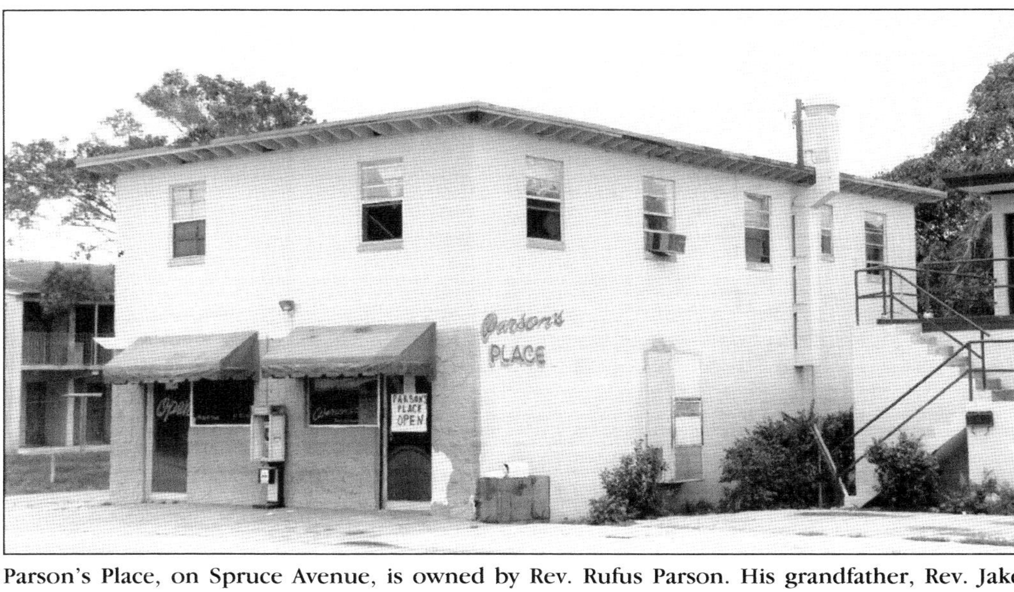

Parson's Place, on Spruce Avenue, is owned by Rev. Rufus Parson. His grandfather, Rev. Jake Parson, built it in the 1950s. This building housed a furniture store and eateries, and it is now a restaurant.

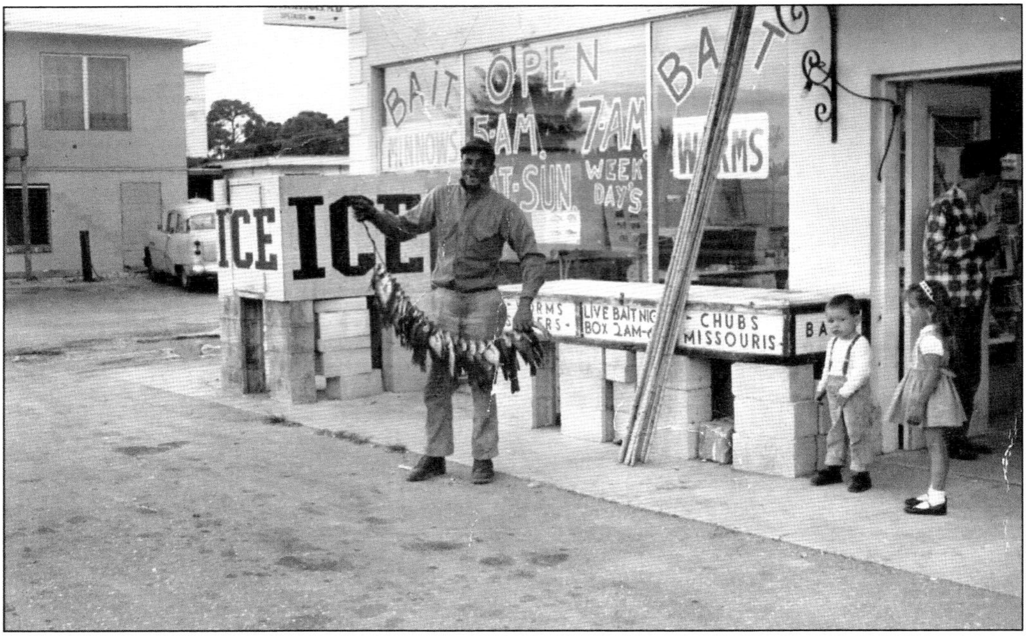

Emanuel Jimerson went fishing and made a great catch in this April 1962 photo.

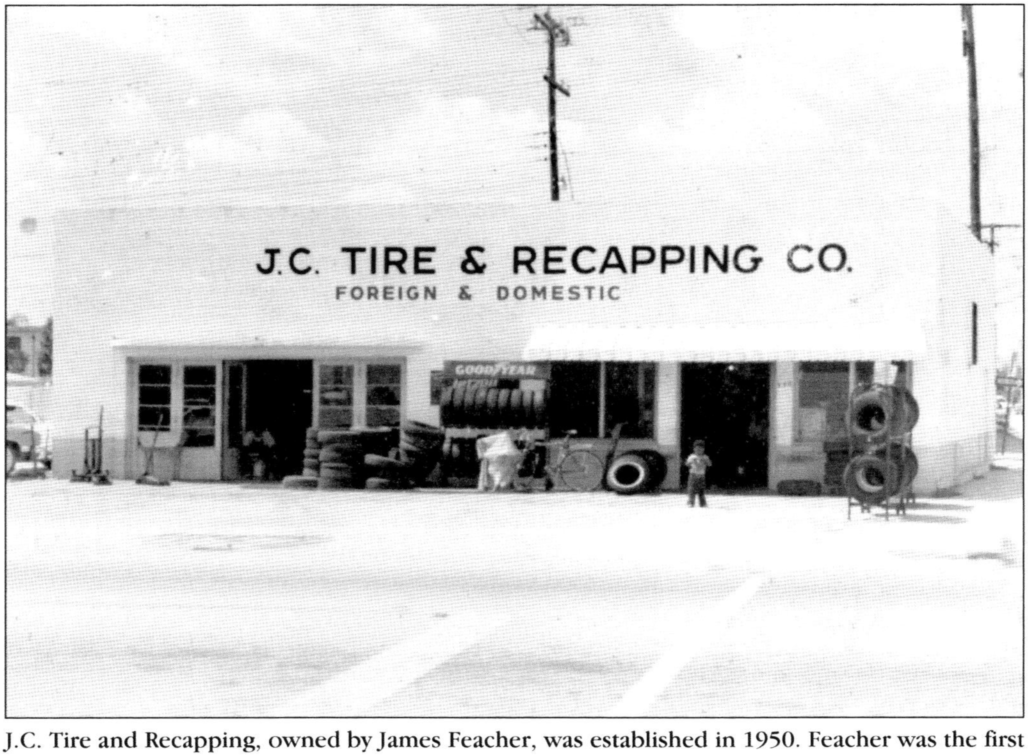

J.C. Tire and Recapping, owned by James Feacher, was established in 1950. Feacher was the first African American in the community to get an SBA loan for business.

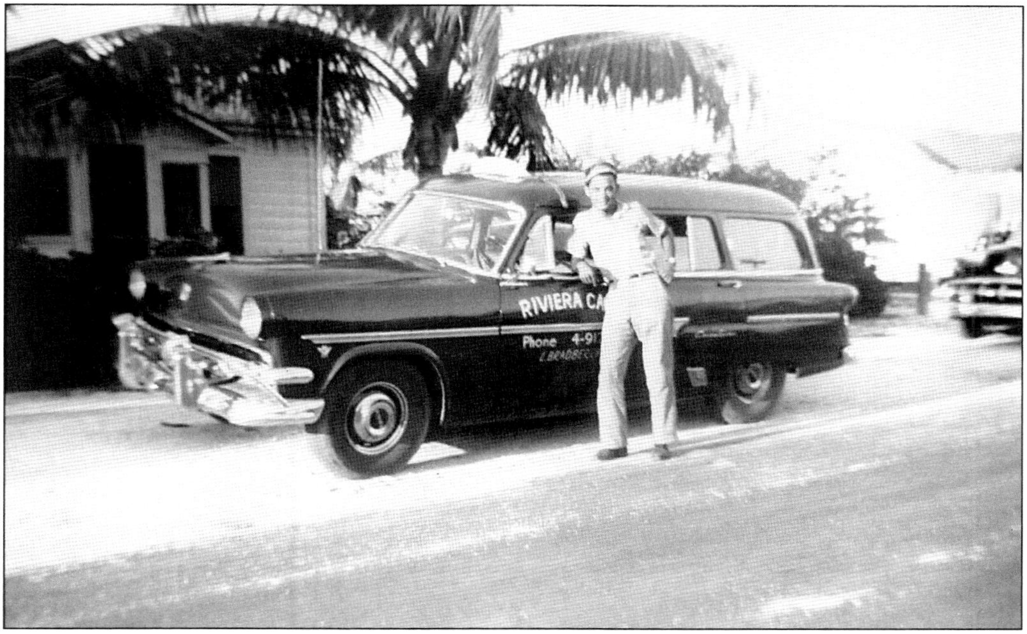

Carol Fisher Cab Service is run by Carol Fisher, the son of pioneer William Howard Fisher.

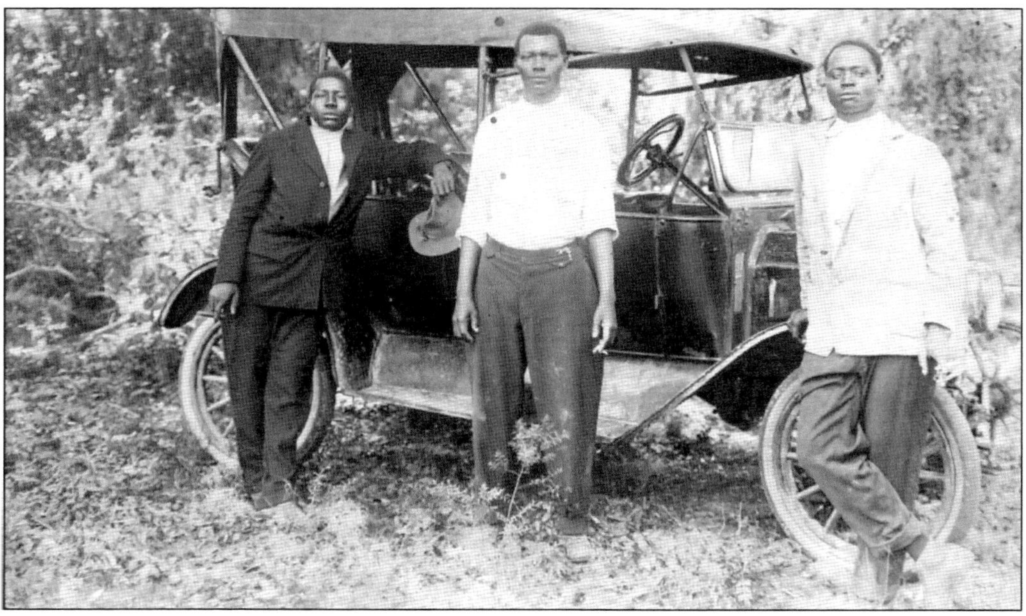

The first person to own his own automobile in Pleasant City was Frederick "Fred" Ferguson, who purchased a new Cadillac in 1935. Often, the employer would purchase a new automobile and give the old one to the employee rather than trade it in.

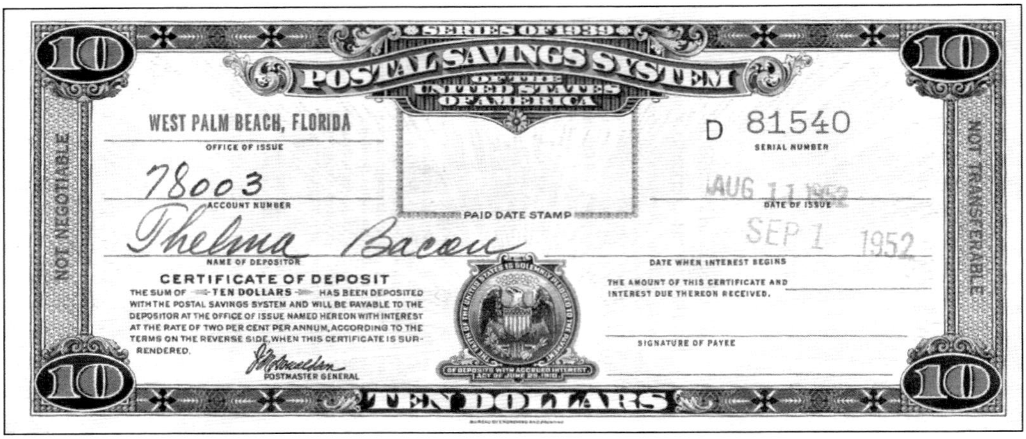
SERIES OF 1939

POSTAL SAVINGS SYSTEM OF THE UNITED STATES OF AMERICA

10	NOT NEGOTIABLE	NOT TRANSFERABLE	10

WEST PALM BEACH, FLORIDA
OFFICE OF ISSUE

D 81540
SERIAL NUMBER

78003
ACCOUNT NUMBER

PAID DATE STAMP

AUG 11 1952
DATE OF ISSUE

Thelma Bacon
NAME OF DEPOSITOR

SEP 1 1952
DATE WHEN INTEREST BEGINS

CERTIFICATE OF DEPOSIT

THE SUM OF —TEN DOLLARS— HAS BEEN DEPOSITED WITH THE POSTAL SAVINGS SYSTEM AND WILL BE PAYABLE TO THE DEPOSITOR AT THE OFFICE OF ISSUE NAMED HEREON WITH INTEREST AT THE RATE OF TWO PER CENT PER ANNUM, ACCORDING TO THE TERMS ON THE REVERSE SIDE, WHEN THIS CERTIFICATE IS SURRENDERED.

POSTMASTER GENERAL

THE AMOUNT OF THIS CERTIFICATE AND INTEREST DUE THEREON RECEIVED.

SIGNATURE OF PAYEE

OF DEPOSITS WITH ACCRUED INTEREST ACT OF JUNE 25, 1910

TEN DOLLARS

For many years, African Americans were not permitted to make bank deposits unless they were of the middle class. Most people who had money to save used the U.S. Postal Savings System. The first black bank opened in West Palm Beach in the early 1970s. The First Prudential Bank did not survive more than six years.

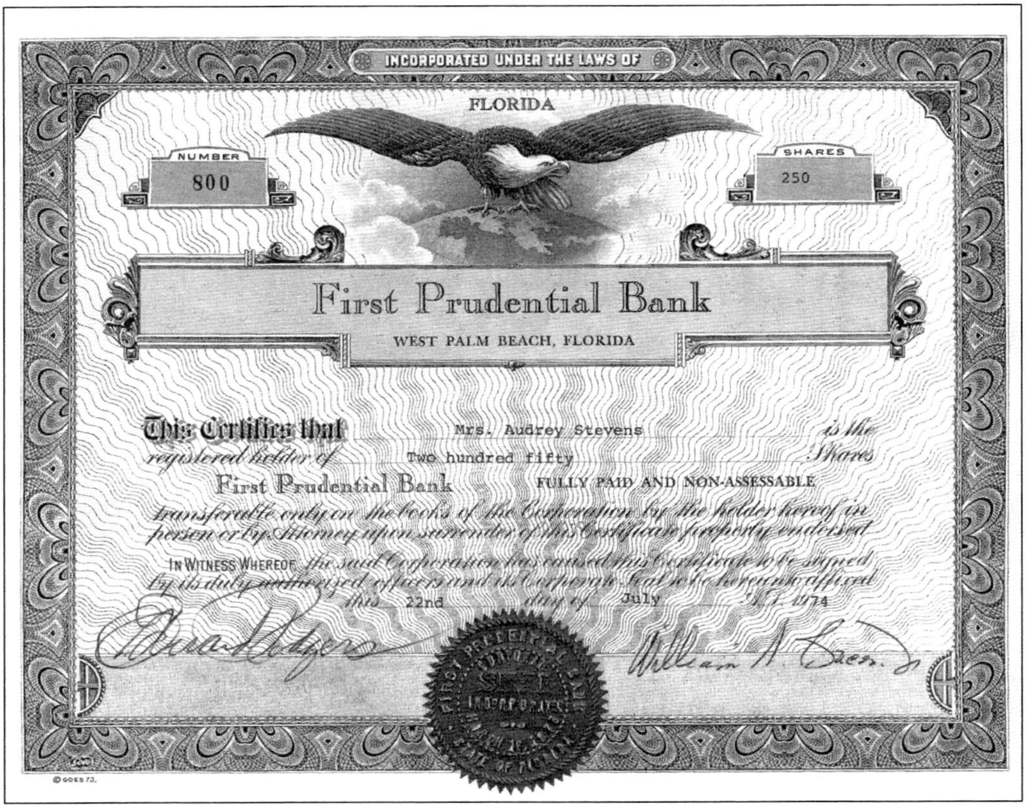
INCORPORATED UNDER THE LAWS OF

FLORIDA

NUMBER 800

SHARES 250

First Prudential Bank

WEST PALM BEACH, FLORIDA

This Certifies that Mrs. Audrey Stevens is the registered holder of Two hundred fifty Shares

First Prudential Bank FULLY PAID AND NON-ASSESSABLE

transferable only on the books of the Corporation by the holder hereof in person or by Attorney upon surrender of this Certificate properly endorsed.

In Witness Whereof the said Corporation has caused this Certificate to be signed by its duly authorized officers and its Corporate Seal to be hereunto affixed this 22nd day of July A.D. 1974

© GOES 73.

Six

EVENTS

A few of the events that have impacted the lives of Pleasant City residents most notably are the Hurricane of 1928, World War II, the Civil Rights Movement, integration of schools and public facilities, the introduction of beauty and talent pageantry, African arts, and community reunions. Only two Pleasant City residents served in World War I—Thomas Culpepper and Frank Singleton. The shock of Pearl Harbor brought drastic changes to our community. Civil Defense wardens reminded residents to turn off the lights during "black-outs." Food and gasoline were rationed. Charlie Foxx Sr. was a flight instructor assigned to instruct the first black Army Air Corp of 13 cadets at Moton Field, Tuskegee, Alabama. Five of the group became Army Air Force pilots. These men and others became the flying 99 Pursuit Squadron. Jeff Burns Sr. fought with the 761st Tank Battalion, the "Original Black Panthers." They were decorated with a Presidential Unit Citation in 1978. Virginia Jefferson Melvin was an army nurse, and Gladys Crawford was the first female to enter service from Pleasant City, serving in the U.S. Air Force.

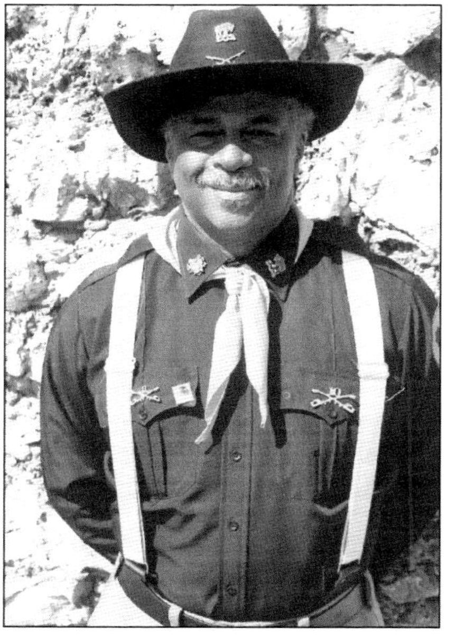

The Heritage Gallery presented the Living Legends, including a buffalo soldier group and the Triple Nickles (African-American paratroopers) to thousands of high school students in three schools in Palm Beach County. Shown here is Lee Reddick.

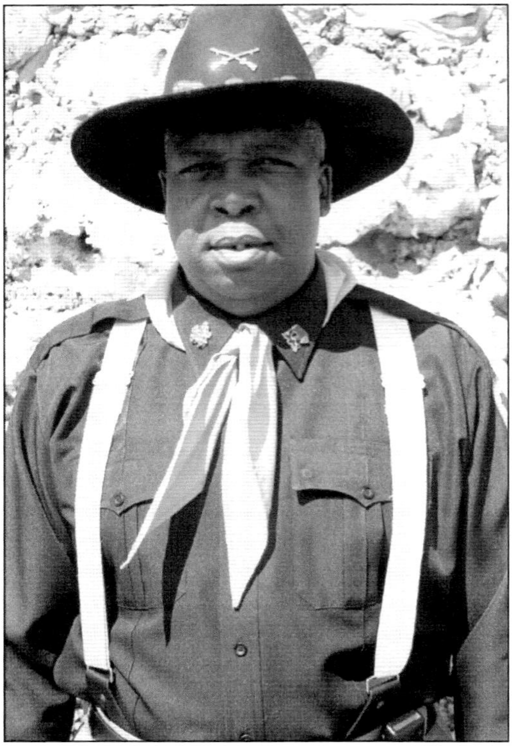

Frank Bell Jr. is a member of the Tampa, Florida unit of the Buffalo Soldiers.

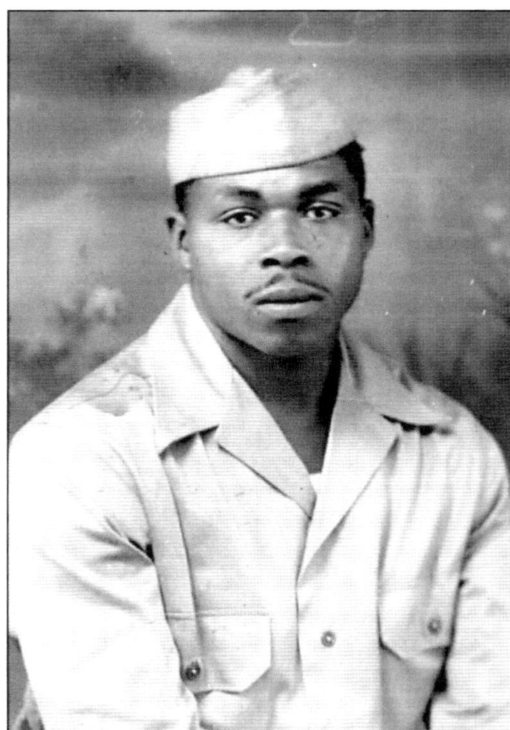

Paul Elkins, the son of Albertha Elkins Price, was drafted and loaded on a bus at Curry Park and taken to Camp Blanding, Florida, and other military centers during World War II. He served in the European Theater of Operation.

Andrew Jimerson was the fourth son in the Jimerson family called into service. He served in the army during the Korean Conflict.

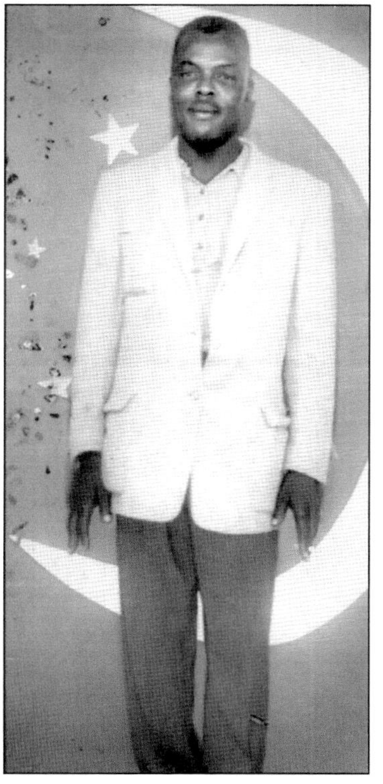

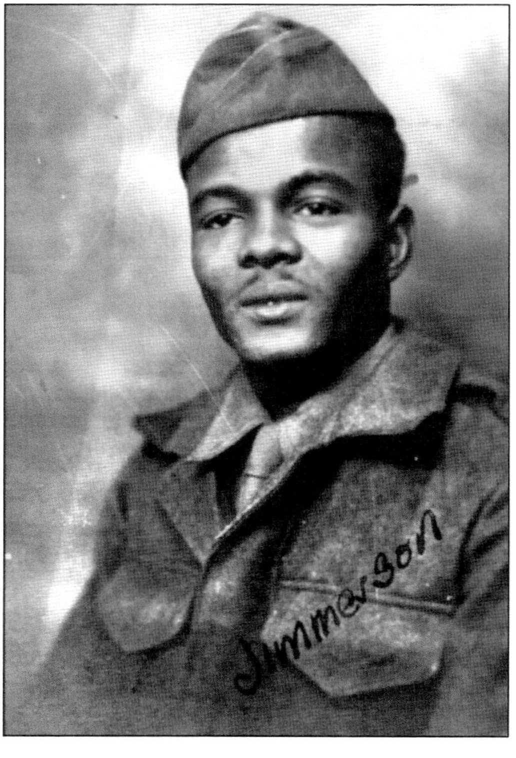

Emanuel Jimerson served in the South Pacific. When he returned home, he married Alma Seymour. They had four children: Emanuel Jr. Diann, Jessica, and Charlton.

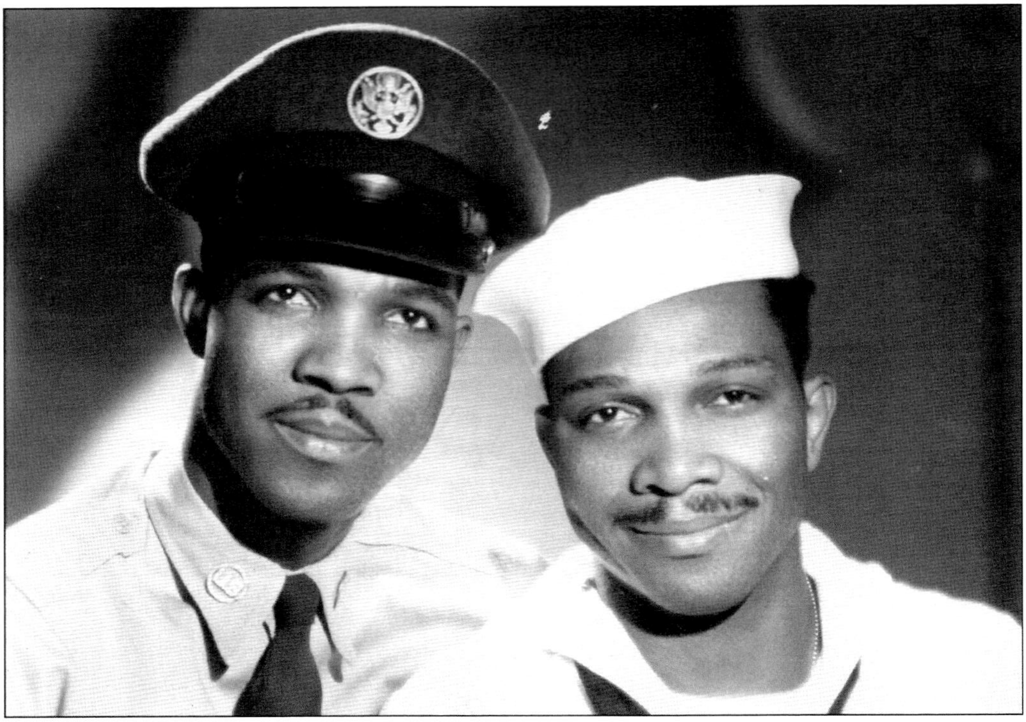

Joseph and Lionel Broxton are sons of the late Joseph and Theresa Broxton. They chose the army and navy. They both returned home safely to marry a rear families—Joseph had two sons and Lionel, four daughters.

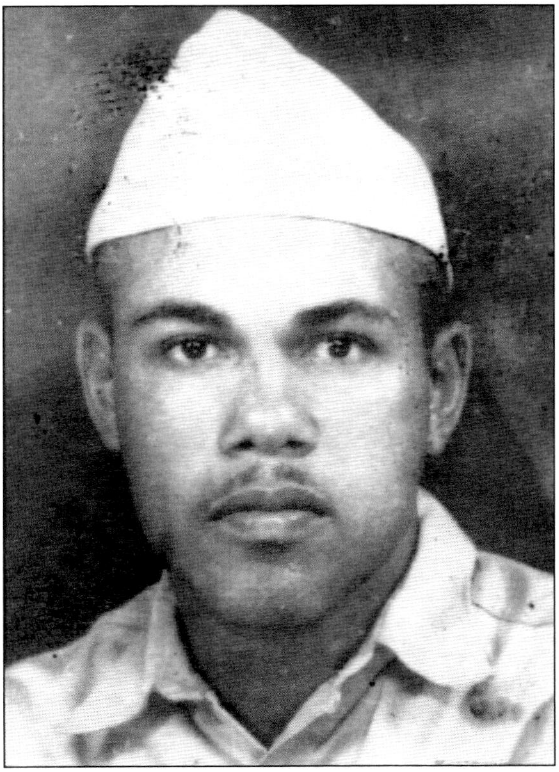

Benjamin Fernandez was the youngest son of pioneers William and Mary Fernandez, who were residents of Cheerful Street.

Henry Fernandez was among the first draftees to leave on the bus from Curry Park going to Camp Blanding.

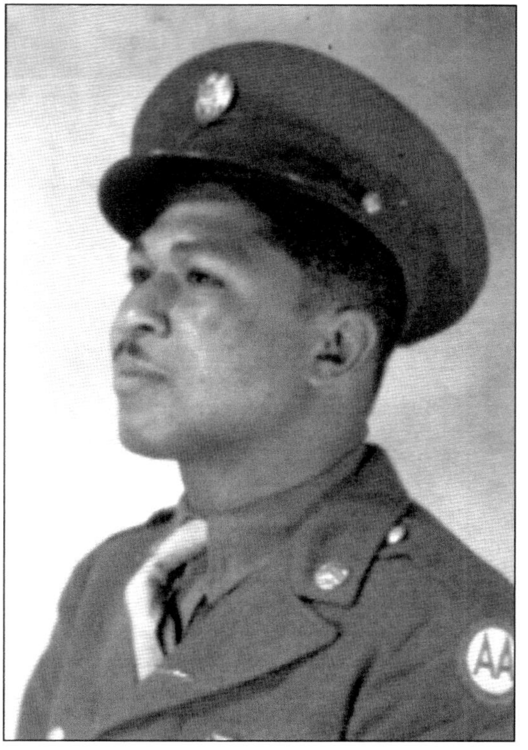

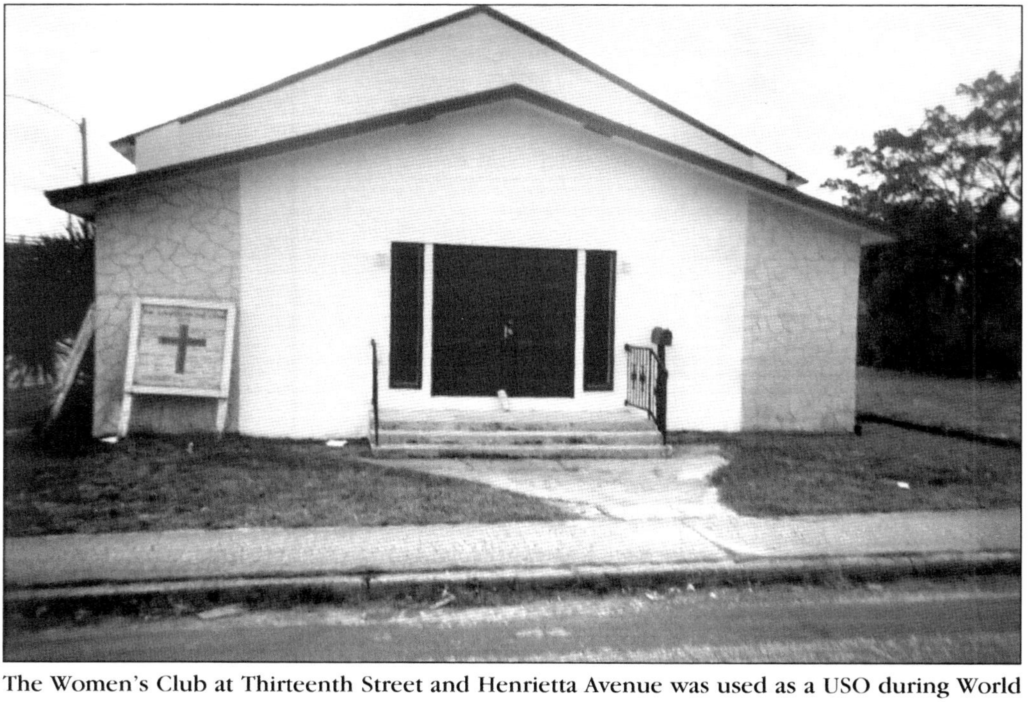

The Women's Club at Thirteenth Street and Henrietta Avenue was used as a USO during World War II. The building is now the Church of Christ.

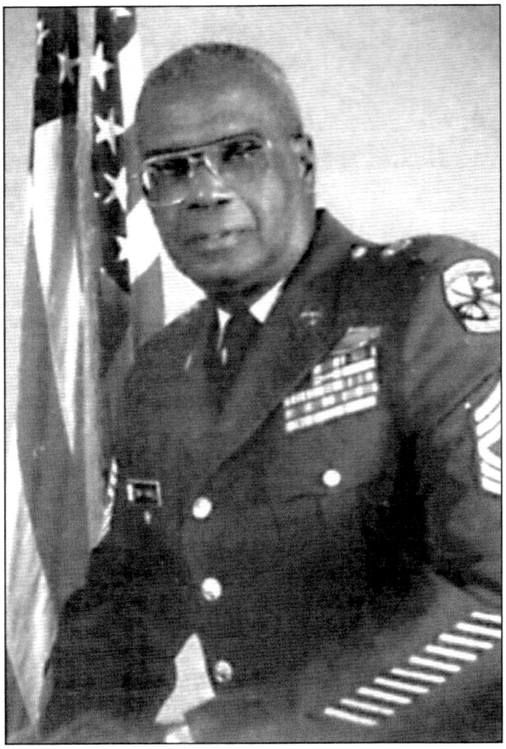

Command Sgt. Maj. Horace Hartman Howell attended elementary school in Pleasant City. He graduated from Industrial High School and attended St. Paul A.M.E. Church. Horace joined the United States Army on June 3, 1943, and proudly served for more than 30 years. Sgt. Maj. Hartman Howell retired June 30, 1976. He served as a junior ROTC program instructor at Lucy C. Laney Comprehensive High School and retired after 15 years. He was married to Dollie Mae Major for 35 years, and they had three sons and two daughters.

below left: Born and reared in Pleasant City, Tommy Holmes was the grandson of pioneer Roxy Frierson and son of Juanita Holmes.
below right: James C. Samuel served in Operation Desert Storm. He is the son of the late Carol and Lanier Samuel and grandson of pioneers William and Mary Fernandez.

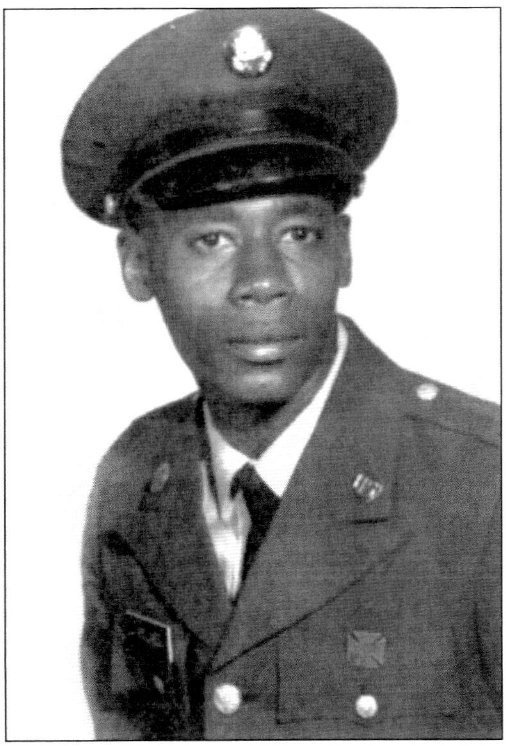

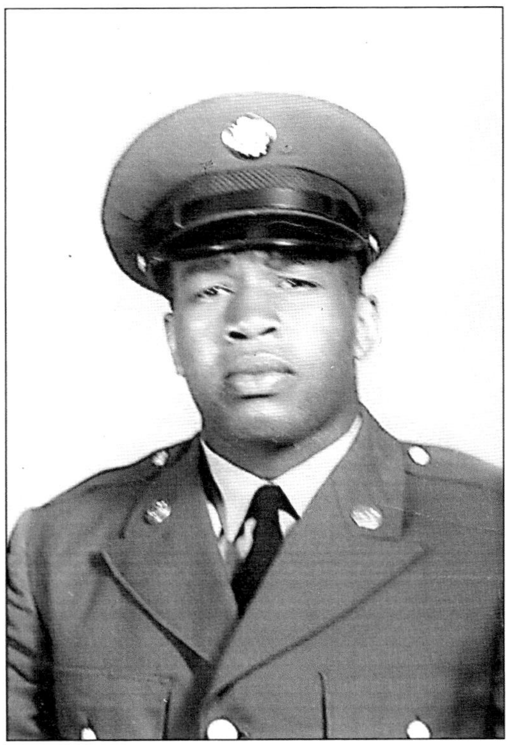

Jeffrey Lee Jackson was the grandson of pioneers Edward and Frances Jimerson and the son of Jeffrey Lee and Ruby Jackson. He spent more than 31 years in military service, as did Choice James, who served in Europe, Korea, and Vietnam.

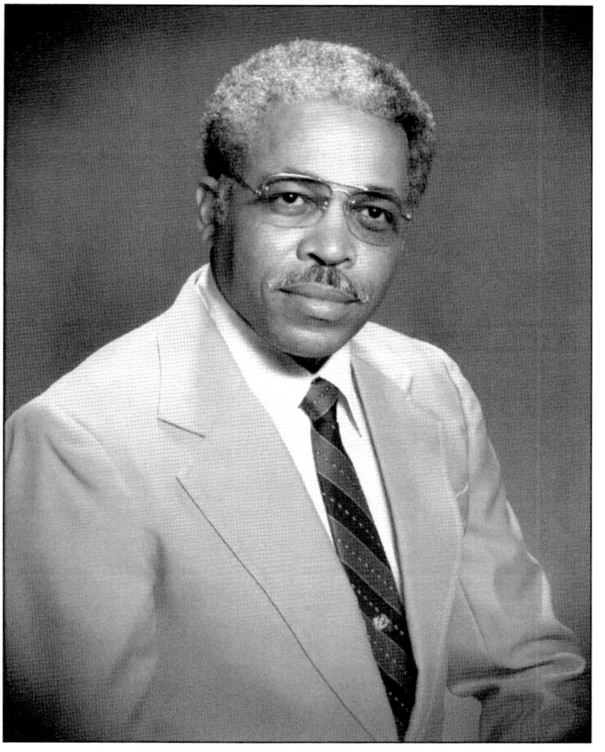

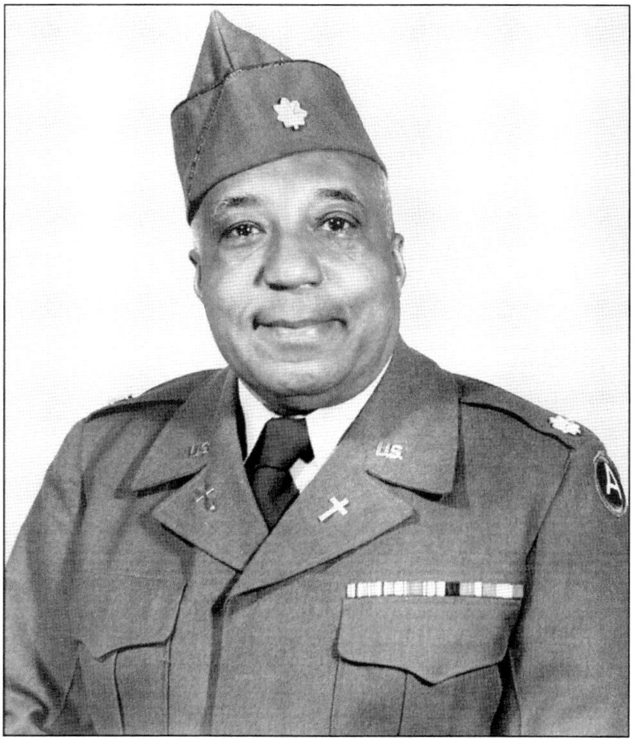

The highest ranking military officer from Pleasant City, Lt. Col. David L. Brewer was born in Sanford, Florida. He received a bachelor's degree from Morehouse College, a degree in theology from Oberlin School of Theology, and a master's degree from Columbia University. He taught at Florida Memorial College for 12 years. In 1943, he entered the military and attended Chaplain's School at Harvard. He served at Fort Lee, Virginia; Korea; Japan; and Fort Bragg, North Carolina.

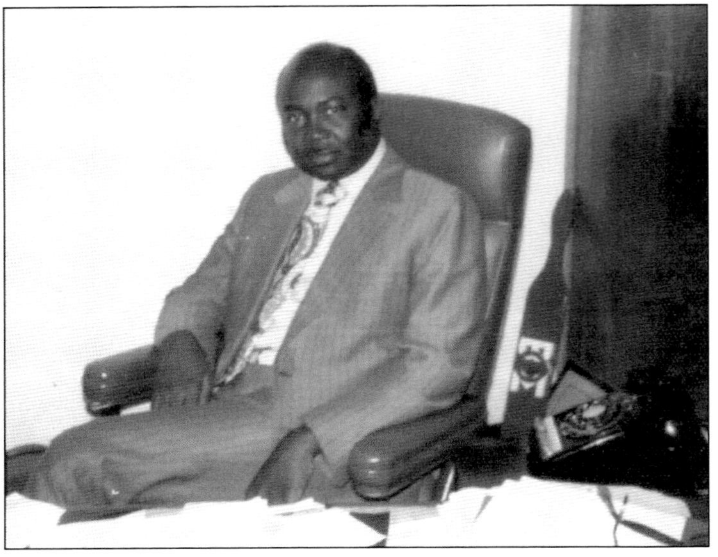

Attorney F. Malcolm Cunningham (1927–1978) came to Palm Beach County and opened his law practice in 1953. He was elected to the Riviera Beach City Council in 1962 and served three terms. The African-American Bar Association in Palm Beach County bears his name.

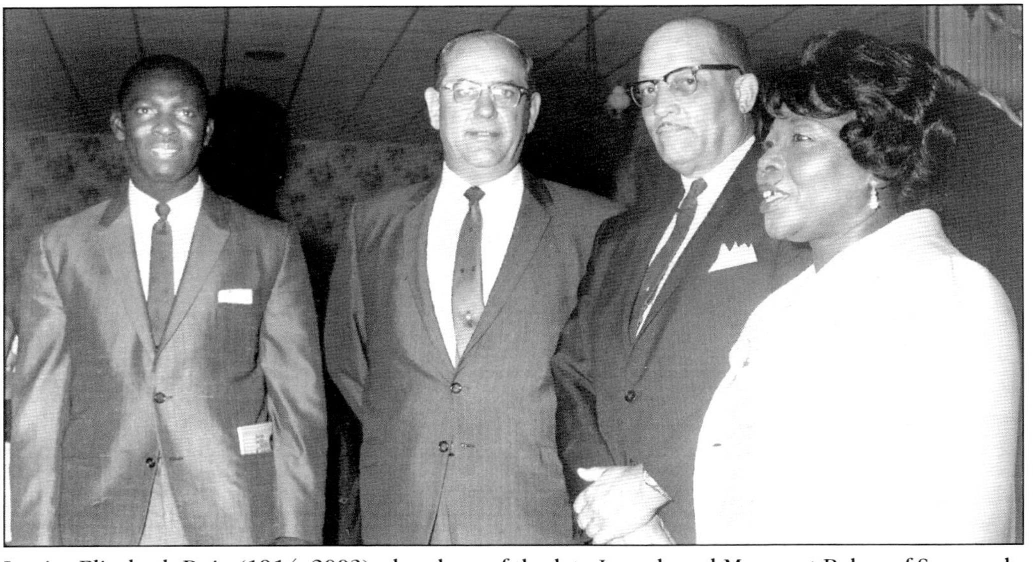

Louise Elizabeth Buie (1914–2003), daughter of the late Joseph and Margaret Baker of Savannah, came to Florida in 1925. In 1937, she joined the local branch of the NAACP and worked her way up from the entertainment, membership, and finance committees to assistant secretary to president in 1954, a position she held until 1968. She worked for African Americans' right to vote in Democratic primaries with the Palm Beach County Voter's League. Through voting came new schools, African-American policemen, and improved streets and other facilities. Suits were filed to open public golf courses and other facilities, and restaurants and hotels were opened through the Council of Human Relations. Mrs. Buie has gone into every area—education, public facilities, housing, labor, voting rights, and penal institutions—with dedication and the hope that African Americans will enjoy the same rights and privileges as others. Mrs. Buie had the Skypass Bridge over the Port of Palm Beach at Riviera Beach dedicated in her honor in 2004. Pictured above are, from left to right, Roderick Stevens of Stevens Brothers Enterprises; Dan Gaynor, County Commission chair; Herbert H. Tate, New Jersey Civil Rights attorney; and Louise Buie.

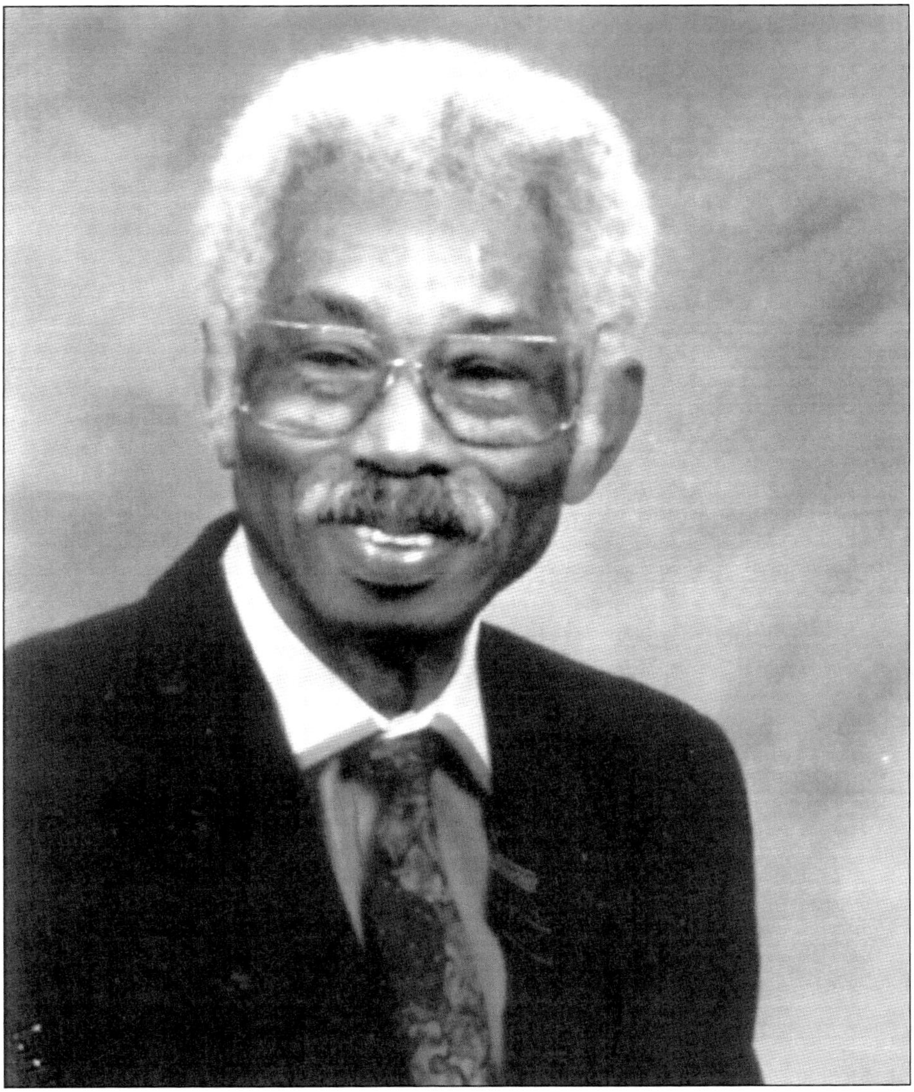

William Meredith Holland Sr. was born in Live Oak, Florida, on February 6, 1922. He graduated from Jones High School in Orlando and from Florida A&M University with a bachelor's degree. He served in the army for a short while and attended law school at Boston University in the 1940s. He came to this area in 1954, becoming the first African-American attorney to practice in Palm Beach County. In 1956, Holland took his six-year-old son to Northboro Elementary School in West Palm Beach, less than two miles from his home, but was politely refused entry. Holland filed suit against the school district and filed a class action suit on behalf of all African Americans in 1958. Token integration took place in 1961, when four black students entered a white school. By 1973, the system was fully integrated. Holland worked diligently to integrate the transportation system to and from the airport and opened golf courses, swimming pools, playgrounds, beaches, and fair housing. He served as a municipal judge in Riviera Beach from 1973 to 1977. Amid death threats, this Civil Rights pioneer remained steadfast in his efforts to bring change in Palm Beach County. He is the first African American in Palm Beach County to have a building named in his honor, the Fulton-Holland School District Service Center.

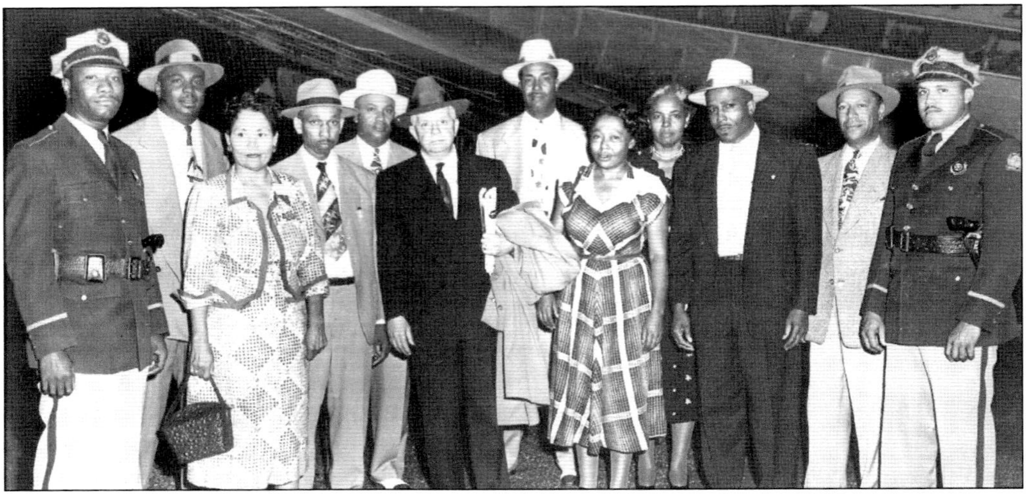

Walter White, president of the NAACP, visits the Palm Beaches. Pictured are, from left to right, Officer Primus Green, Wyle Blye, Ann Brewer, unidentified, Sheriff Burney, Walter White, unidentified, Annie L. Motley, unidentified, a Central Life Insurance agent, funeral director George R. Coleman, and Officer Holly Wilson.

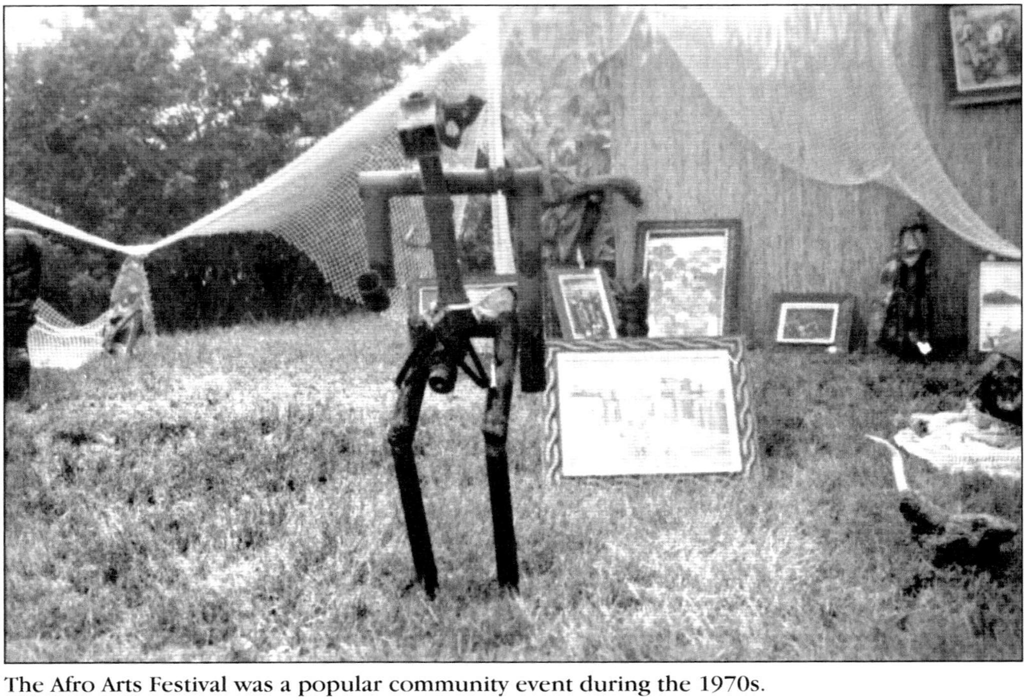

The Afro Arts Festival was a popular community event during the 1970s.

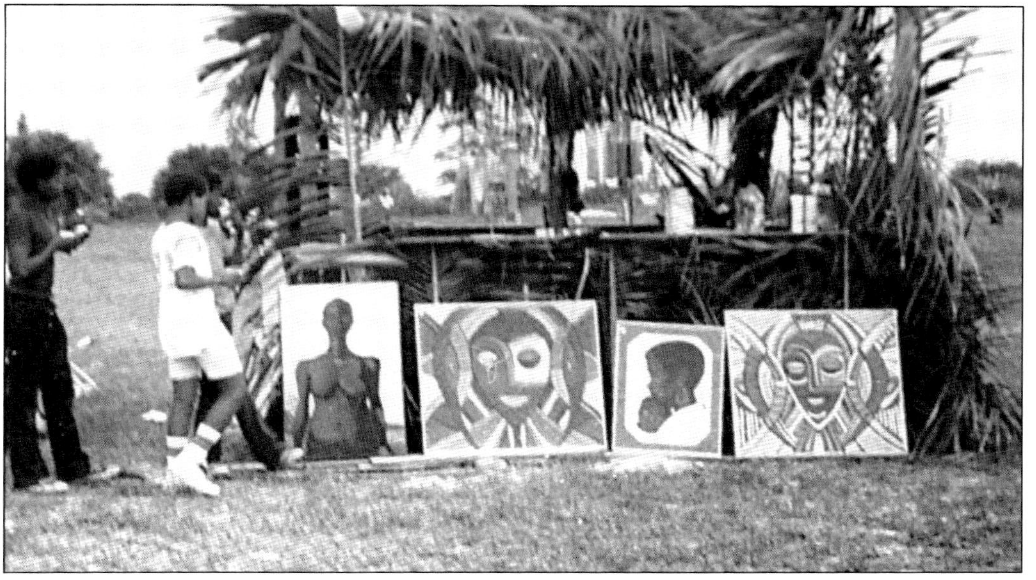

The festival served as an introduction of African art into the community.

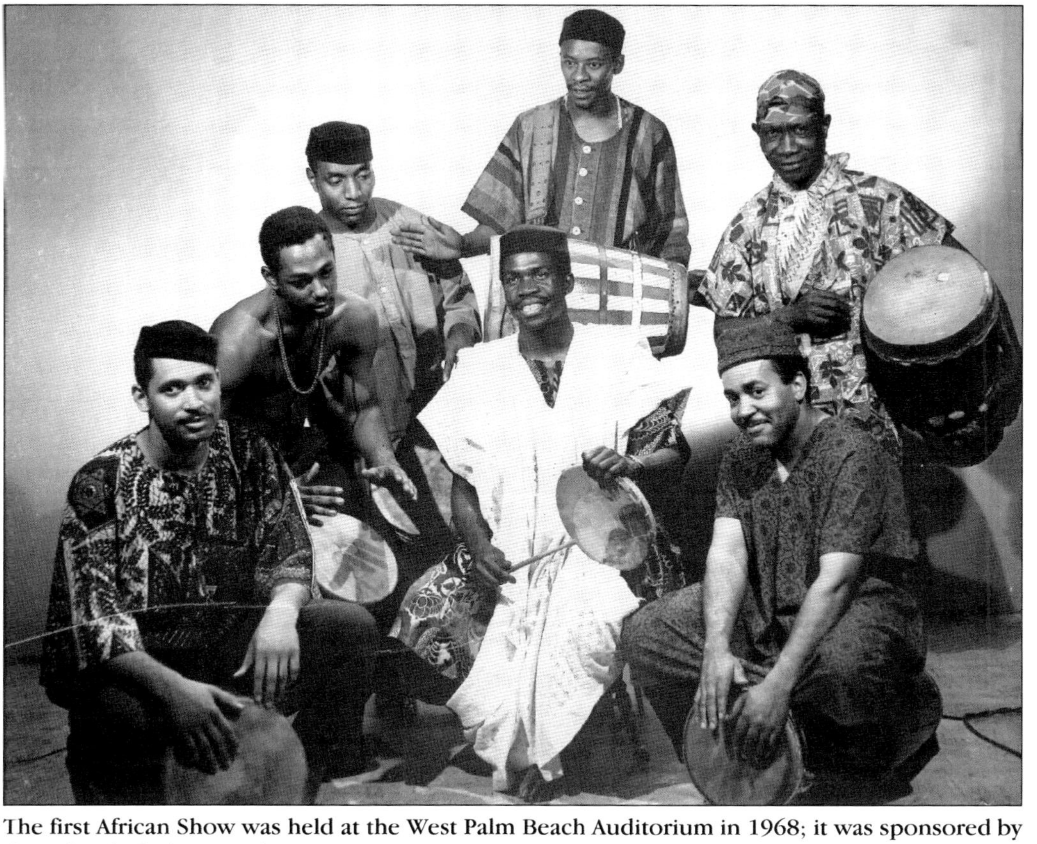

The first African Show was held at the West Palm Beach Auditorium in 1968; it was sponsored by the School of Charm and Dance.

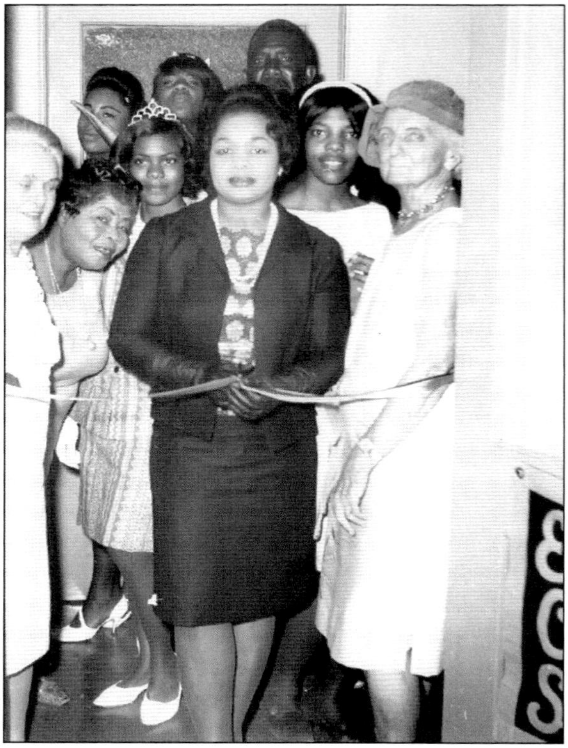

The opening of the School of Charm and Dance in 1967 at 205 Datura Street in West Palm Beach is seen here. Included in the image are Billie Wilson, Elouise Freeman, Audrethia Lowe, "Miss Teen" Brenda Johnson, Ada Stretcher, ribbon-cutter Everee Jimerson Clarke, Beverly Jimerson, and John Freeman.

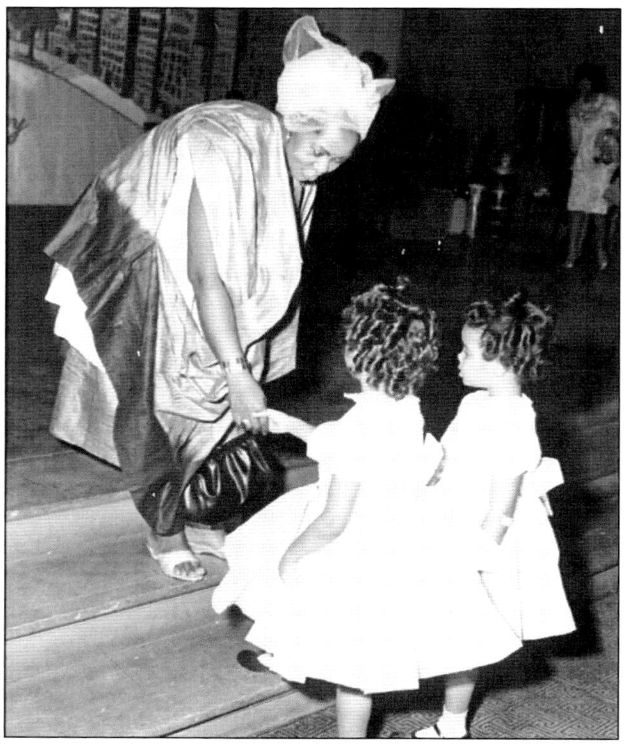

The Clarke sisters, Renee and Frances, meet to talk about dance with one of the performers of the African Ballet.

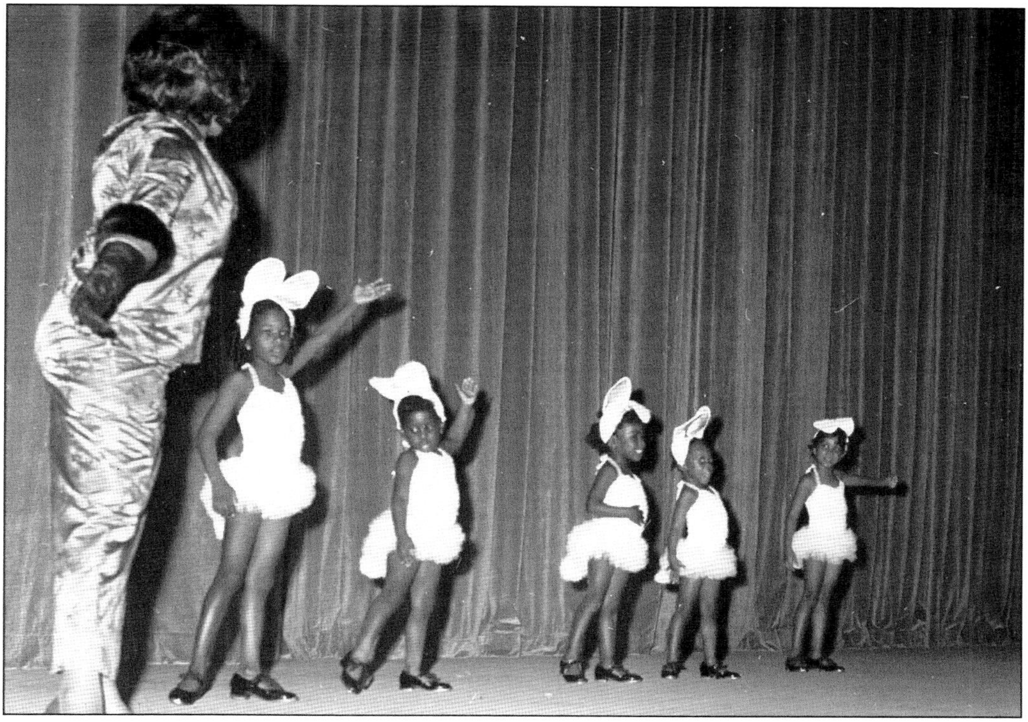

At the West Palm Beach Auditorium in June 1968, the "cute little bunnies" are, from left to right, Gia Tyus, Lena Locke, Mitzi Thomas, Cassandra Wilson, and Nicki Sims.

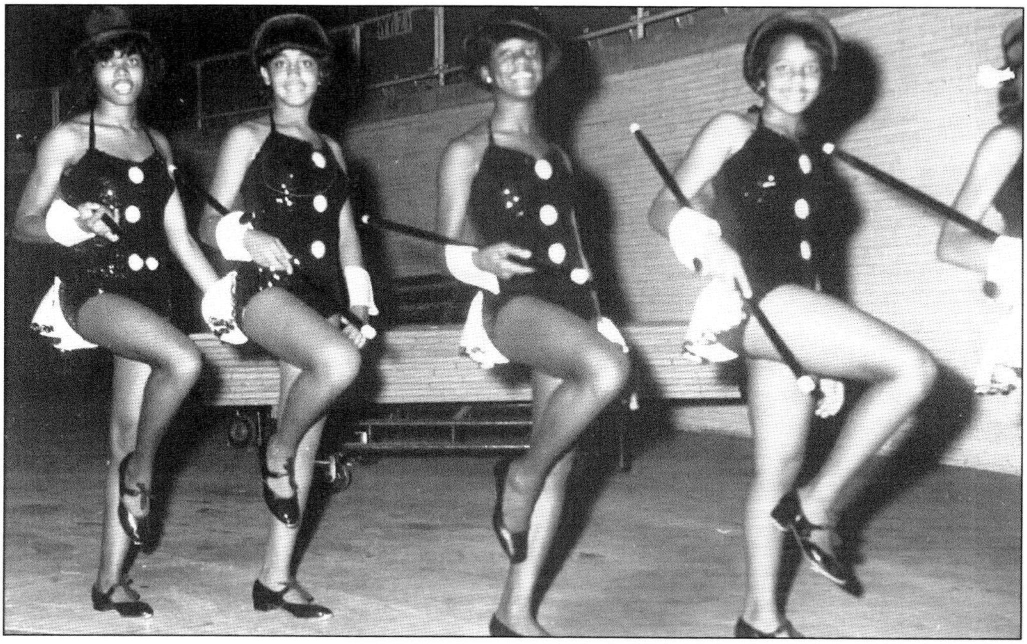

High steppers on stage at the West Palm Beach Auditorium in 1967 are, from left to right, Regina Bryant, Cheryl Harper, Marlena Owens, and Frances Clarke.

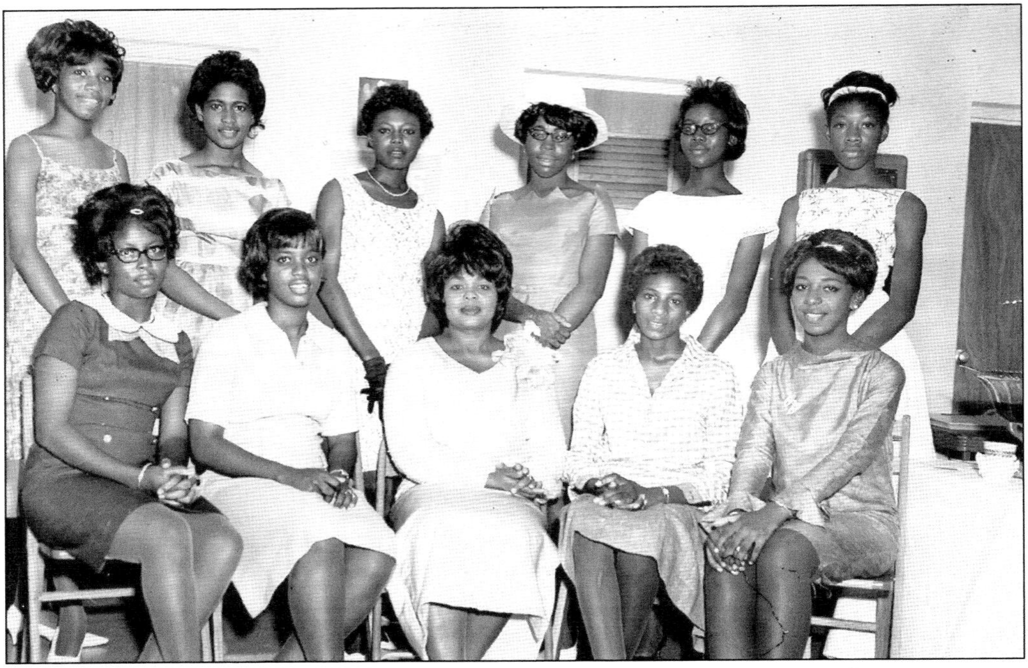

Entries for the first Miss Teen Pageant Florida in 1965 were, from left to right, (front row) Karen Cunningham, Joyce Ratcliff, Everee Clarke, Carrie Gamble, and Veta Moses; (back row) Trinette Rolle, Ana Marie Brunson, Brenda Rolle, Claretta Reid, Linda Smith, and Dianna Ross.

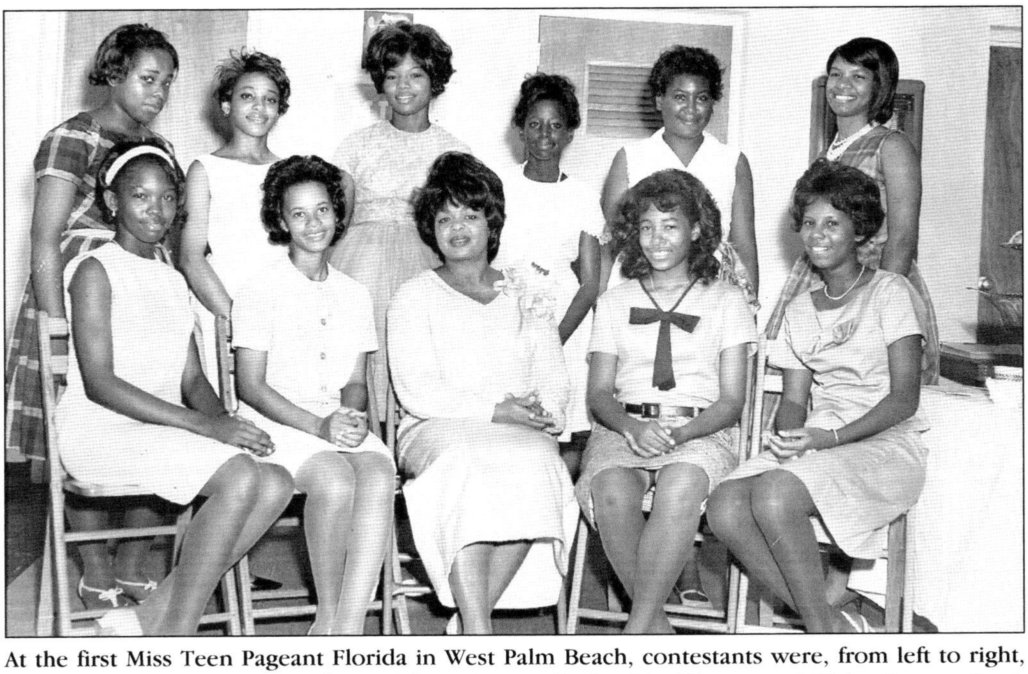

At the first Miss Teen Pageant Florida in West Palm Beach, contestants were, from left to right, (front row) Toni Gatlin, Pamela Bradshaw, Everee Clarke, Rita Wester, and Vivian Bryant; (back row) Sandra Taylor, four unidentified people, and Glenda Stevens.

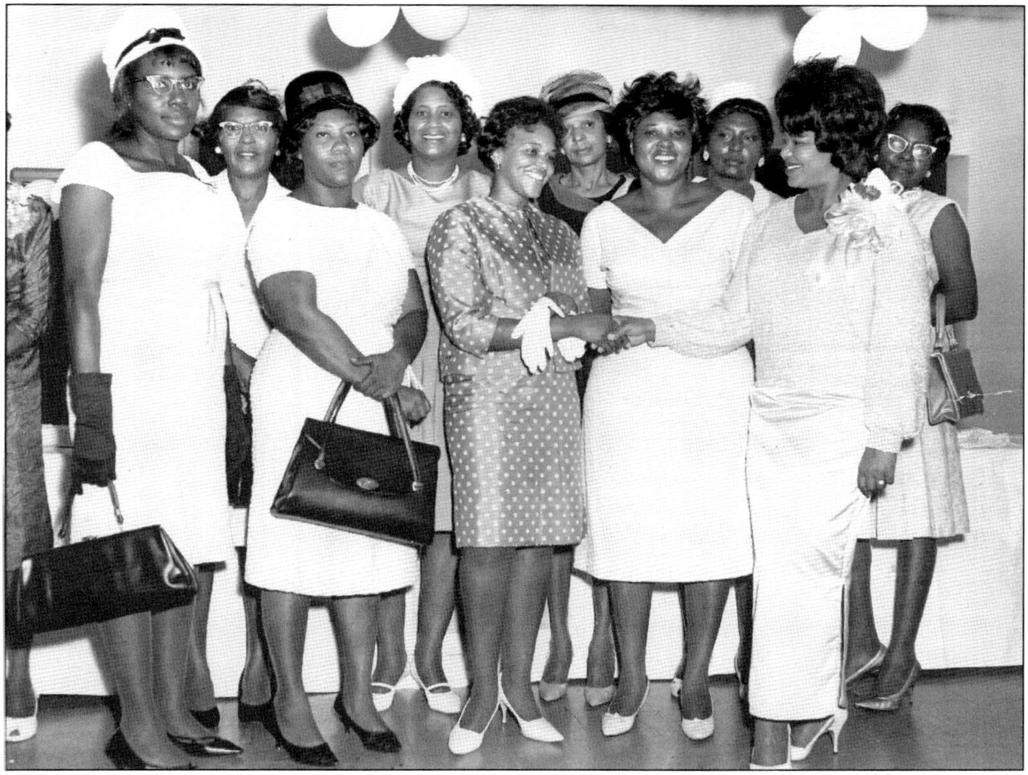

At the first Miss Teen Pageant Florida in 1965, the pageant mothers pose for a photograph.

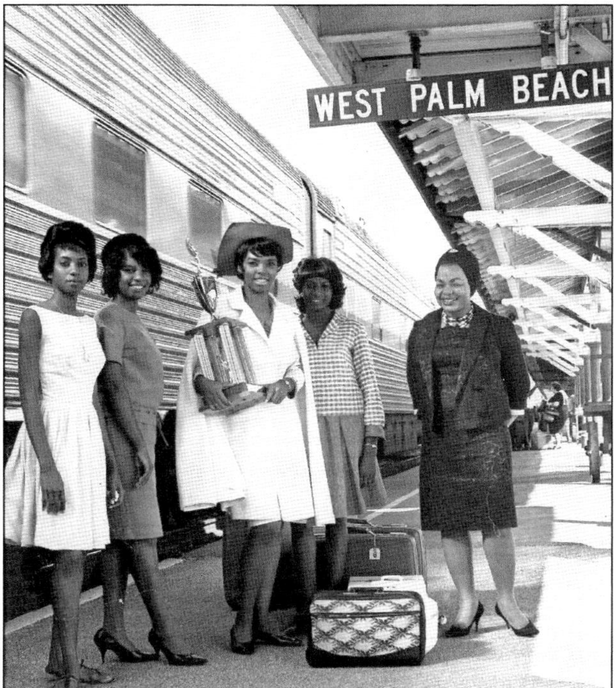

Miss Teen New Jersey arrives in West Palm Beach for the first Miss Teen Pageant Florida in 1965. From left to right are Deatra Wright, Glenda Stevens, Miss Teen New Jersey Norrice Canady, Carrie Gamble, and Everee Clarke.

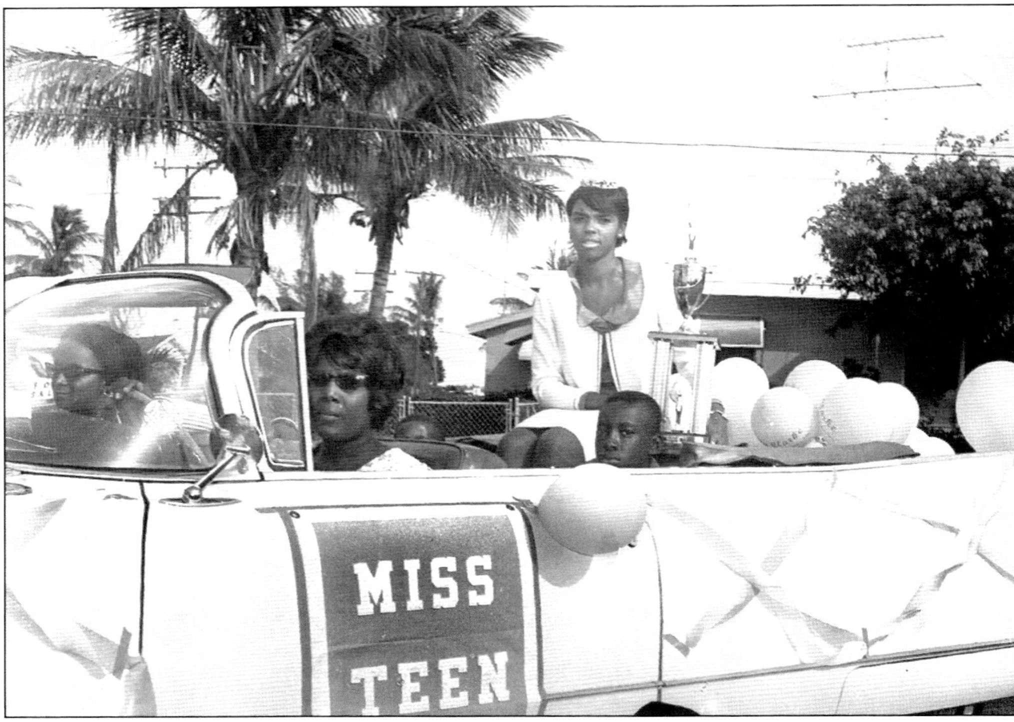

Norice Canady, Miss Teen New Jersey, rides in a West Palm Beach motorcade in 1965. Also in the car are driver Alzalee Colbert, Rosie Lee Jones, and Tommy Holmes.

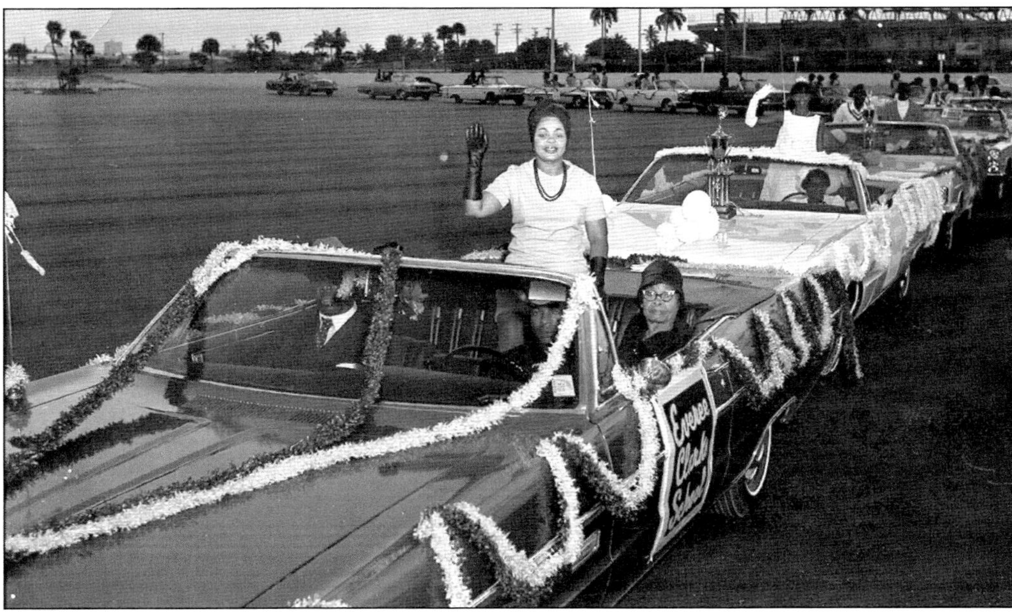

Two city motorcades were held to promote the Miss Teen pageant. The motorcade began in West Palm Beach and travelled to Riviera Beach. This picture shows the long motorcade around the West Palm Beach Auditorium, where the pageant was held.

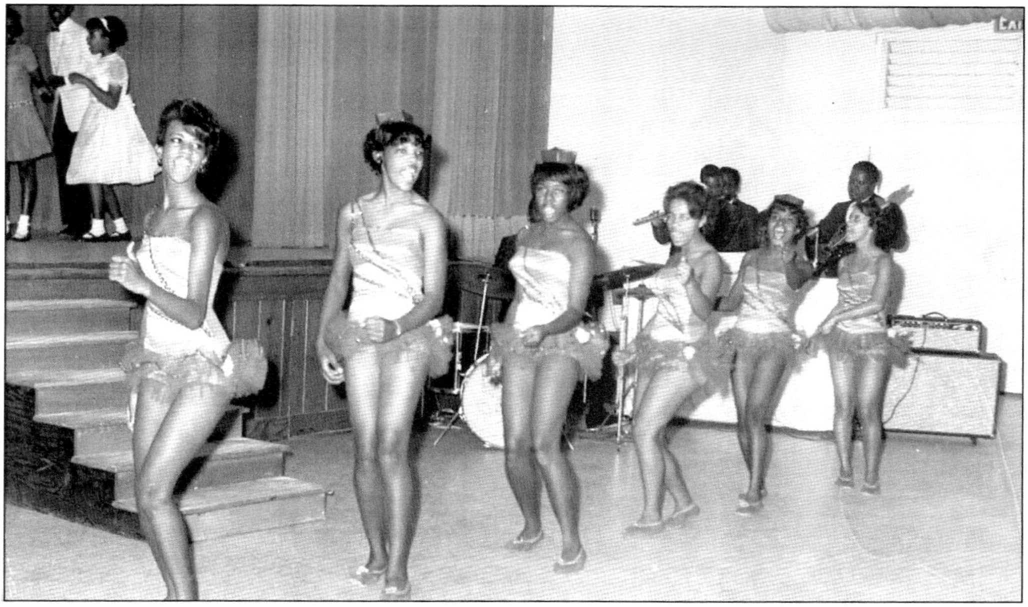

Here are Miss Teen Dancers at the Colonades Beach Hotel in 1967. From left to right are Pat Harris, Brenda Johnson, Jessica Jimerson, Rita Wester, Cynthia Joseph, and Pamela Bradshaw. Music at the event was by the Ray Nelson Group. Orville Lawton is dancing on stage with two junior contestants.

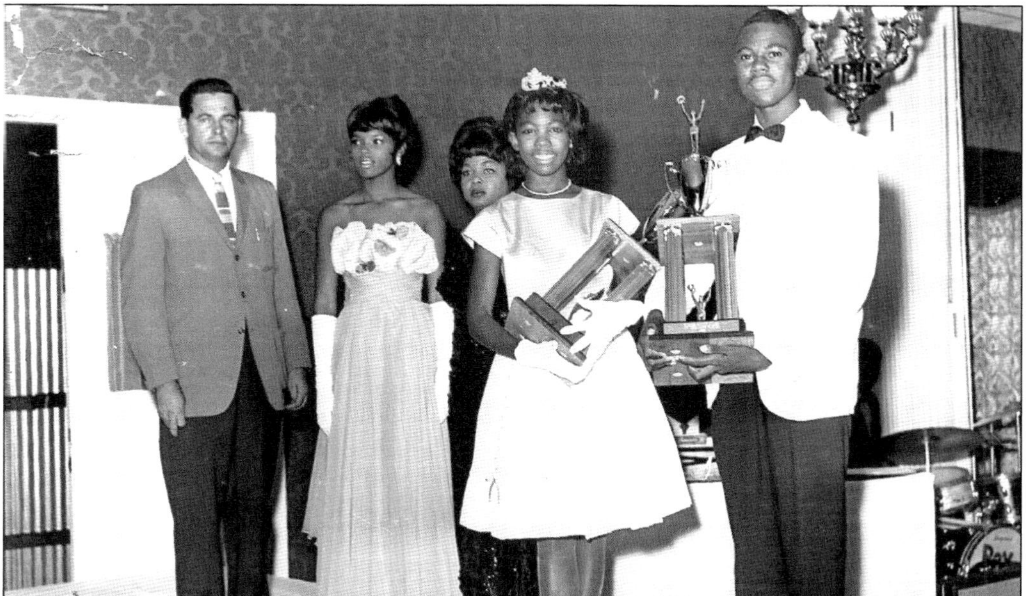

The first Miss Teen–Mr. Debonair event in Florida was held at Captain Alex's Restaurant in Riviera Beach. From left to right are Riviera Beach mayor Jake Bozman, Miss Teen New Jersey Norice Canady, pageant director E.J. Clarke, Miss Teen Florida Gwendolyn "Toni" Gatlin, and Mr. Debonair Florida Orville Lawton.

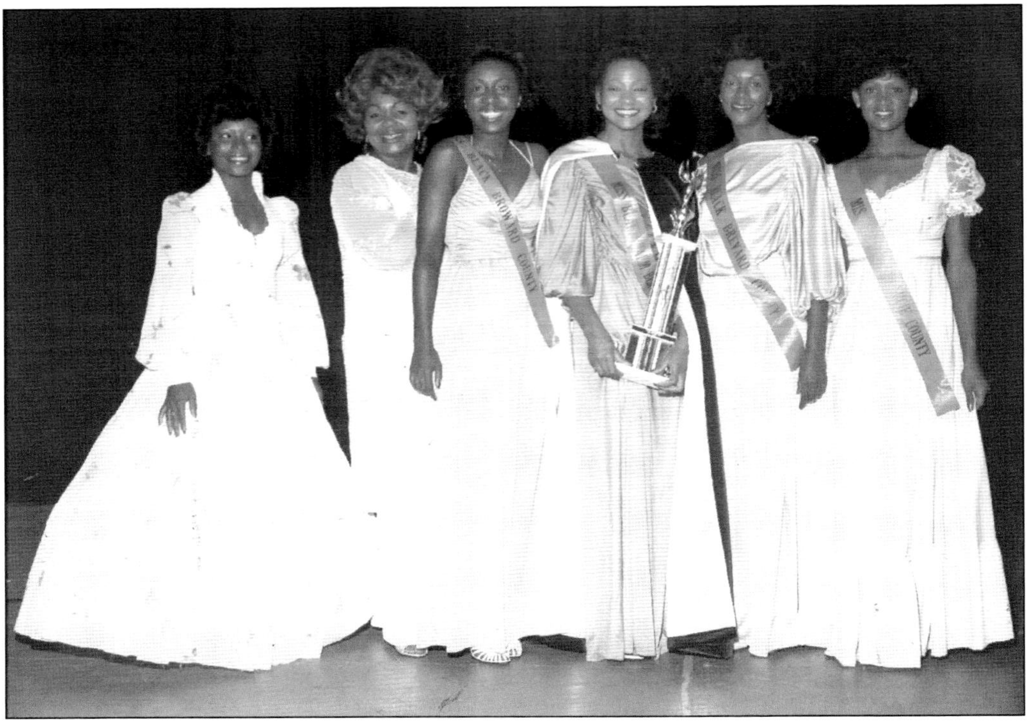

The winners in the Miss Black Florida Pageant 1979 are, from left to right, Miss Black America Hattie Rolle, Everee Clarke, Miss Black Florida (National Pageant) 1978 Debra Howard (Miss Broward County), Miss Palm Beach County Carla Warren, Miss Brevard County Donna Kitchen, and Miss St. Lucie County Brenda Gamble.

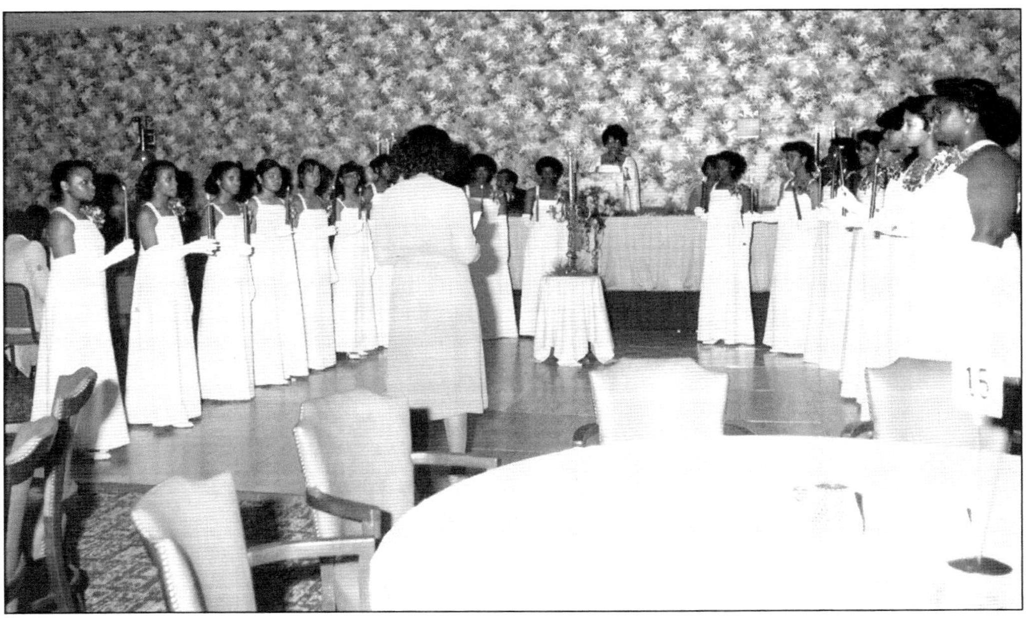

Shown here is the induction ceremony at the Elegante International Teen Club in 1981.

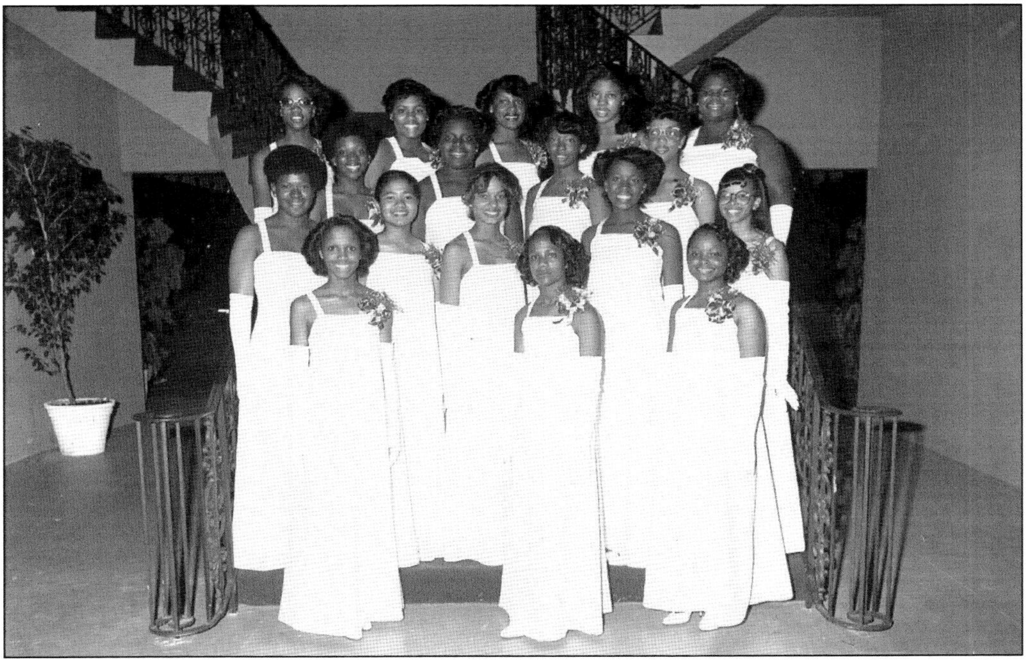

Included in this photo are Lavette Pittman, Denise Cone, Anita Jackson, Jana Tullus, Mimi Oliver, Eva Hill, Tamela Daniels, Lisa Pittman, Tina Johnson, Alva Bell, Gavis Ball, Cindy Gassett, Lori Allen, Stephanie Campbell, Rolanda Warren, Andrea Embery, and Dolvanya Mosby.

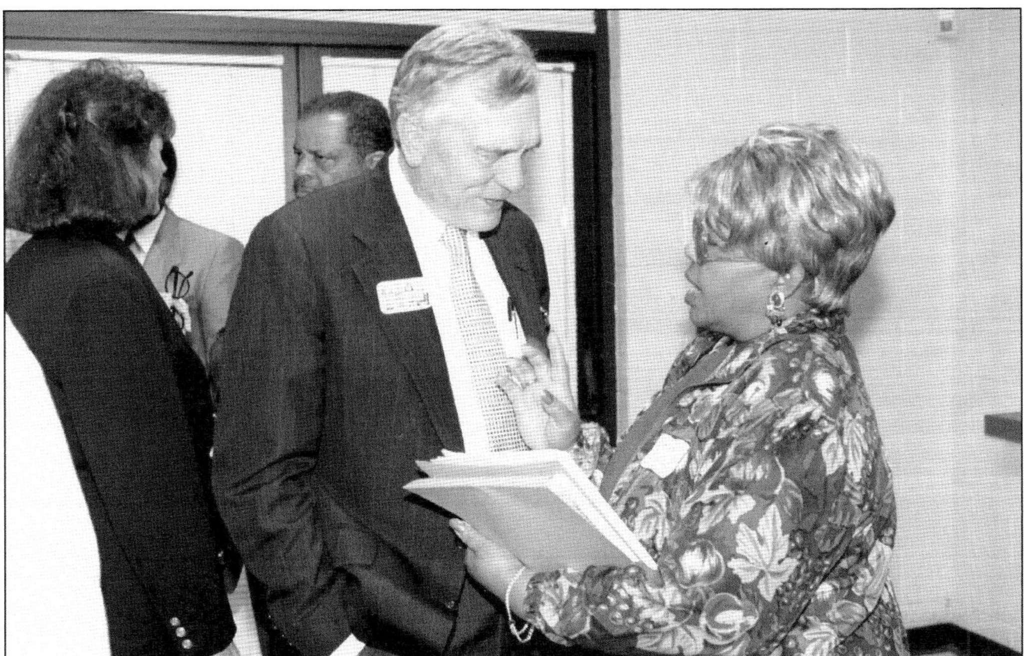

Gov. Lawton Chiles, shown here talking with Everee Clarke, visited a meeting at the Pleasant City Recreation Center in 1995 to receive a progress report on state-funded programs in the community.

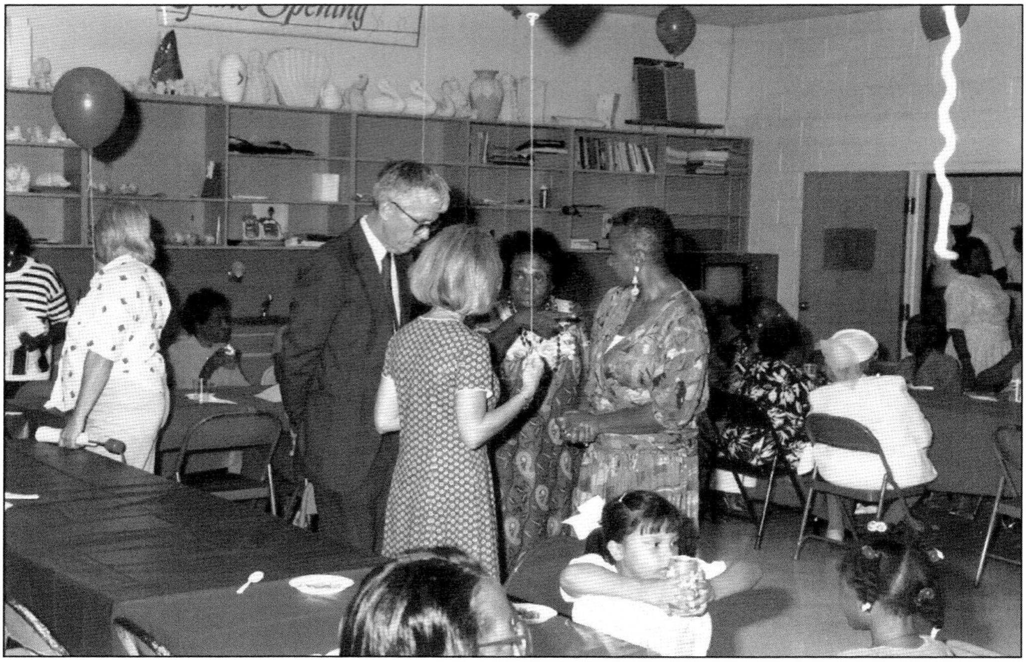

The first Pleasant City Family Reunion took place from July 4 to July 6, 1994. The first assembly was at the Pleasant City Recreation Center. Mayor Joel E. Daves and his wife welcome home former resident Dr. Leah Gaskin Fitchue, standing with Dr. Alice Moore.

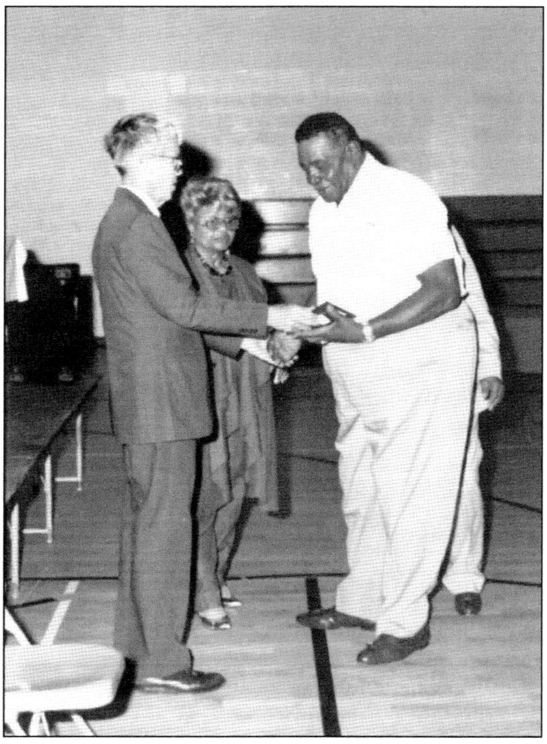

The Pleasant City Family Reunion 1994 honored the pioneers. Mayor Joel E. Daves presents an award to pioneer and businessman Forest Parson.

Elouise Wilson, Dr. Leah Gaskin-Fitchue, and Rosie Lee Jones were guests at Pleasant City Community Reunion 1994.

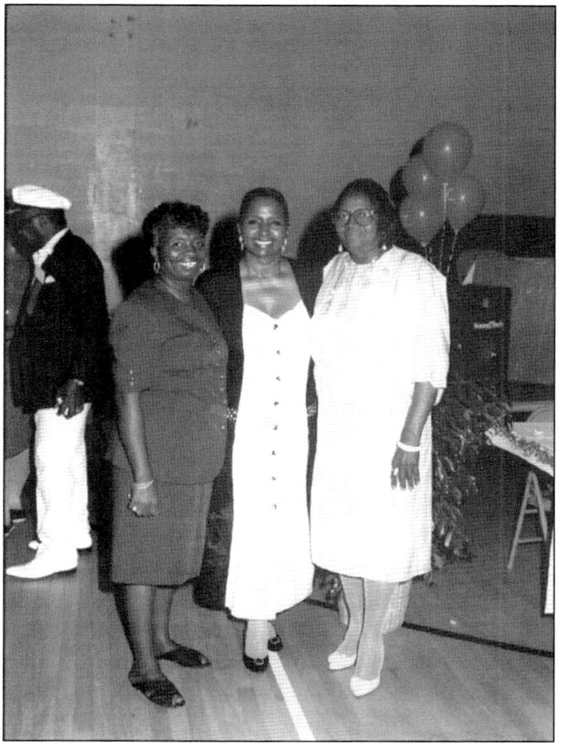

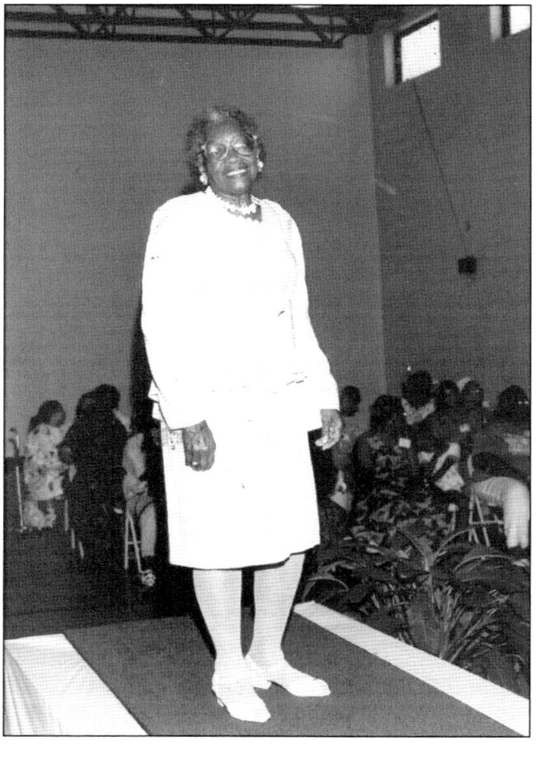

Grecolia Jackson, born and reared in Pleasant City, was a member of the board of directors for the family reunion committee. She had to sacrifice her home to the redevelopment effort to build the new elementary school. She now resides in Daytona Beach with her son.

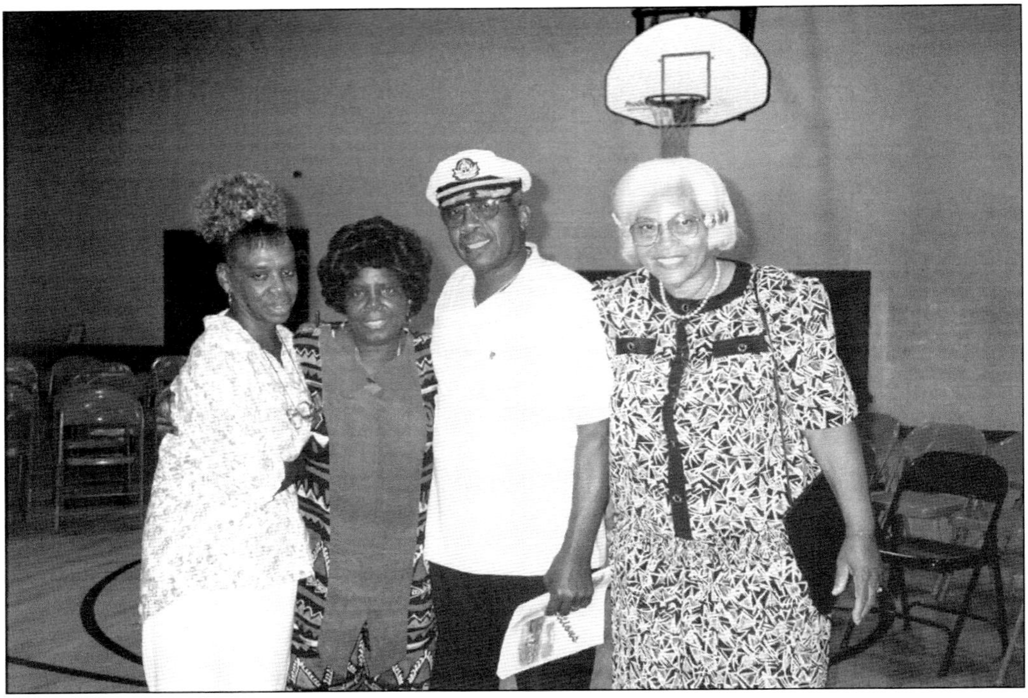

Pictured from left to right are Alice Foster, Olga Wallace Gidion, George Newbold, and Mrs. Isadore Toombs.

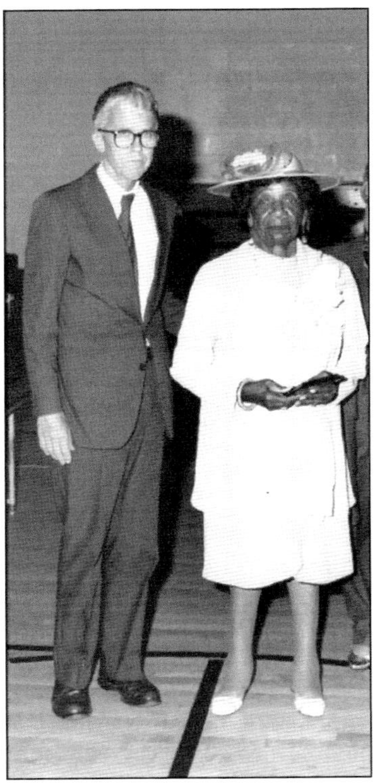

Pleasant City Community Reunion 1994 featured a ceremony in which pioneer Mildred Pryor Burroughs received an award from Mayor Daves.

Pansy Harper, granddaughter of pioneer Millie Gildersleeve, receives an award during pioneer night at the community reunion.

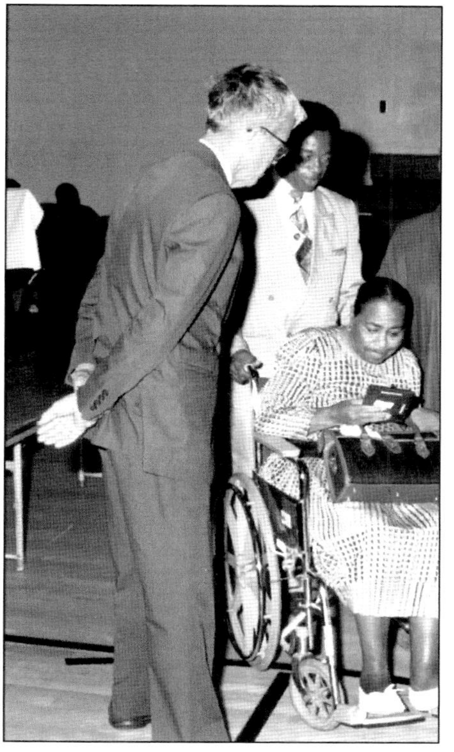

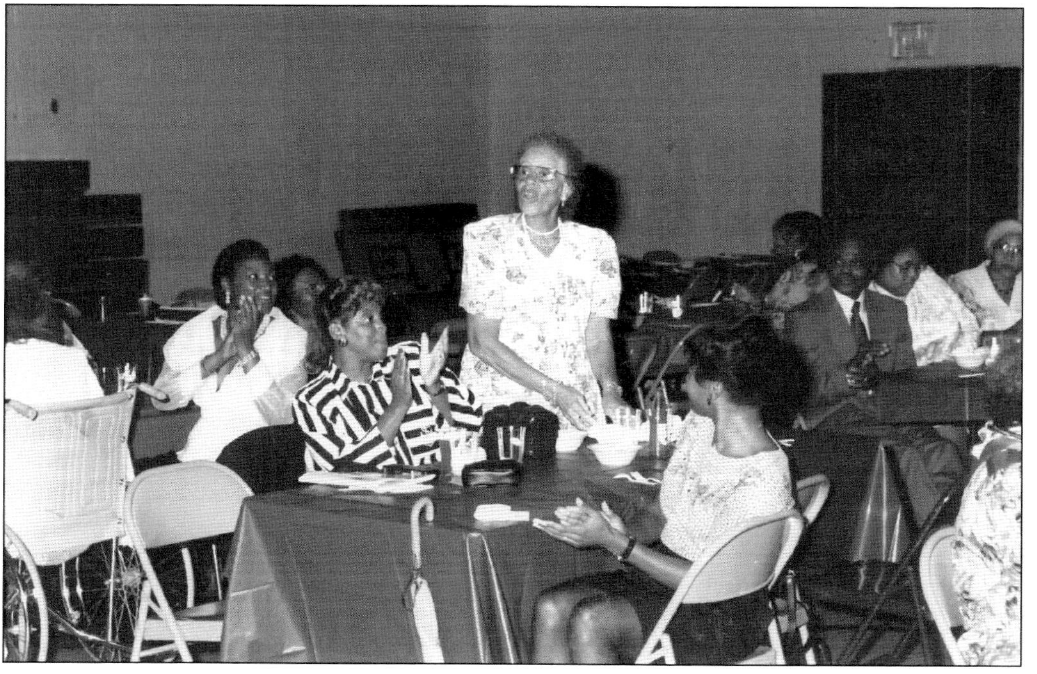

Lula Thomas, the only surviving teacher from the old Pleasant City Elementary School, is applauded at the first Pleasant City community reunion.

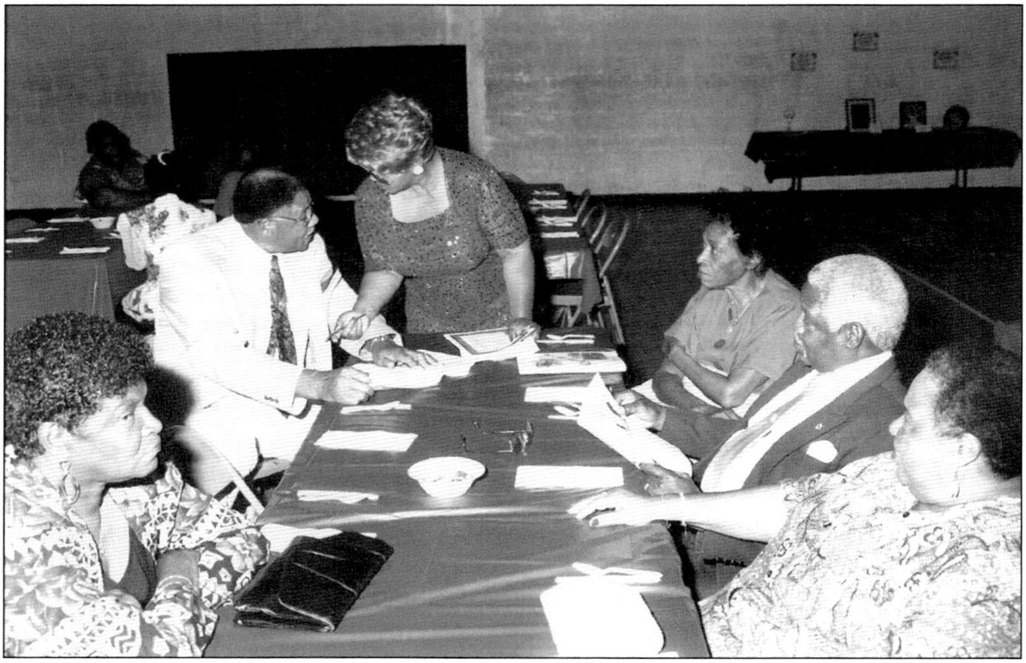

Pictured at Pleasant City Community Reunion 1994 are, from left to right, sister Calli Collier, honoree Dr. Leon Collier, Everee Clarke, sister Bessie Harvey, brother-in-law Al Edden, and sister Lillian Collier Edden.

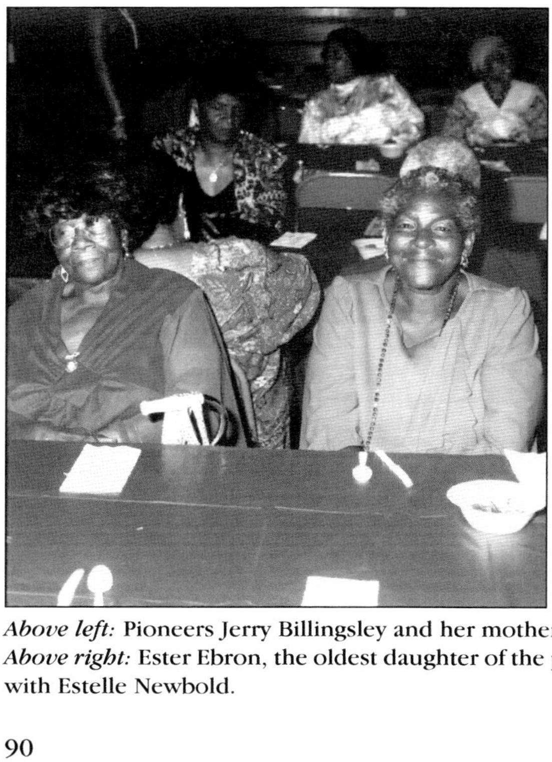

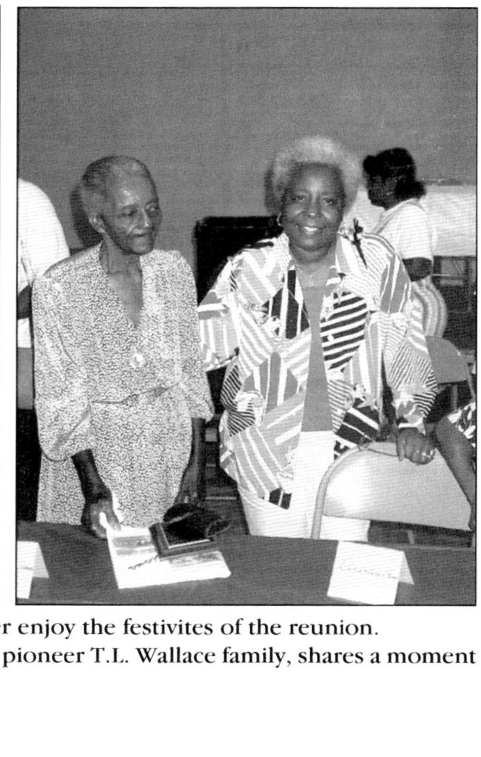

Above left: Pioneers Jerry Billingsley and her mother enjoy the festivites of the reunion.
Above right: Ester Ebron, the oldest daughter of the pioneer T.L. Wallace family, shares a moment with Estelle Newbold.

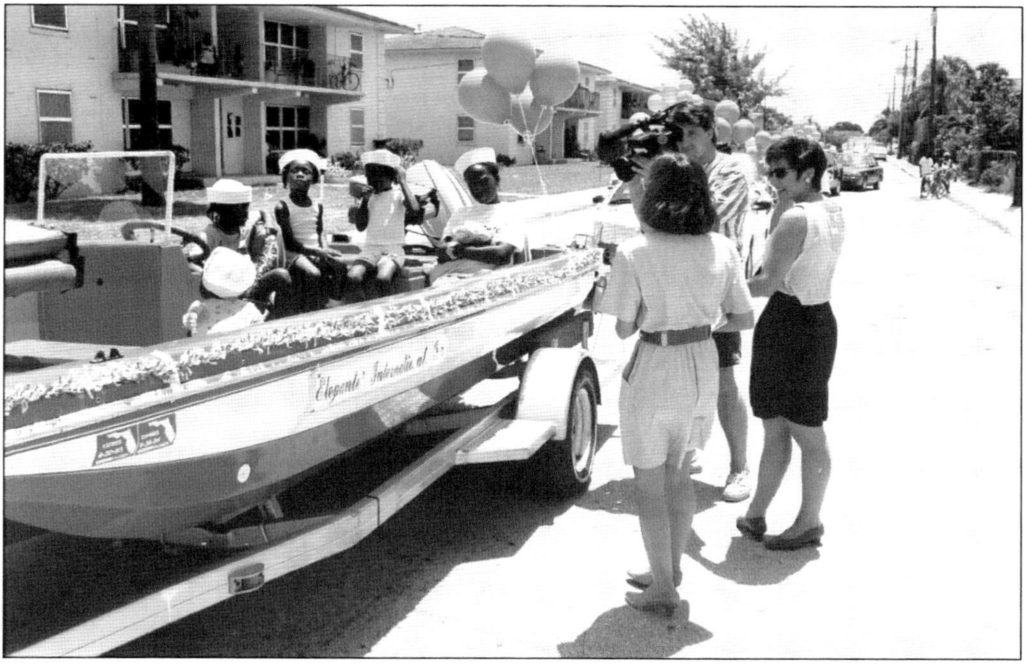

The first Pleasant City Family Reunion was held from July 4 to July 6, 1994. The event brought back to the community Pleasant City residents who had not been home for as many as 40 years.

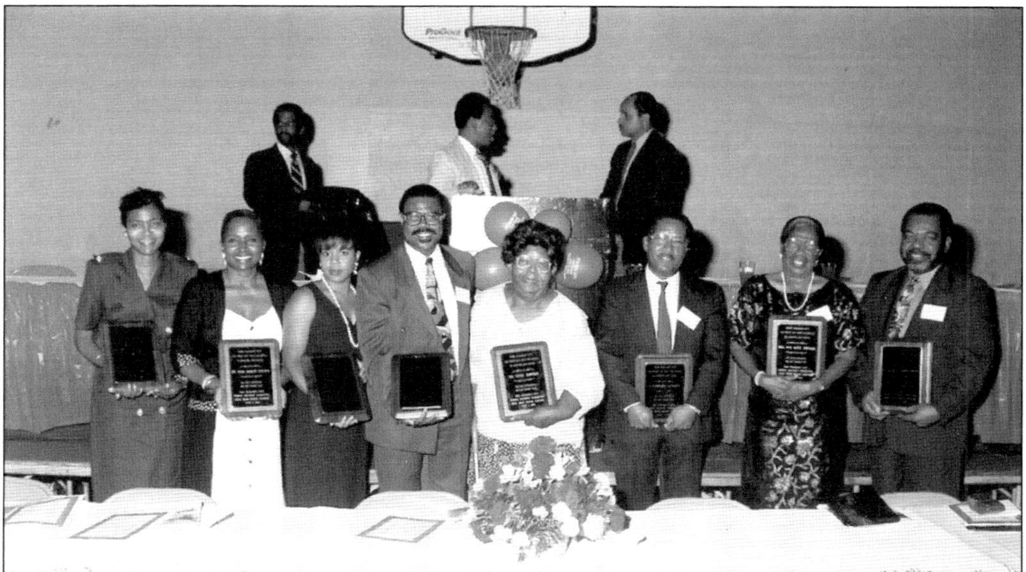

Winners of the Achievement Award of the first Pleasant City Community Family Reunion are, from left to right, Connie Ward, representing Mrs. Inez Peppers-Lovett in Education; Leah Gaskin Fitchue, Religion; Frances Yvette Clarke, Business; Dr. Orville Lawton, the Arts; Mrs. Mary Dawson, representing her son, Dr. Gene Dawson, in Science; J. Edward Kinsey, Housing Development; Mae Alice Daniels-Johnson, Education and Community Service; and Dr. A. Thomas White, director of Human Resources Development of Palm Beach County, Administration.

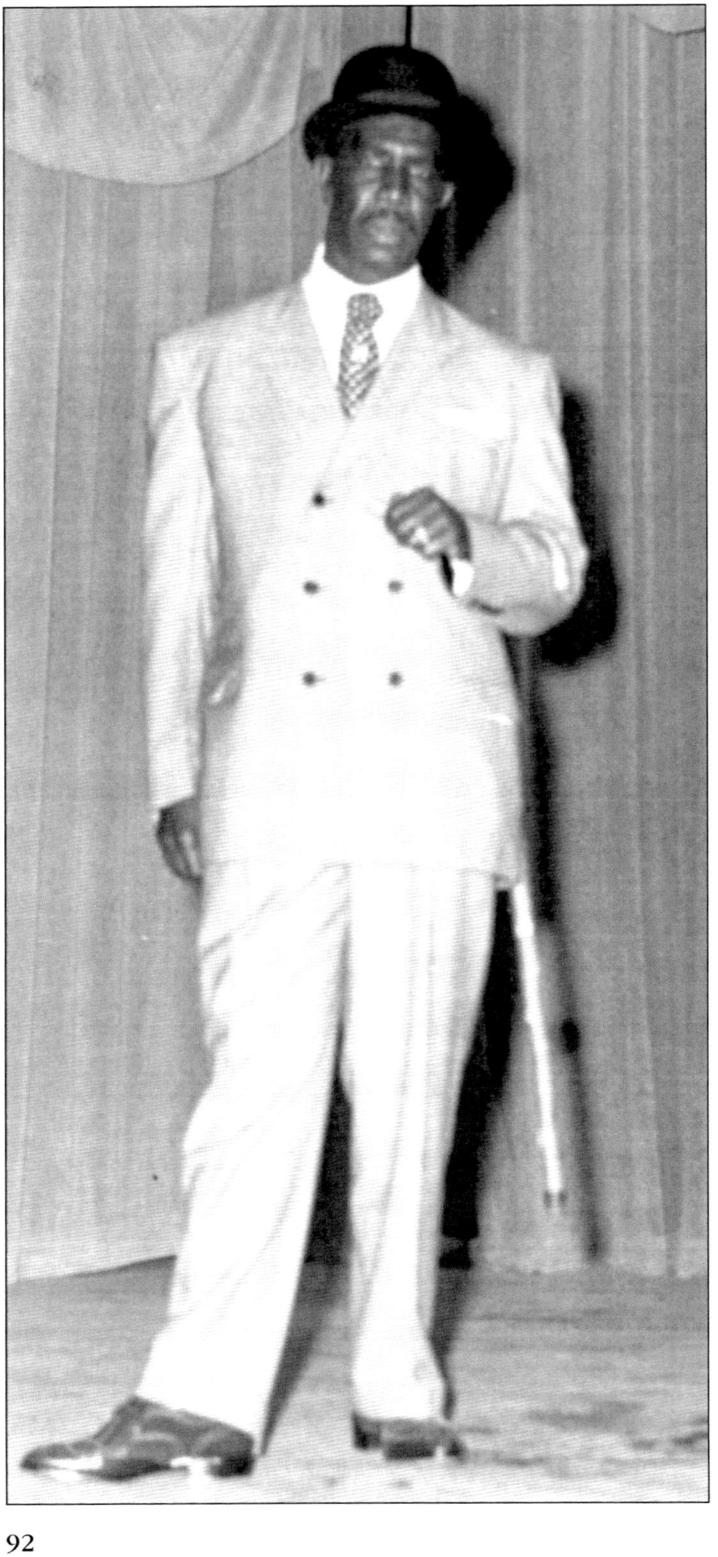

John Freeman was a master chef and fashion model. During the summer, he spent his time at a seaside resort restaurant serving the rich and famous in New Jersey. He was known for his fine clothes and accessories.

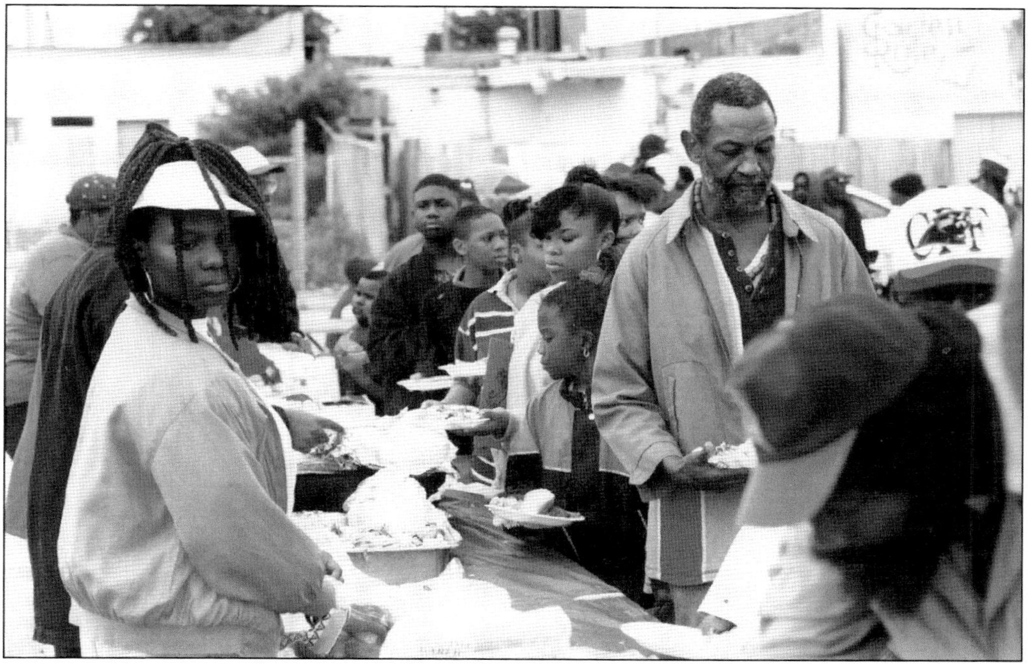

Hundreds of people from all over the city came out to share the holiday spirit in Pleasant City at the 1994 Community Christmas Celebration. Among them were a number of homeless people.

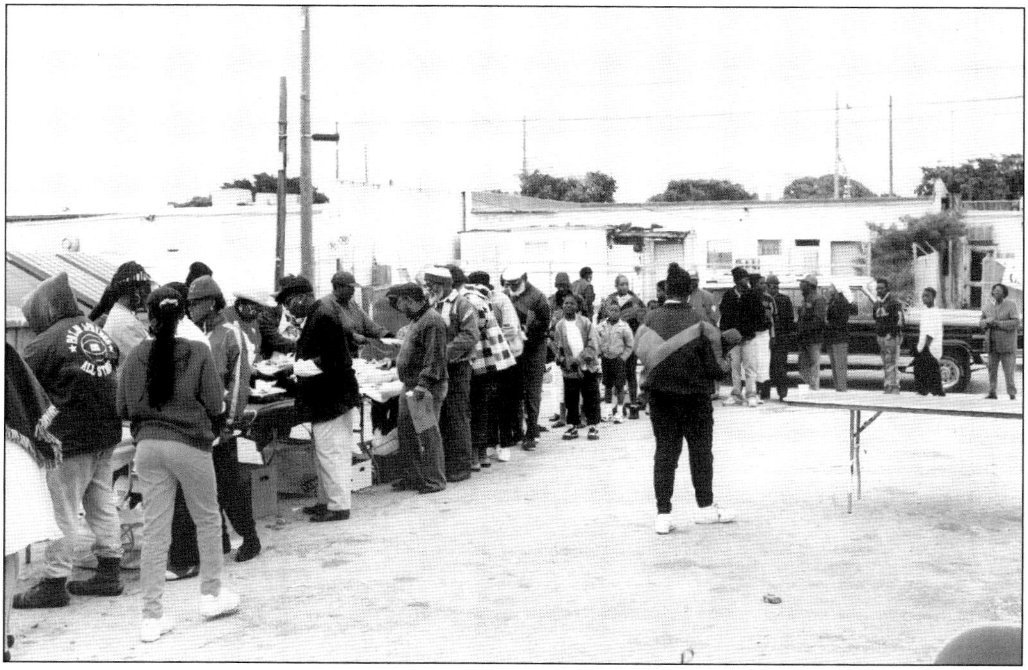

Large crowds and long lines of people wait for the food to be served at the 1994 Community Christmas Celebration.

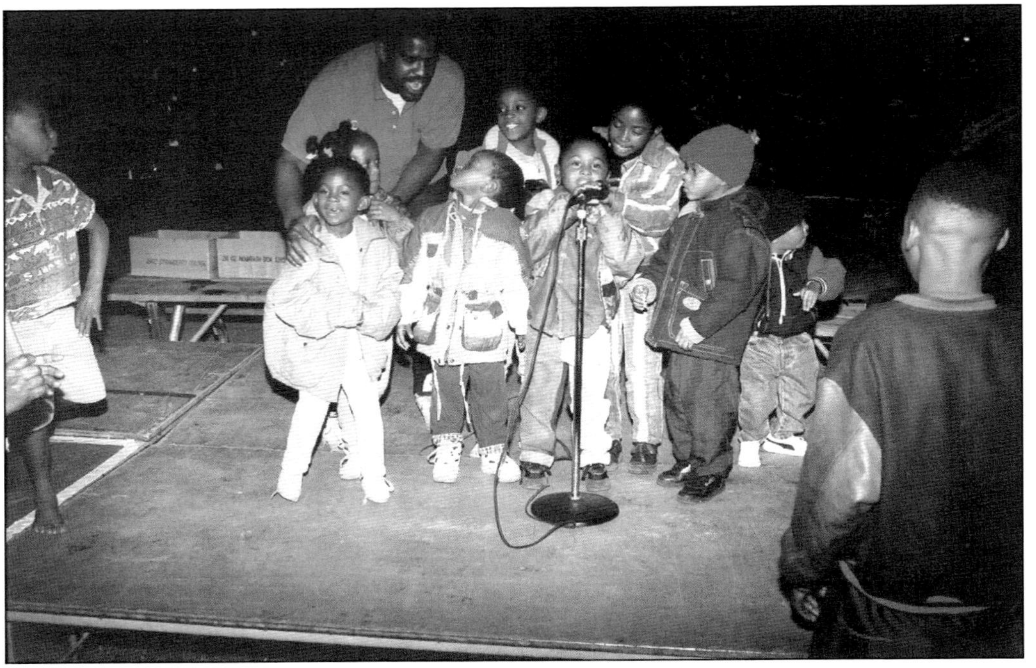

Peter Cleveland encourages youth to participate in singing carols.

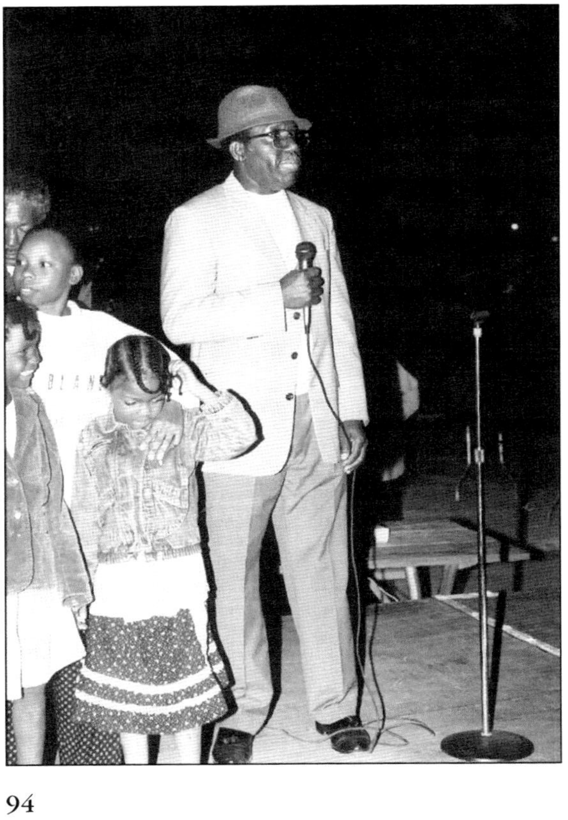

Rev. Joseph Tyson works with an older group of children who want to be in the spotlight.

Young ladies like Annie Potter, shown here, put on their finest to attend church and other special events.

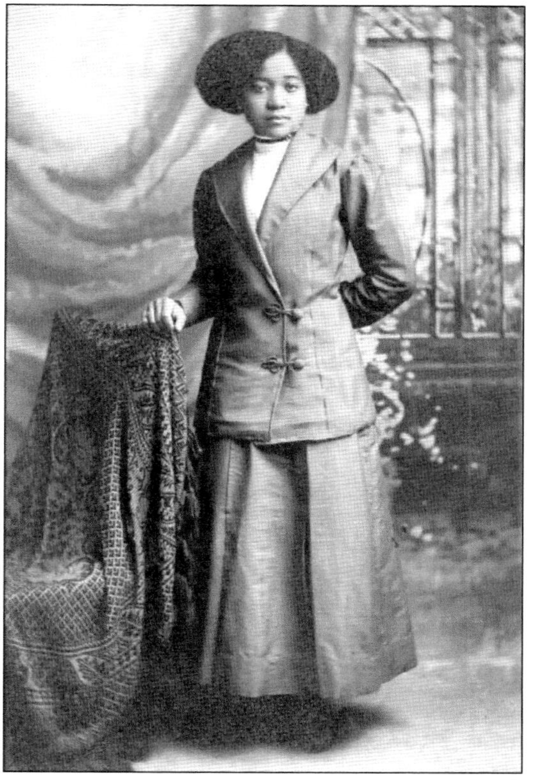

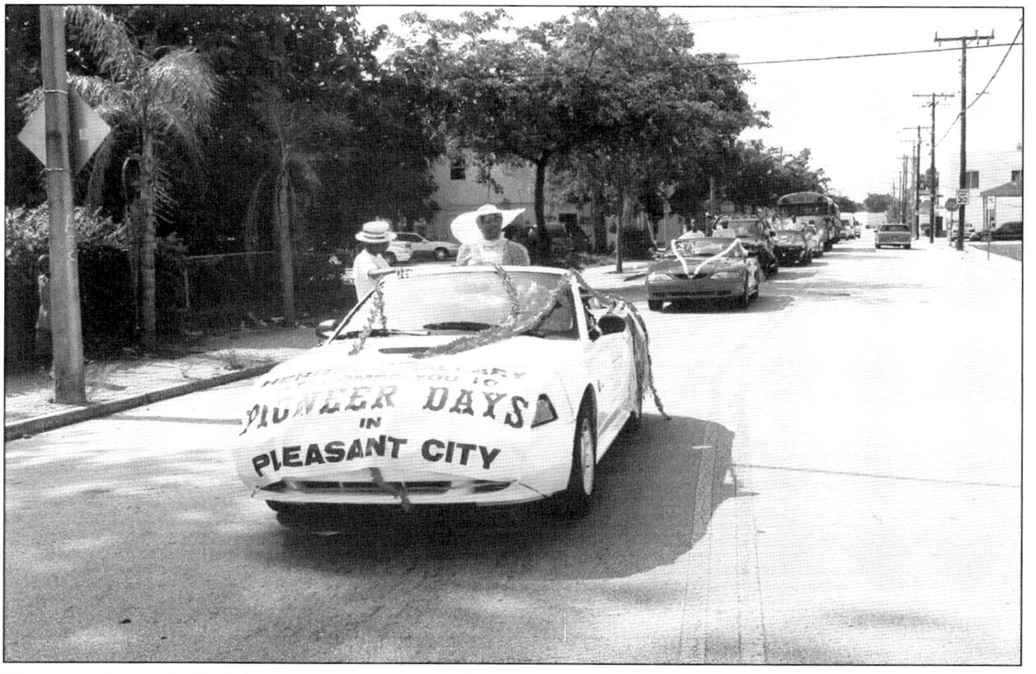

The grand marshal of the Pioneer Day Parade was Mayor Joel E. Daves of West Palm Beach.

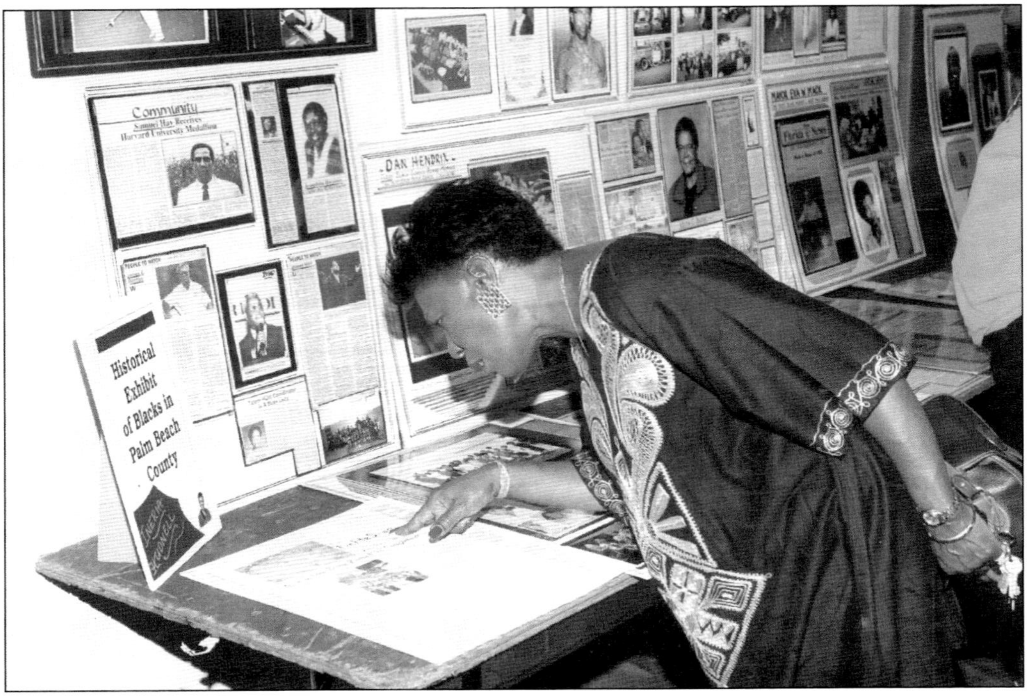

Palm Beach County commissioner Addie Greene visits the Pioneer Day Exhibit in 1999.

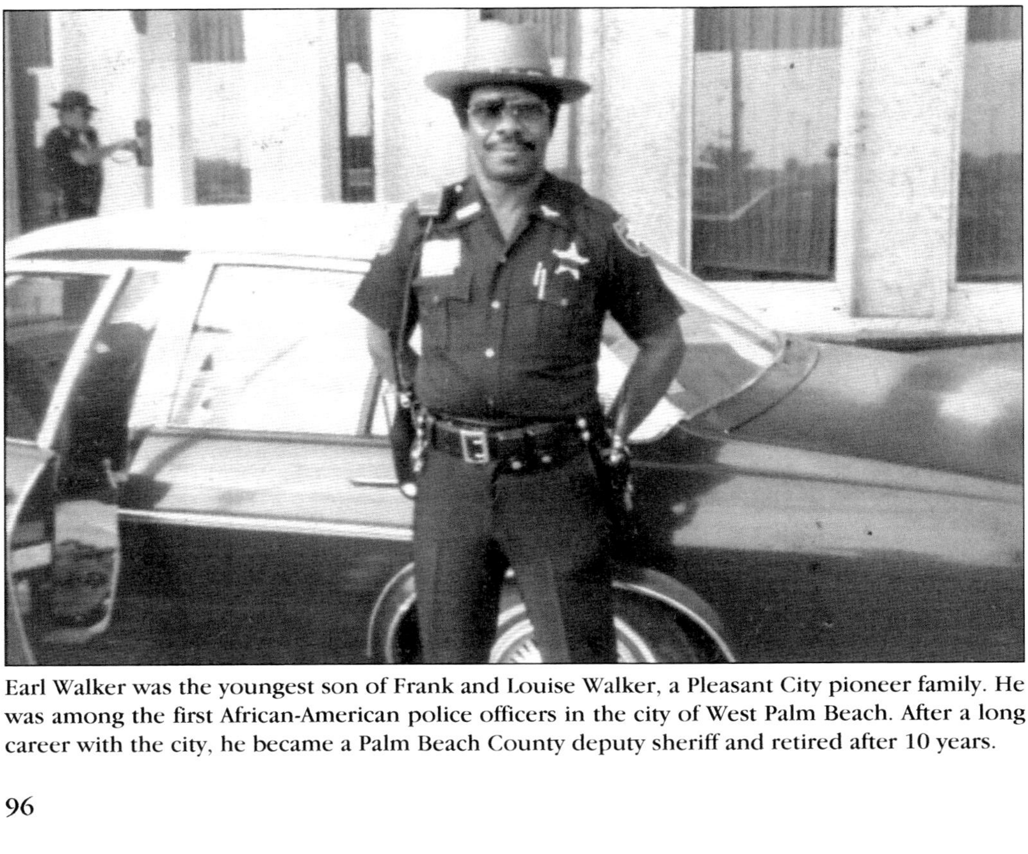

Earl Walker was the youngest son of Frank and Louise Walker, a Pleasant City pioneer family. He was among the first African-American police officers in the city of West Palm Beach. After a long career with the city, he became a Palm Beach County deputy sheriff and retired after 10 years.

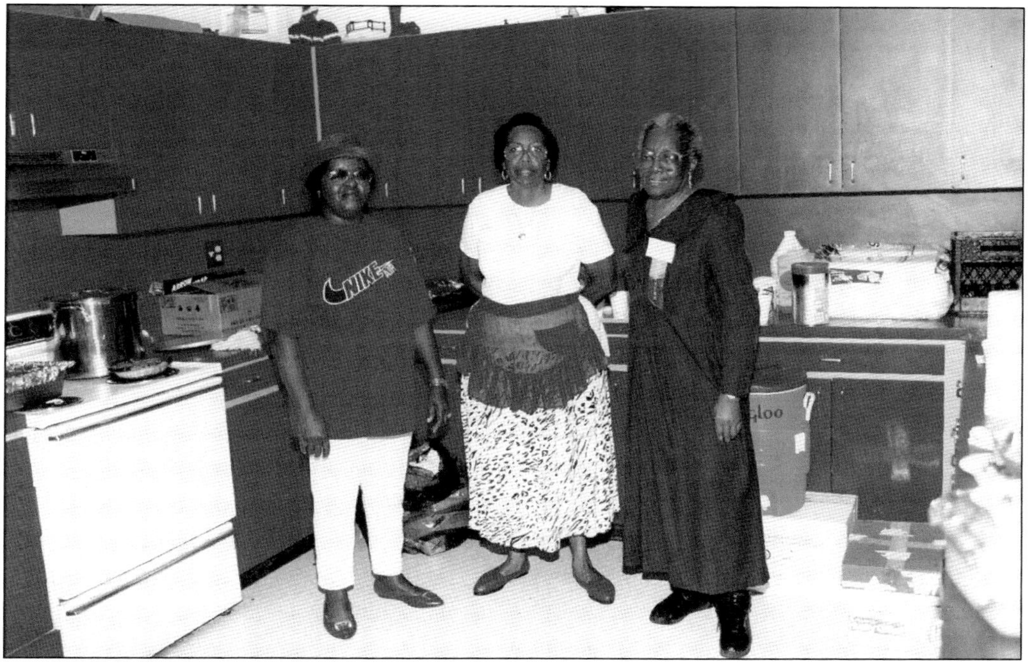

From left to right are Rosetta Whipple Lovett, Grace White, and Grecolia Jackson. They are serving dinner to Pioneer Day activity attendees.

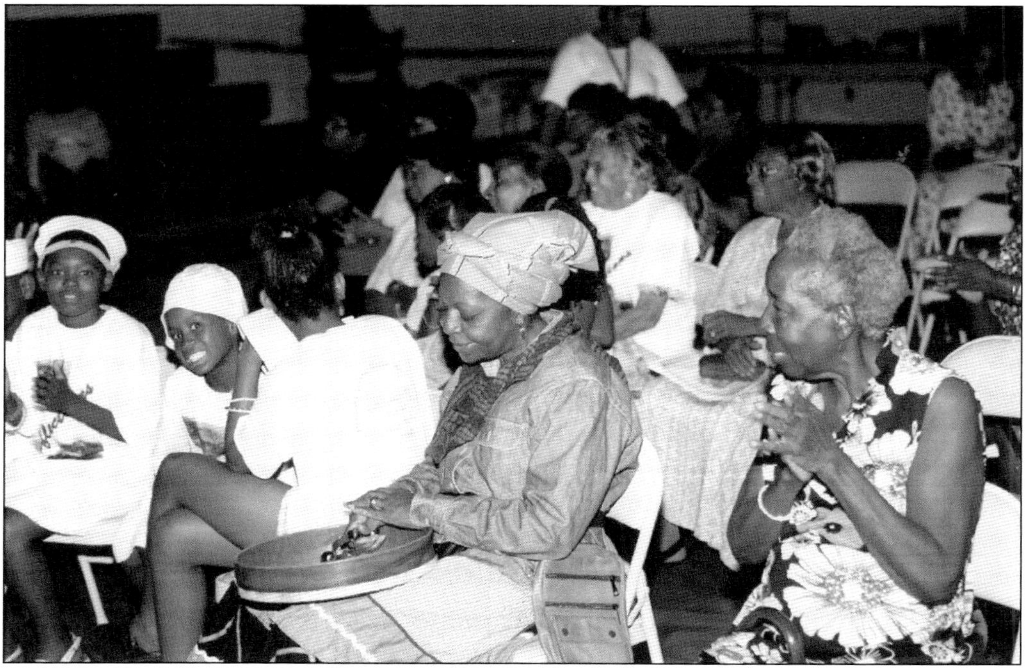

Youth dressed as pioneers participate in drumming experience and the play *Outstanding Women in Black History*.

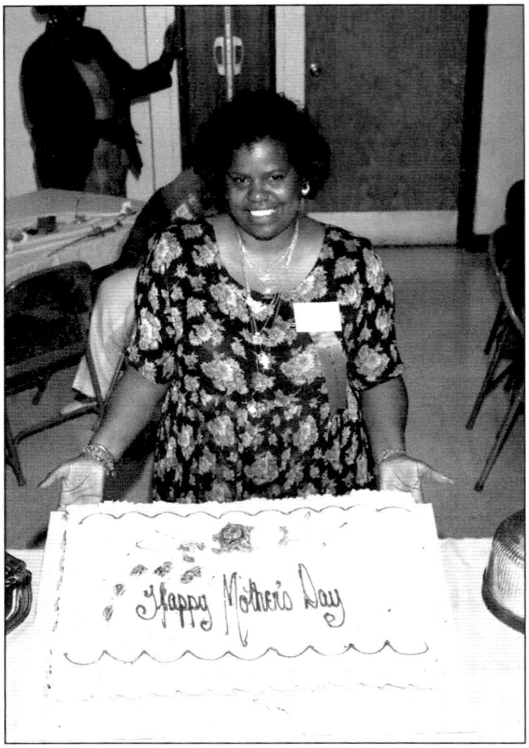

At a Salute to Mothers banquet, Annette Brown serves up Mothers' Day cake. Annette is the secretary at St. John Missionary Baptist Church. This event, held annually, honors the oldest, the youngest, and the mother with the most children.

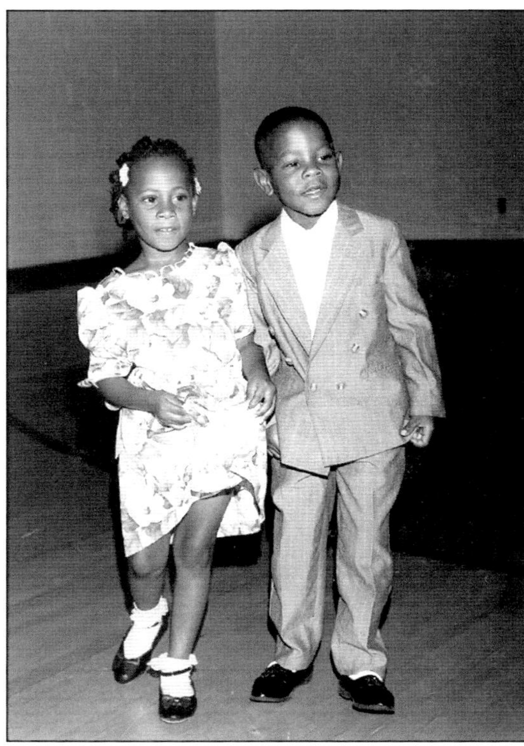

Latrice Nikia Hollis and Larry Wayne Hollis, a brother-and-sister dance team, perform in a Salute to Mothers in 1995. After presenting a rose to each mother attending the event, the children danced and entertained the guests.

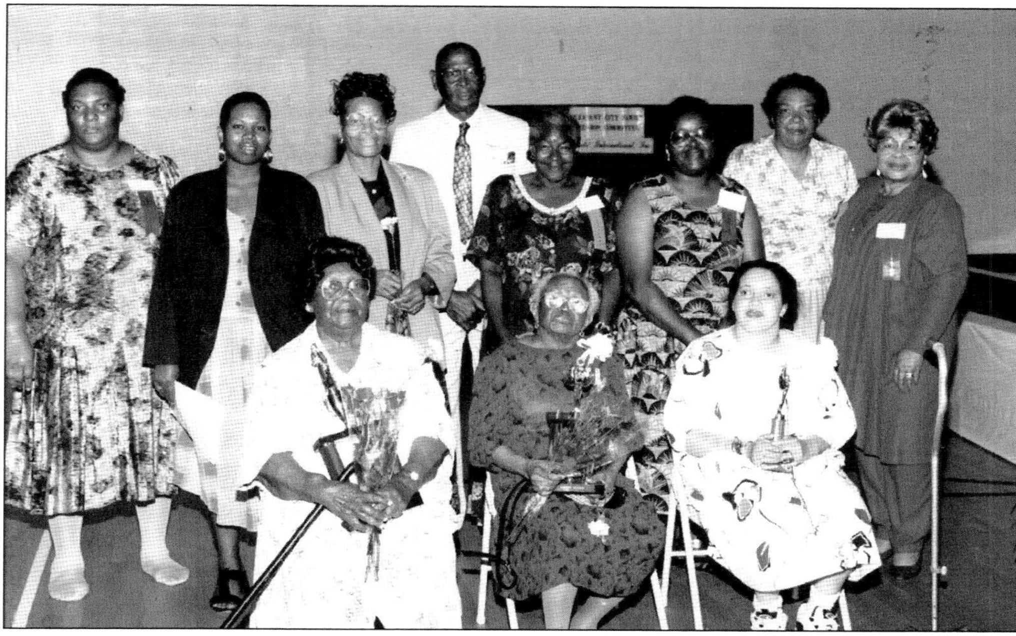

A salute to mothers of all ages is one of the committee programs designed to bring families back together in Pleasant City. From left to right in the front row are Mothers' Day honorees Mrs. Margaret Higgins, Mrs. Lucille Roberts, and Mrs. Isabel Genorio.

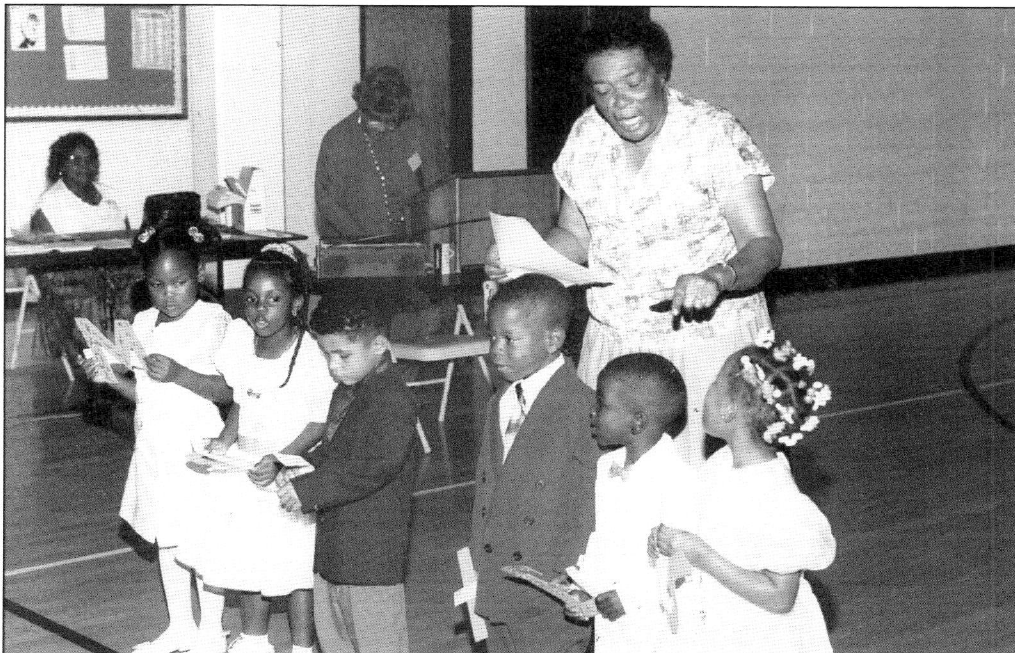

Mrs. Bessie Collier Harvey, youth director, leads the children in singing to mothers. Mrs. Harvey is a retired educator and member of the pioneer Collier family. She grew up in Pleasant City, and her father was pastor of St. John Missionary Baptist Church for many years.

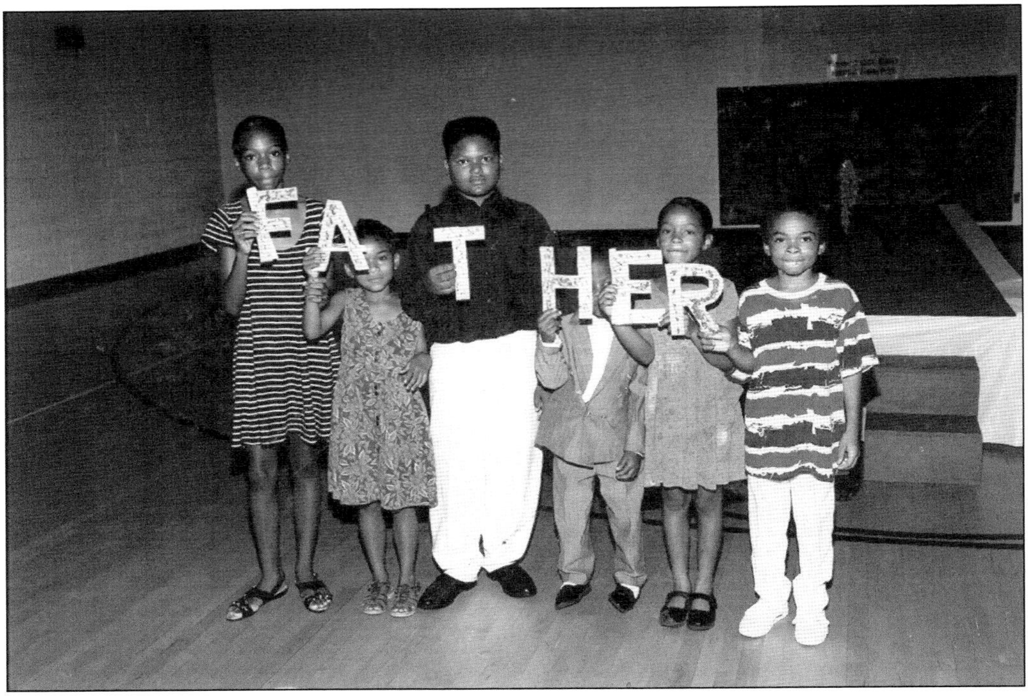

Pictured here is a Father's Day celebration. Father's Day is another important day in the reunion committee's efforts to bring families back together.

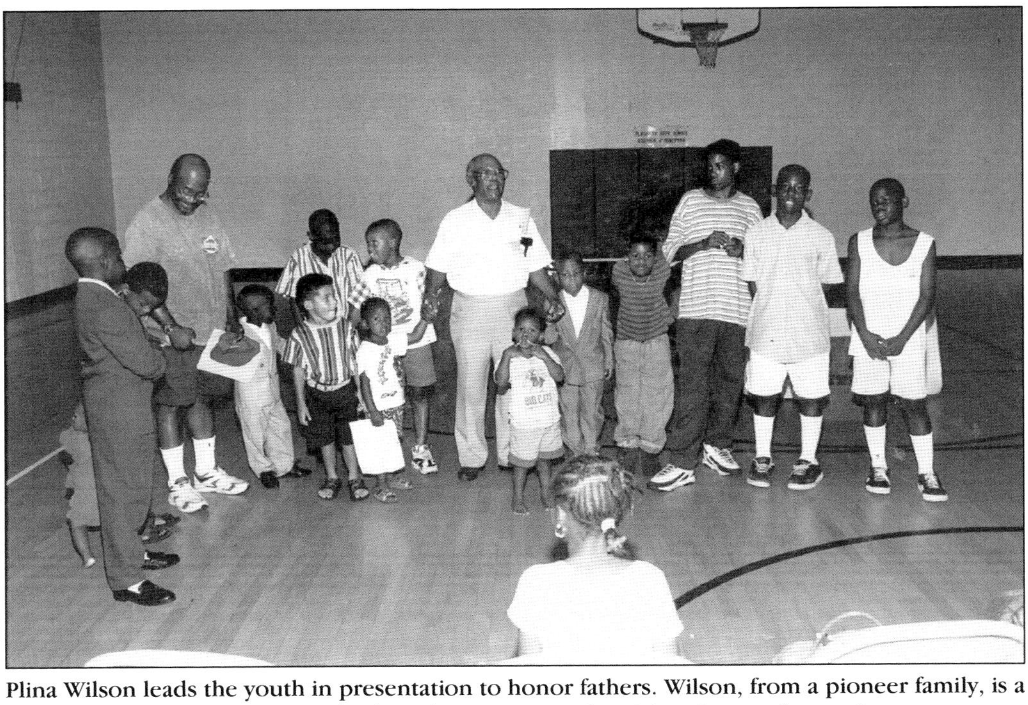

Plina Wilson leads the youth in presentation to honor fathers. Wilson, from a pioneer family, is a retired businessman who gives back to the community by giving time to the youth.

Seven

INSTITUTIONS

The Vanguard Club, the Tri County Chapter of the NBL, the NAACP, the Odd Fellows, and the Prince Hall Lodge with its many units have been the leaders in all aspects of community life.

The most powerful black organization in Palm Beach County was the Vanguard Club, organized about 1910. This group was comprised of the community's leading businessmen and professionals. It heavily impacted all aspects of the black community with close ties and influences with the white community.

This group was dissolved in 1975, when the director of the Urban League urged them to merge the two organizations. By that time, most of the members were ready to retire or had become very busy with their own personal lives. Some members were Clifton G. Dyson, Dr. J. Russell Dyett, Dr. Warren Collie, Carl Robinson, Dr. Robert L. Smith, Samuel Fluellen, Rufus Chester and E.J. White Sr.

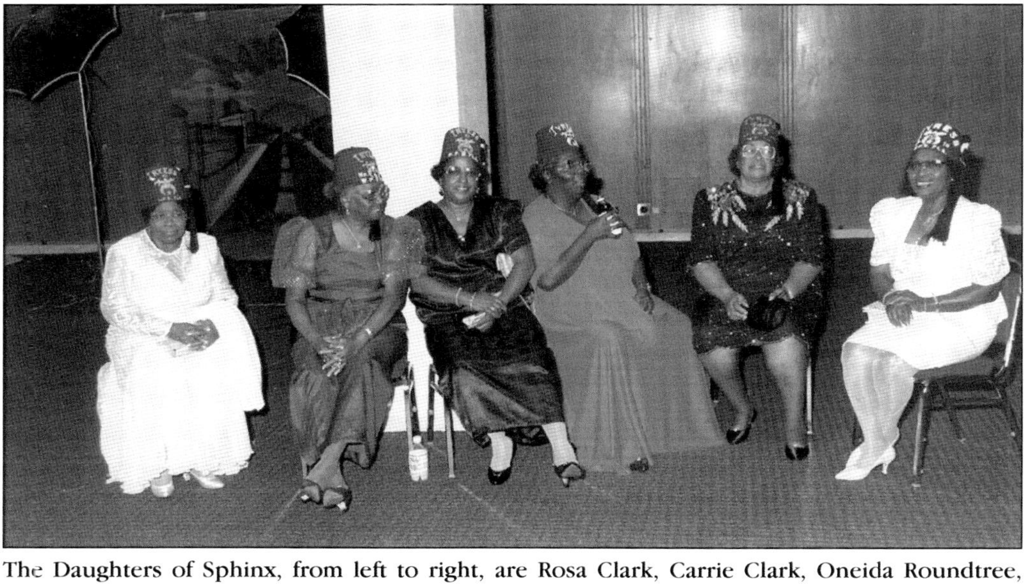

The Daughters of Sphinx, from left to right, are Rosa Clark, Carrie Clark, Oneida Roundtree, Florence Hays, Elizabeth Rivers, and Blanch Crawford.

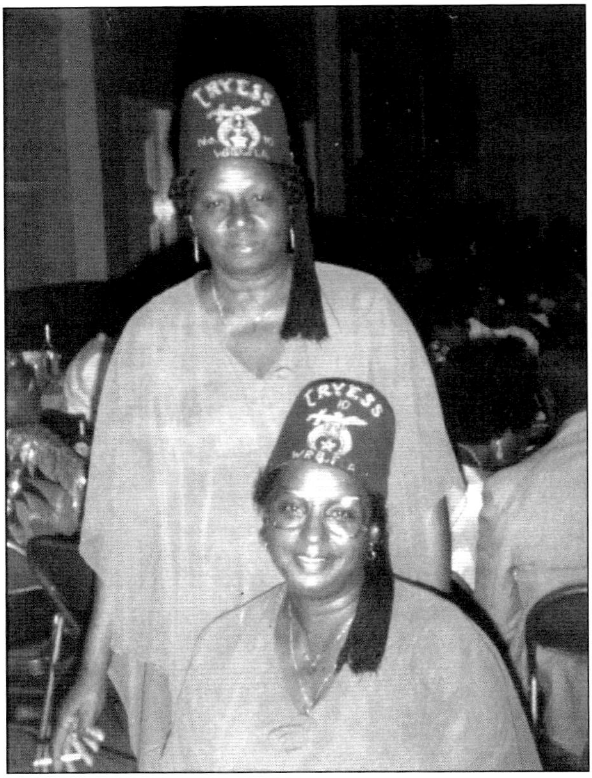

Daughters of Sphinx Carrie Clark and her daughter Oneida Roundtree are pictured here. The Daughters of Sphinx are a unit of the Prince Hall Lodge. Their program is educational and benevolent. They provide services and scholarships for deserving youth.

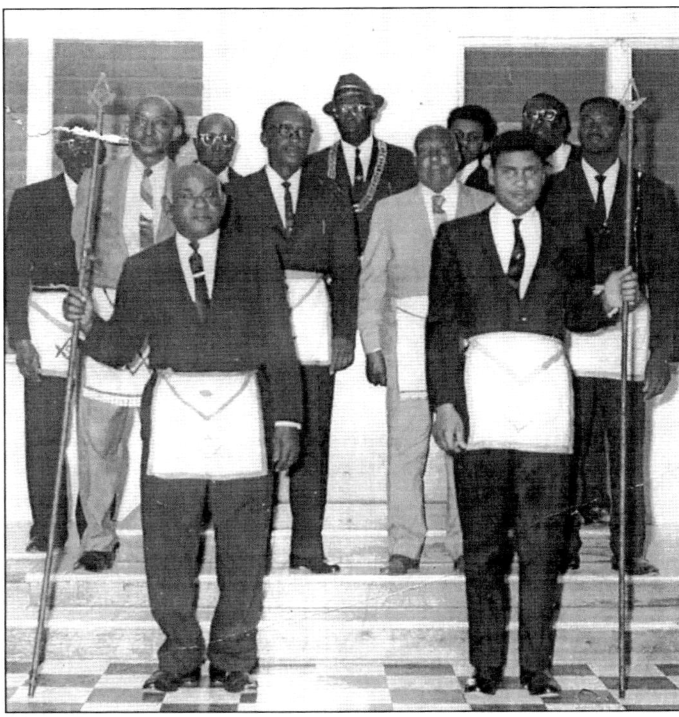

Masons of Rising Star Lodge 67 include Ruben C. Madison, James Frances, U.S. Pittman, Samuel Hodges, Col. David Brewer, John Evans, Stonewall Phillips, T.L. White, Charlie Nunn, Ernest Taylor, and Marshall Paulk.

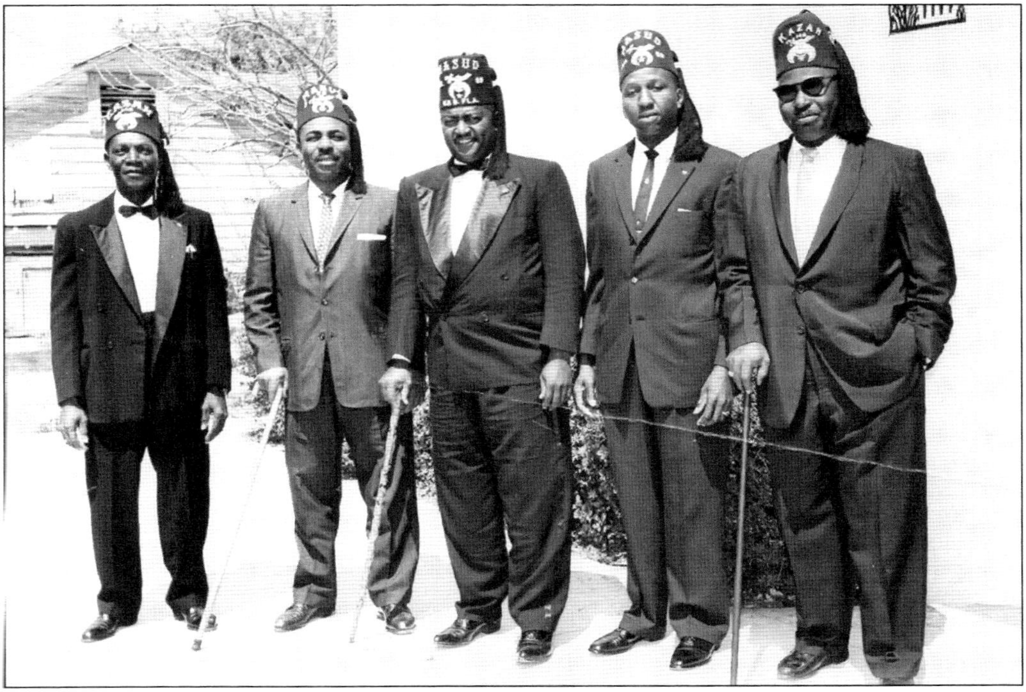

Shriners Masud Lodge 69 is, from left to right, Sam Bracy, Eugene Stevens, William Mercer, James Arnold, and Leonard Stevens.

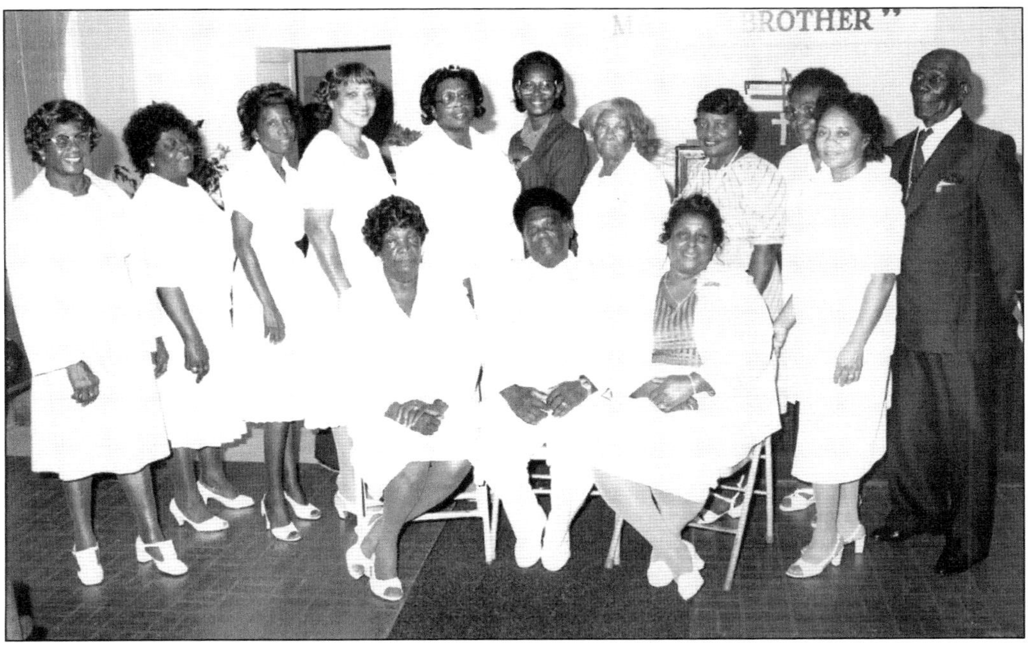

Calanthes of the Prince Hall Lodge pictured here include Lillie Mae Hamilton, Carlton Woods, Florida Brown, Betty Stringer, Rose Dawson, Pearl Felder, Beulah Davis, Rheba Johnson, Mrs. Boone, Betty Stringer, and Mr. Boone.

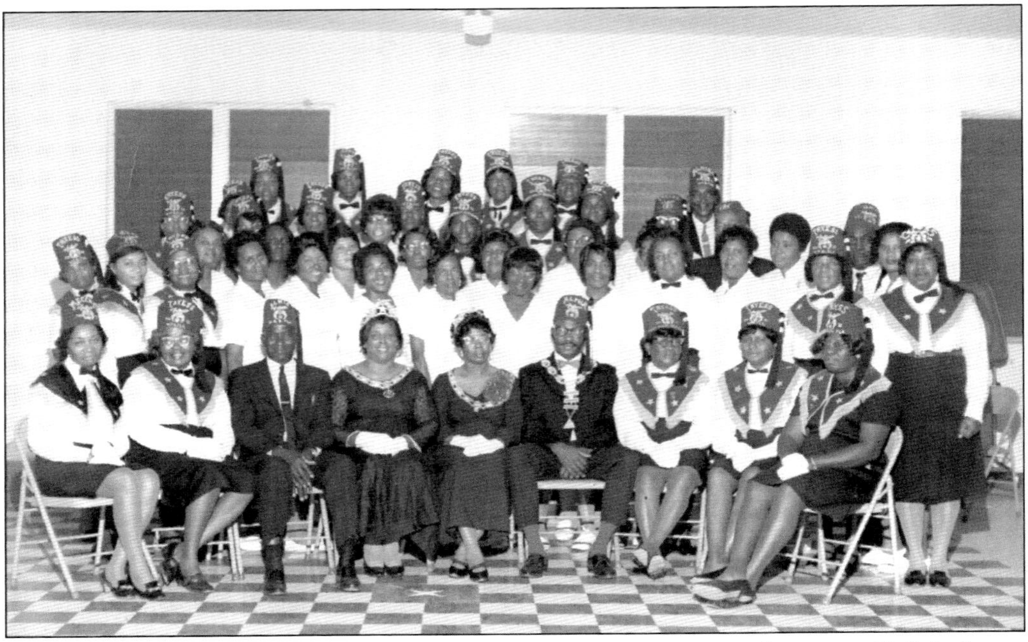

The Nobles of the Mystic Shrine and Daughters of Sphinx meet at the Prince Hall Lodge at Twentieth Street and Spruce Avenue. Among those pictured here are Aretha Randolph, Annie Pearl Bell, C.C. Harvey, Florida Brown, Zanie Chance, Robert Hall, Corine Mainor, Carrie Clark, and Dessie Christian.

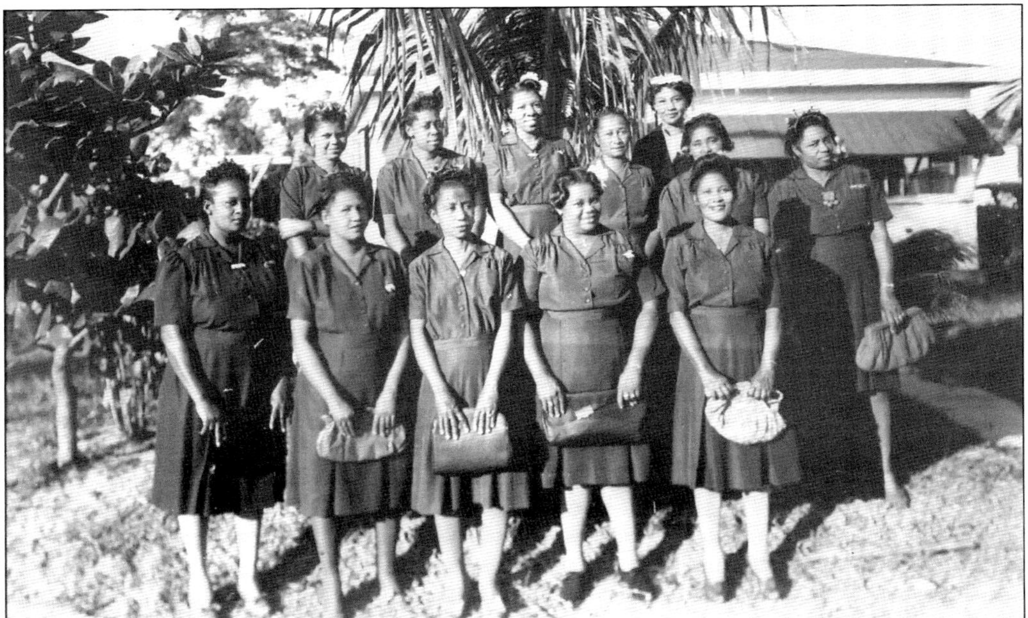

Neighborhood clubs were an independent element in the community during the 1940s. These ladies kept abreast of the issues affecting their neighborhood and sought to bring peaceful solutions to problems.

Eight

The Heritage Gallery

The Heritage Gallery was established in 1996 by the Pleasant City Family Reunion Committee. The gallery honors the pioneers through authentic photographs, documents, artifacts, and memorabilia. The committee sponsors historic tours and performances.

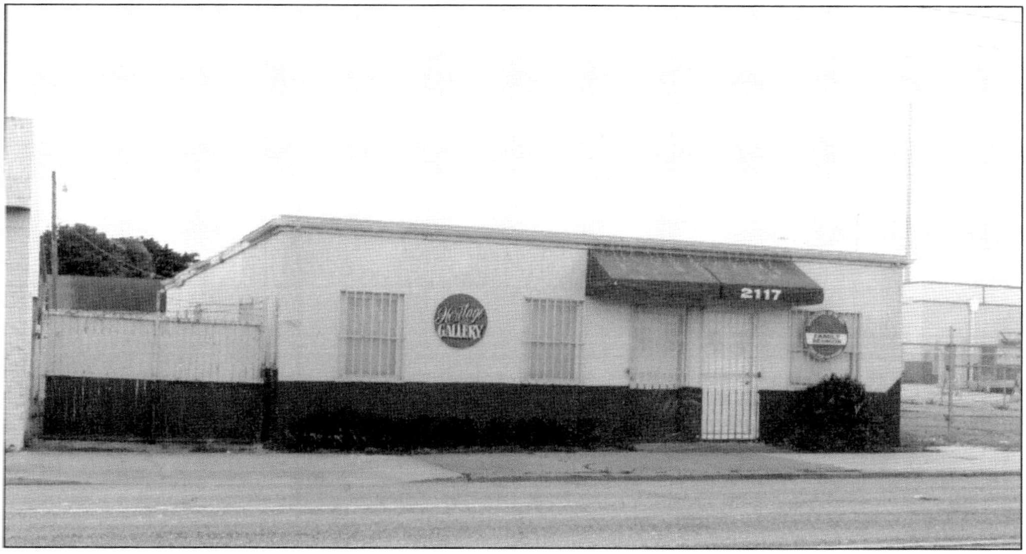

The Pleasant City Heritage Gallery, located at 2117 North Dixie Highway, was established by sons, daughters, and lineage of the pioneers in 1996. It includes works of art, books, magazines, videotapes, and catalogs on such subjects as self-improvement, health, business, and family relations. Oral histories, periodicals, artifacts, and books used by the pioneers, some more than 100 years old, are also held there. The Achievers' Corner features photographs of residents who have excelled in their careers and endeavors in various fields. The gallery features permanent and traveling artists and exhibits.

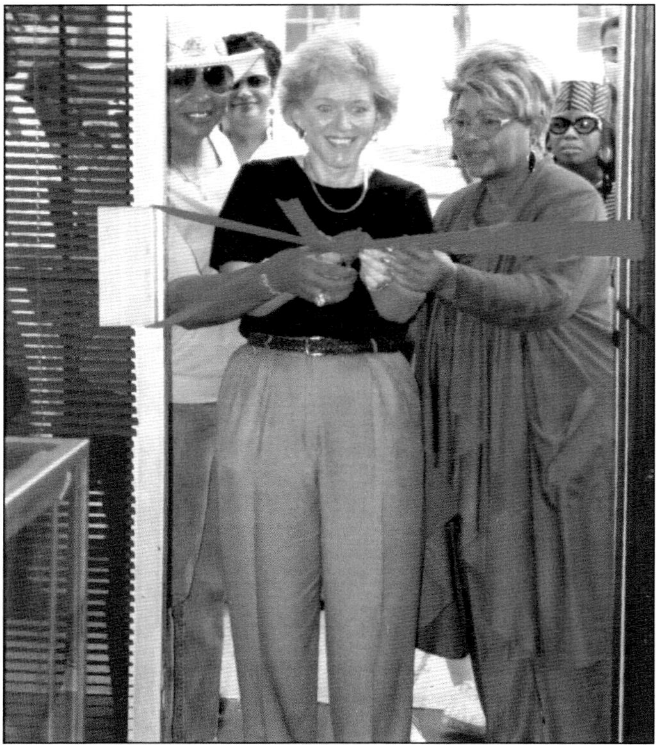

Mayor Nancy C. Graham, City Commissioner Mary Hooks, and executive assistant to the mayor Gloria Shuttleworth are ready for a ribbon cutting ceremony at the grand opening of the Heritage Gallery on September 21, 1996.

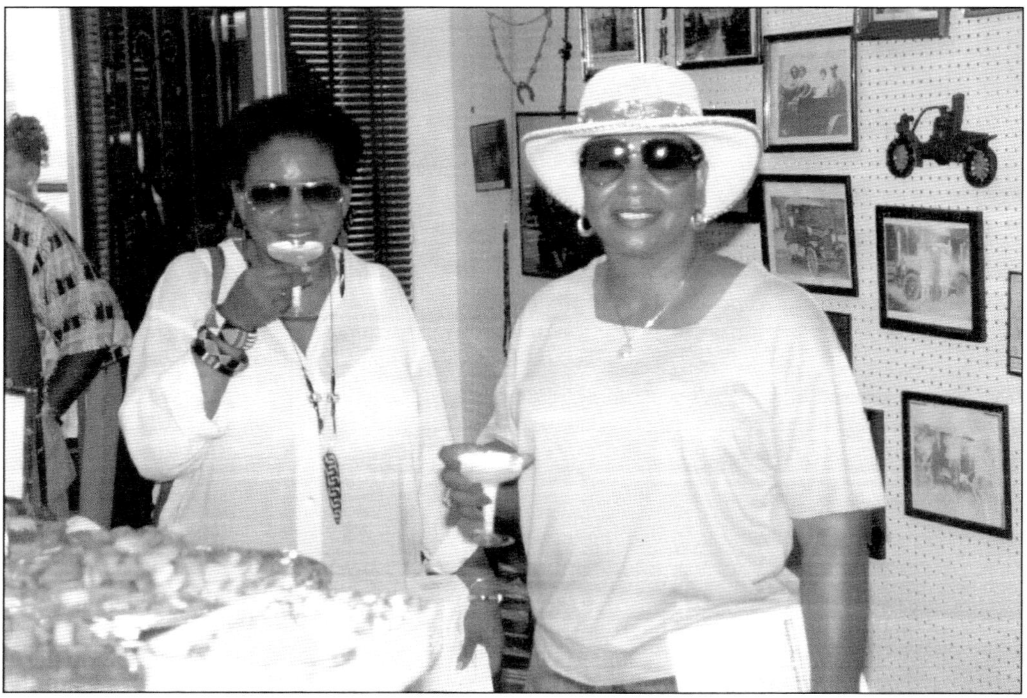

Gloria Shuttleworth and Commissioner Mary Hooks sample refreshments.

Shown are John and Virginia Brooks, Heritage Gallery Board members.

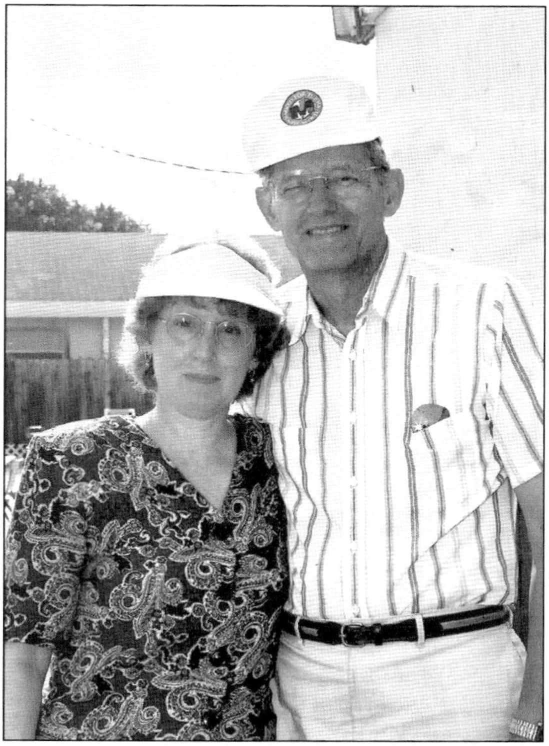

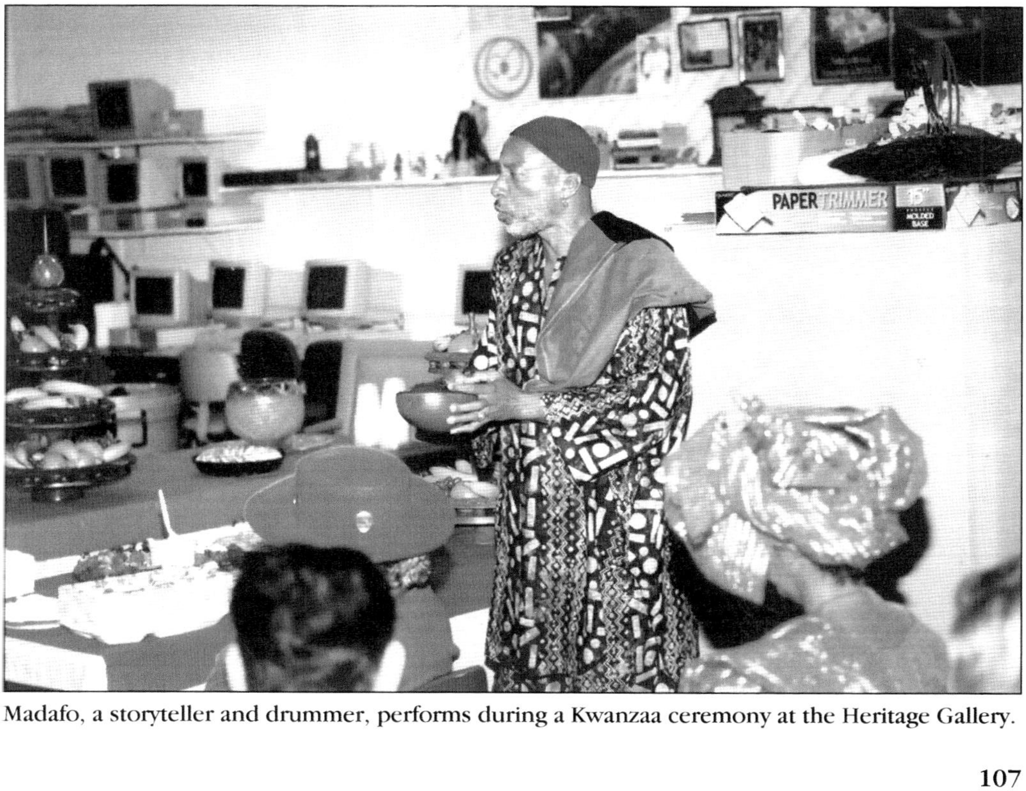

Madafo, a storyteller and drummer, performs during a Kwanzaa ceremony at the Heritage Gallery.

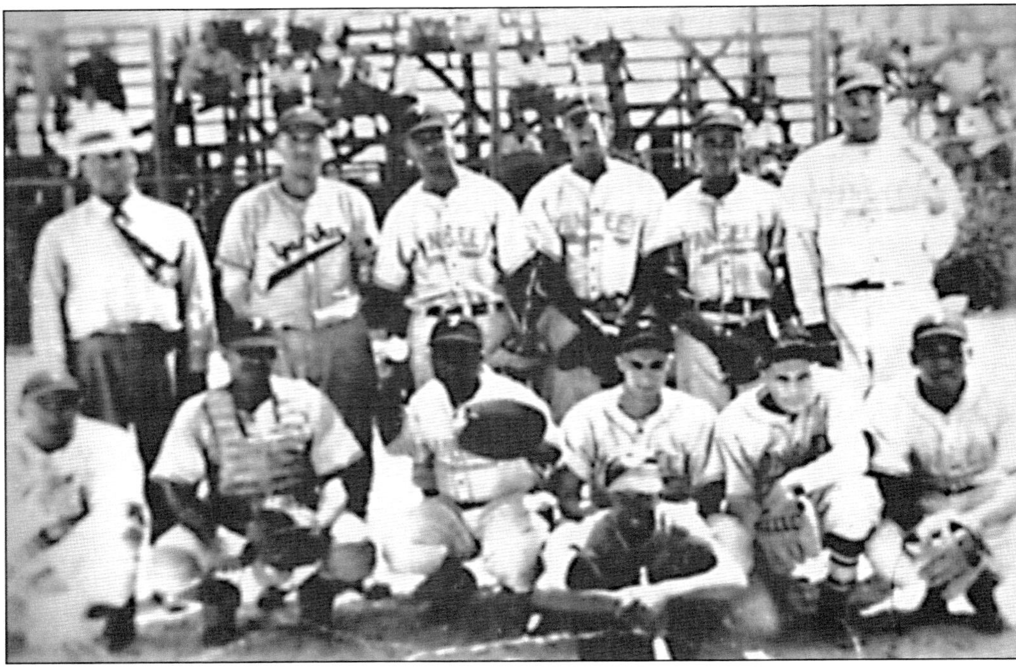

Members of the West Palm Beach Yankees baseball team in this photo are Shamrock, Hamm, Tommie Simmons, David Deal, Mike Hicks, and Johnnie Williams, Pow Wow Walker, Sammie Gardner, Mike, Frank Scruggs, and Connie Green. Owner Bill Etham is also pictured.

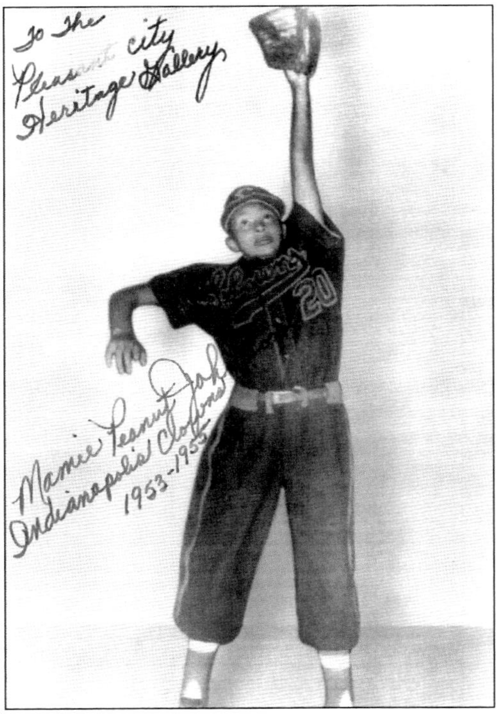

Mamie "Peanut" Johnson is the only living female player from the Negro League. She played with the Indianapolis Clowns from 1953 until 1955. She now resides in Washington, D.C.

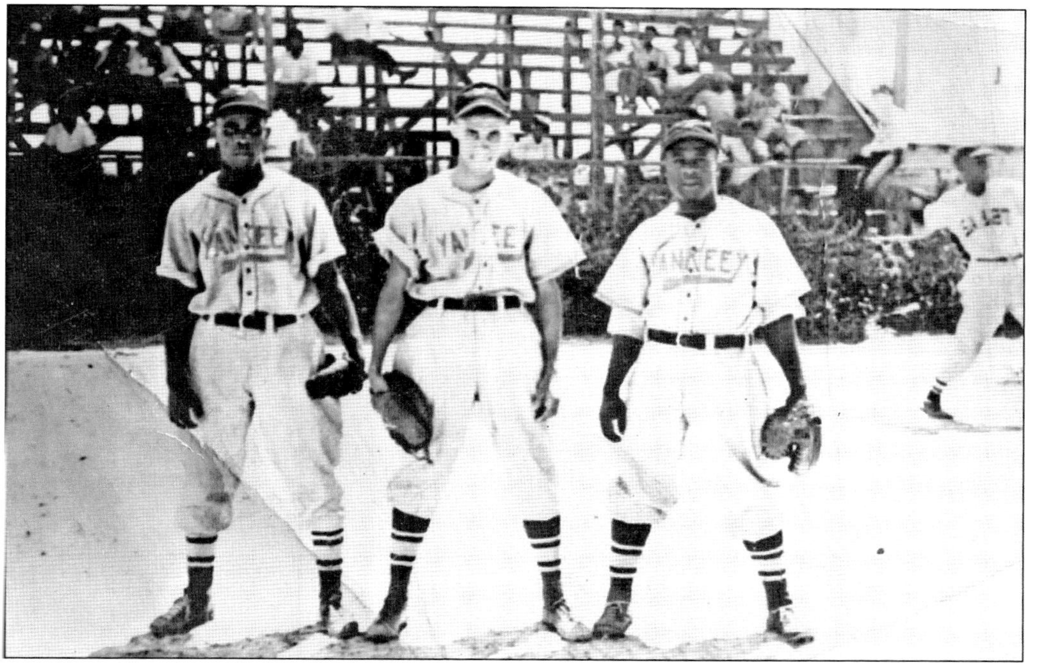

Three members of the West Palm Beach Yankees in the 1940s are pictured here. From left to right are Frank Scruggs, David Deal, and Tommie Simmons.

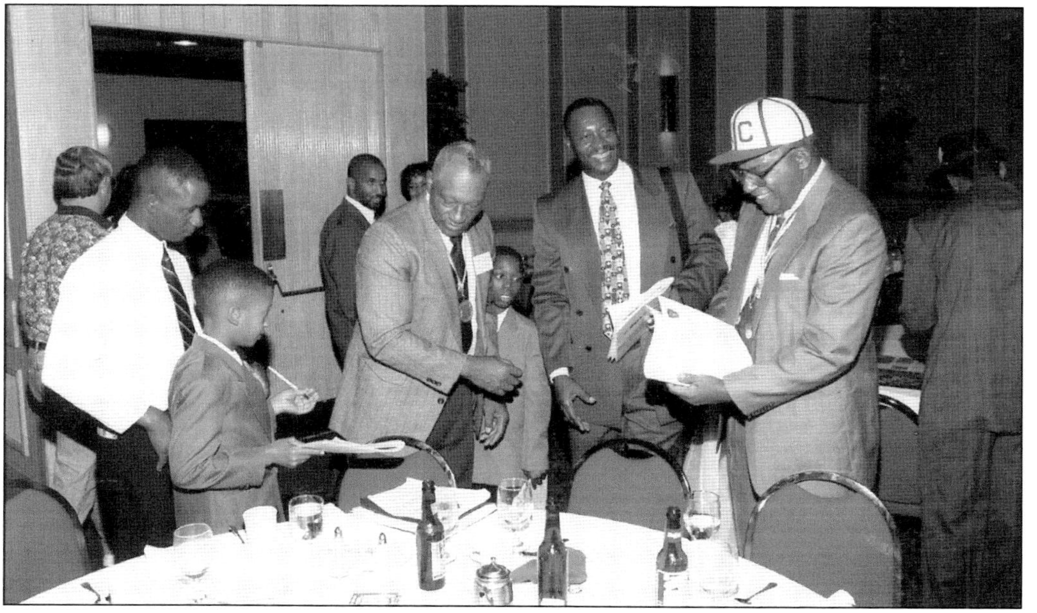

Bob Mitchell (far right with baseball hat), a native son, now lives in Tampa. He is the public relations coordinator for the Living Legends of Negro Baseball League, professional ballplayers from the early days of the game. They played with Jackie Robinson, Larry Doby, and Satchel Paige, but they never received the big money. They have recently won a big fight to receive a pension from the major leagues.

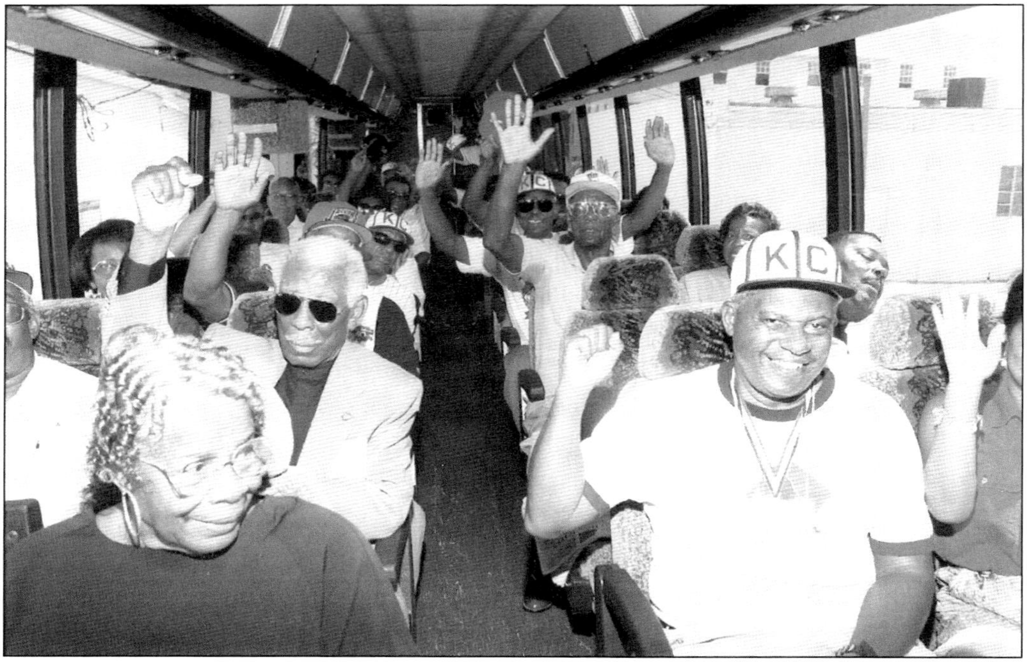

Sponsored by the Pleasant City Family Reunion Committee, Inc. and the Heritage Gallery, Living Legends of Negro Baseball League visited the Palm Beaches in August 1997. Shown are players on the tour bus being transported to the Montreal Expos Club House for a welcome party.

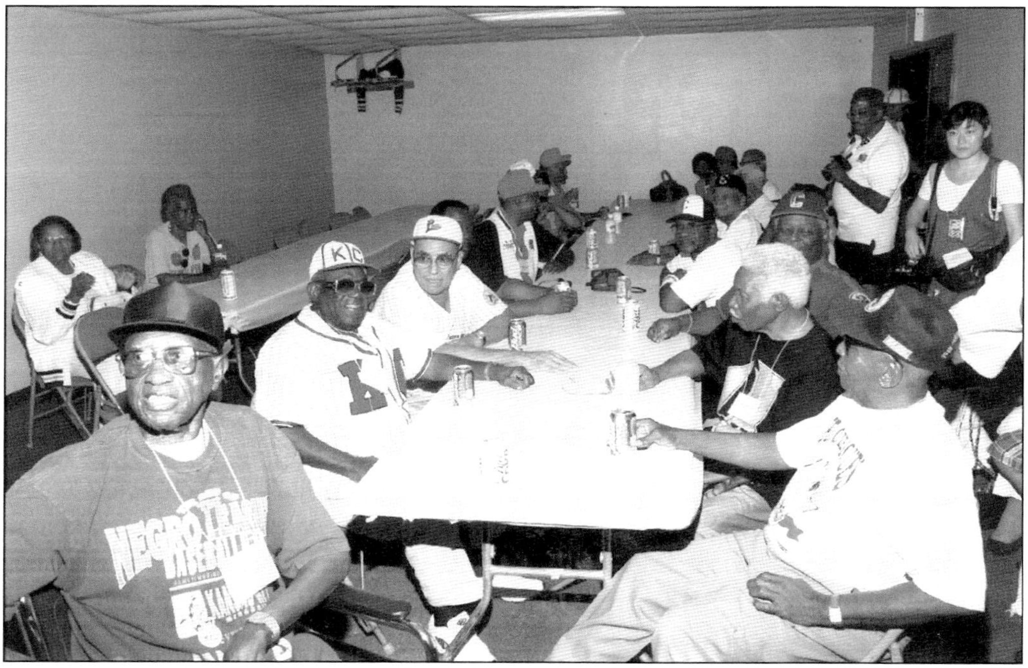

These men played with Jackie Robinson and Satchel Paige, but they never earned the money of the big times.

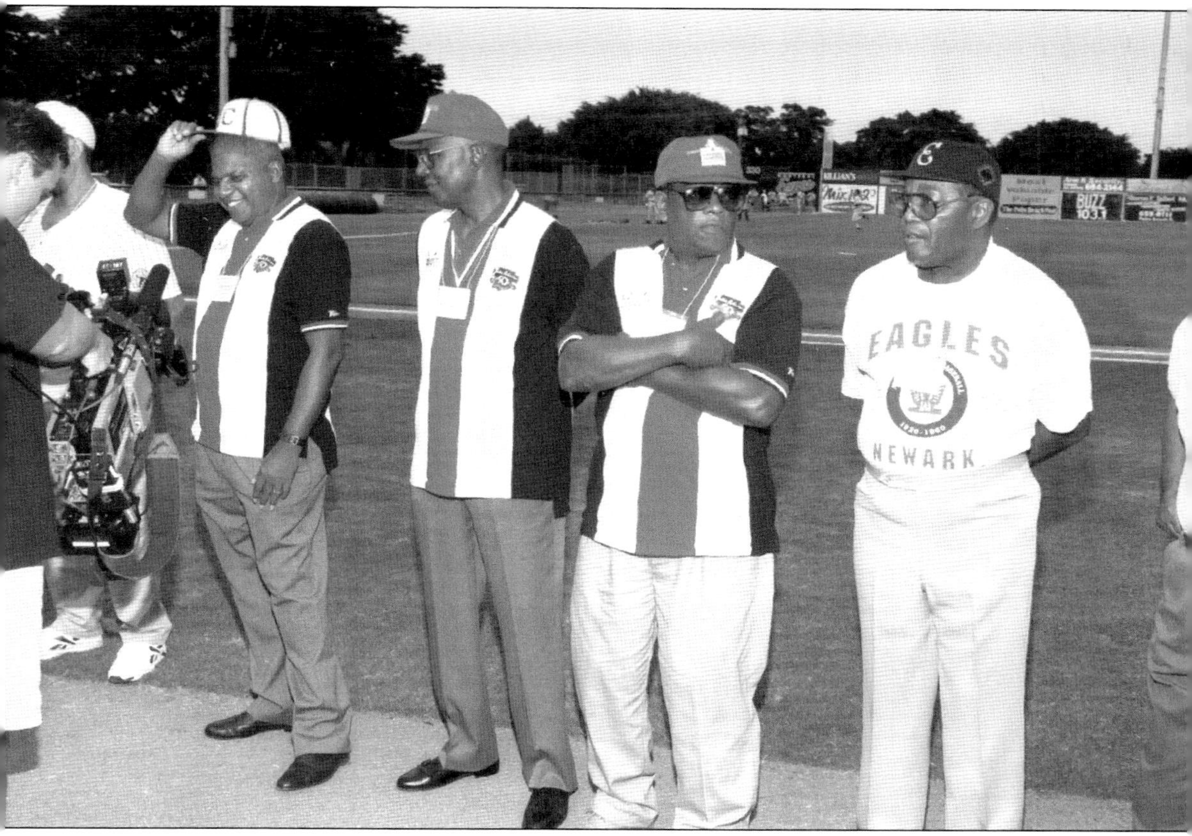

Members of the league received recognition at the final baseball game played at the West Palm Beach Stadium. A new stadium was opened in Jupiter and is named for auto dealer Roger Dean.

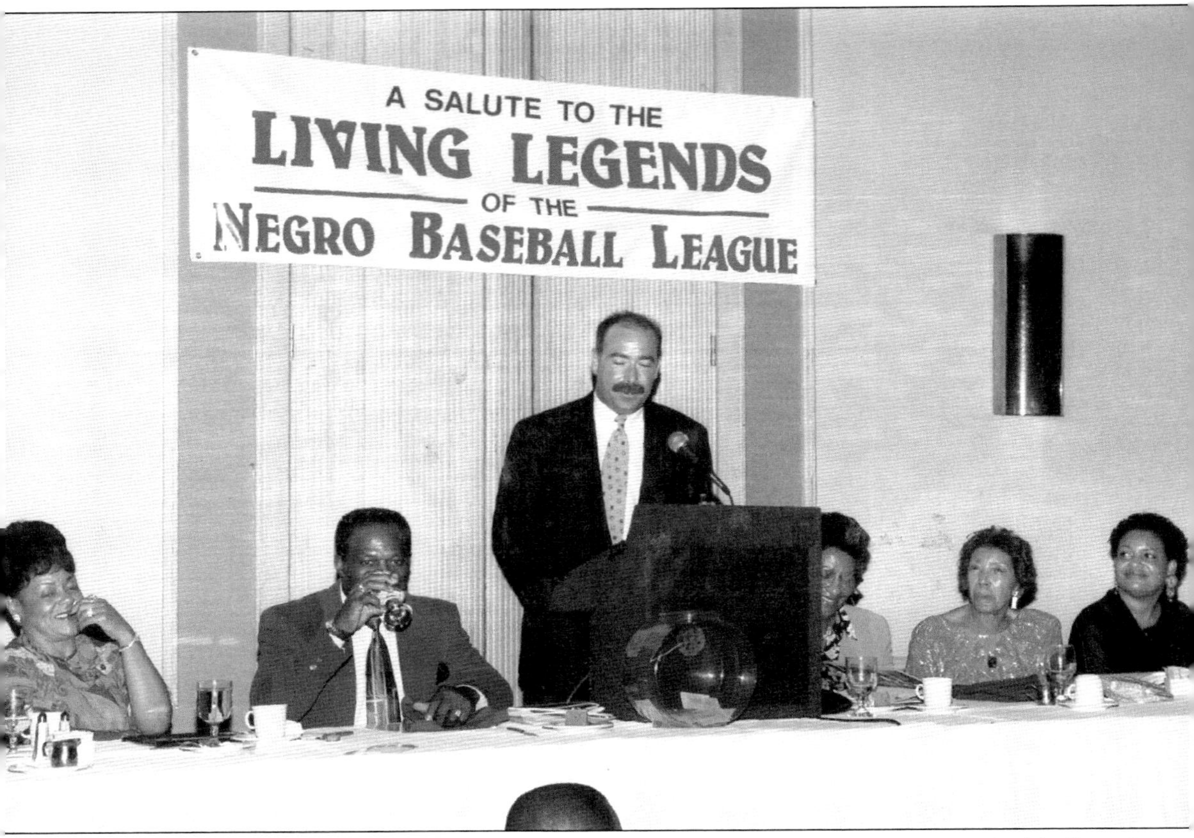

The awards banquet was held at the Omni Hotel in 1997 where players autographed balls and programs. From left to right are Mrs. Lou Brock; Hall of Famer Lou Brock; Robert Rabenecker, stadium manager; Maude Ford Lee, county commissioner; Clara King Williams, Riviera Beach mayor; and other guests. The Pleasant City Family Reunion Committee and Heritage Gallery sponsors historic programs that are not readily available to the Pleasant City community. In 1997, they brought 28 of these legendary players to West Palm Beach to expose them to the community for three days. They were honored at a banquet at the stadium. They visited high schools, held press conferences, and attended receptions to honor them and expose them to thousands.

Nine

ACHIEVERS

Pleasant City has always had outstanding achievers. The pioneers were not just common laborers. Many were professionals, very skilled in their trades—they were architects, engineers, doctors, educators, boat builders, and yachtsmen. Because of their interest in education, this continues through their lineage.

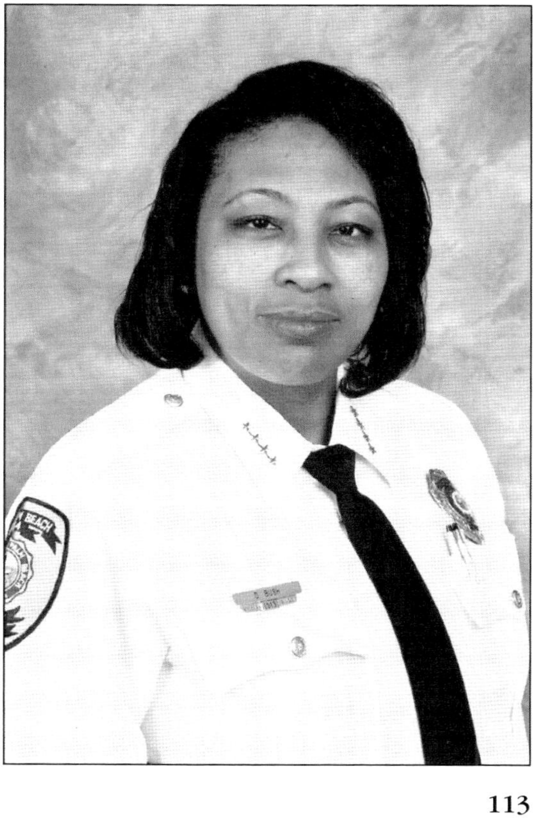

History was made in the city of West Palm Beach on Monday evening, January 5, 2004, when city commissioners joined Mayor Lois Frankel in naming Delsa Bush chief of the city's 419-member police department. Chief Bush, who had been a police captain since 1999, is the first African American and the first female head of Palm Beach County's largest city police department, joining only three or four other African-American women department heads in America.

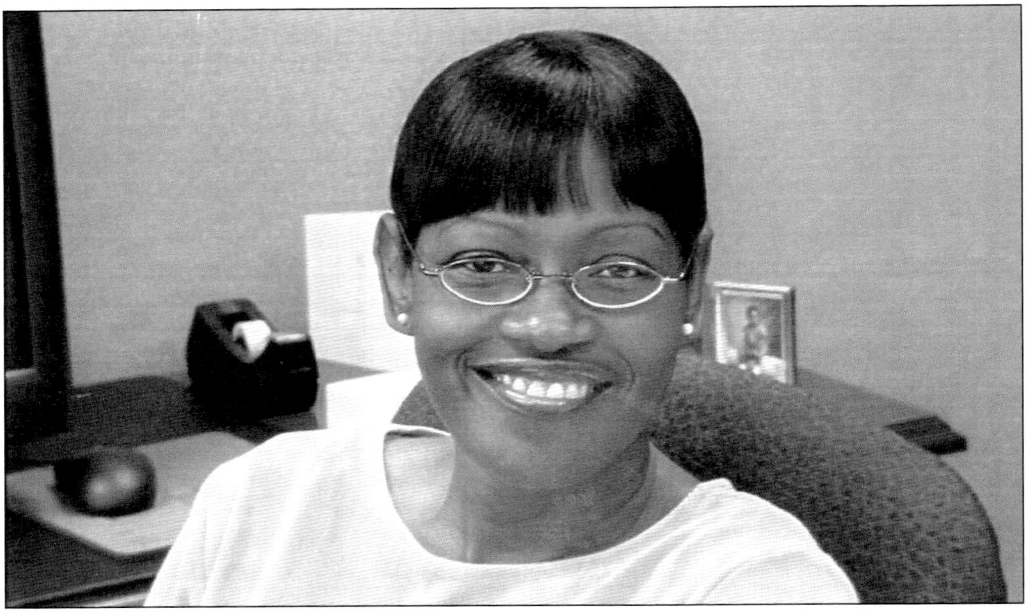

Faye Outlaw is the assistant administrator to St. Lucie County. She is the first African American to hold this post. Outlaw was community development manager in West Palm Beach for 12 years and director of economic and community development in Ft. Lauderdale for five years. She is a graduate of Bethune Cookman College with bachelor's and master's degrees in public administration from Howard University. She has two sons, Napolean and Jarel.

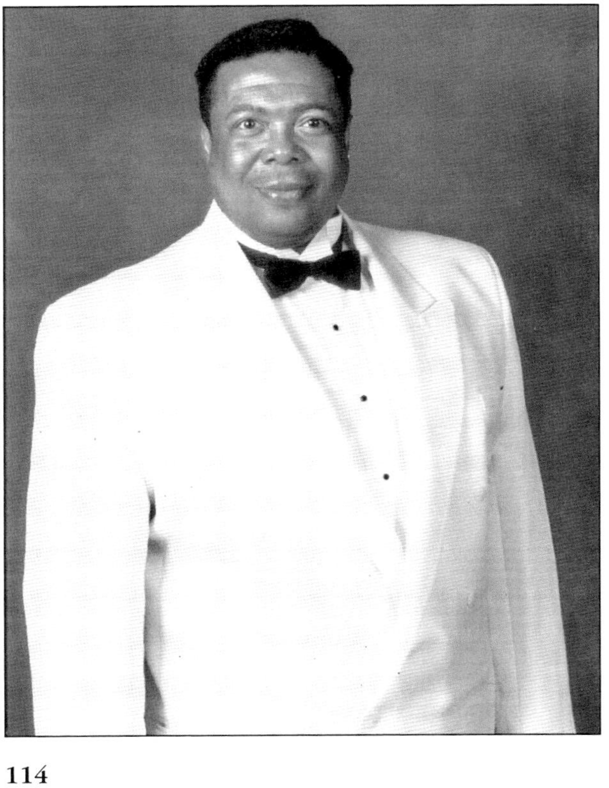

Dr. Rufus Jimerson Jr. is the son of Rufus Osten Jimerson Sr. and grandson of pioneers Rev. William and Mrs. Cynthia Jimerson. He is director of student teaching and assistant professor of education at Lincoln University in Oxford, Pennsylvania. He received his doctorate in education from Rutgers University. He has three master's degrees from Columbia University.

Dr. Leon Alphonso Collier retired from the St. Lucie County School System in 2003, where he had been dean of students and instructor of U.S. history. He earned his bachelor's degree from Florida A&M University and his master's degree from Florida Atlantic University. He did graduate studies at Northwestern University and received a doctorate in education from Florida Atlantic University. He's listed in *Who's Who in Black America* for 1976, 1977, and 1987.

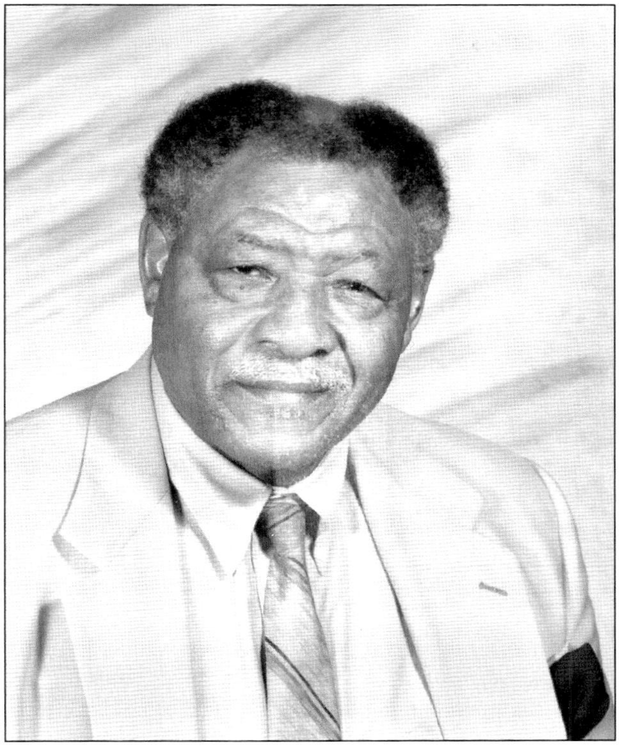

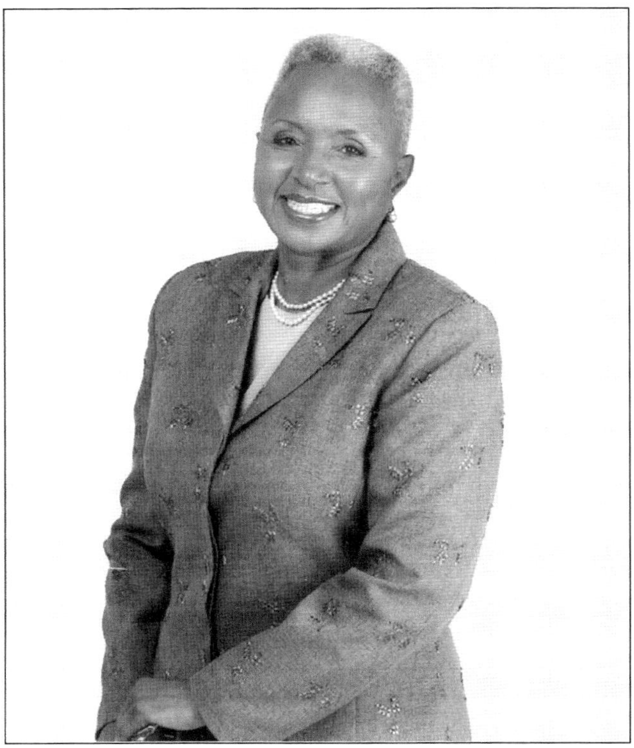

The Reverend Dr. Leah Doreatha Gaskin-Fitchue is president of Payne Theological Seminary in Wilberforce, Ohio. She is the first female theological seminary president in America. Dr. Fitchue joined Eastern Baptist Theological Seminary in 1992 as the first full time African-American female faculty member. She was ordained as an itinerant elder in the African Methodist Episcopal Church in 1993. Dr. Fitchue received her bachelor's degree from Douglas College, New Jersey; her master's from Michigan; her Masters of Divinity from Princeton; and her Ph.D. in education from Harvard.

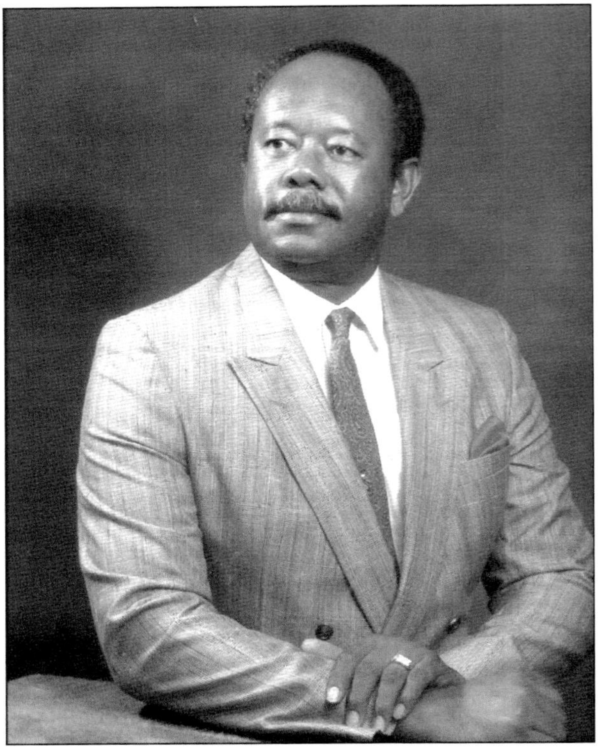

Clifford Bridges retired as the Palm Beach County school administrator. He is chairman of the Civil Service Board for West Palm Beach. He is the son of pioneers Mr. and Mrs. Clifford Bridges Sr.

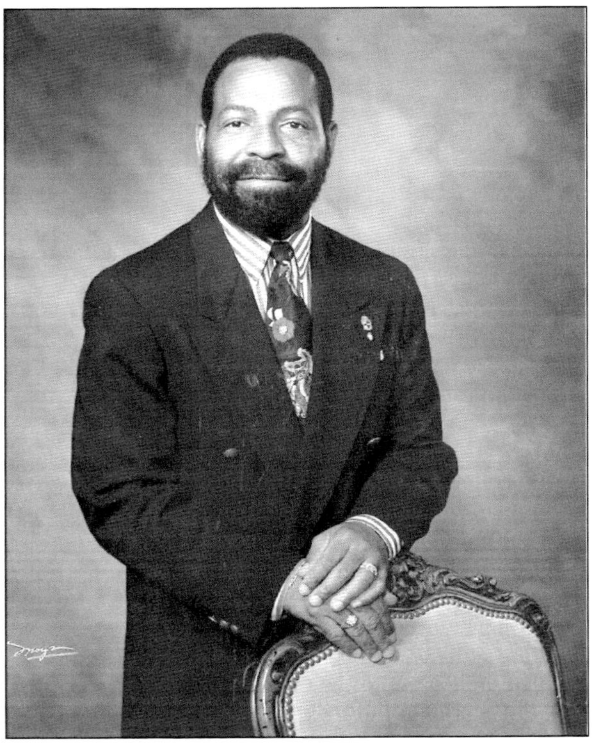

Dr. Charles Eugene White is the son of E.J. and Carmeta Ferguson White, a graduate of Fisk University, Florida Atlantic University, the University of London, and the University of Miami. He is an administrator at Polo Park Middle School in Wellington, Florida. He chairs the Education Advisory Committee in West Palm Beach and the Alpha Phi Alpha Educational Scholarship Foundation, is a member of the Community Relations Committee at the Kravis Center for the Performing Arts, and is president of Alpha Phi Alpha Fraternity.

Terence Bryan White is the son of Charles and Saundra White, grandson of E.J. and Carmeta Ferguson White, and great-grandson of Prince Albert and Frances Rahming Ferguson, pioneers of Pleasant City. He is a graduate of Morehouse College and Georgia School of Professional Psychology, and he is a clinical psychologist at Fern Park Center in Orlando, Florida.

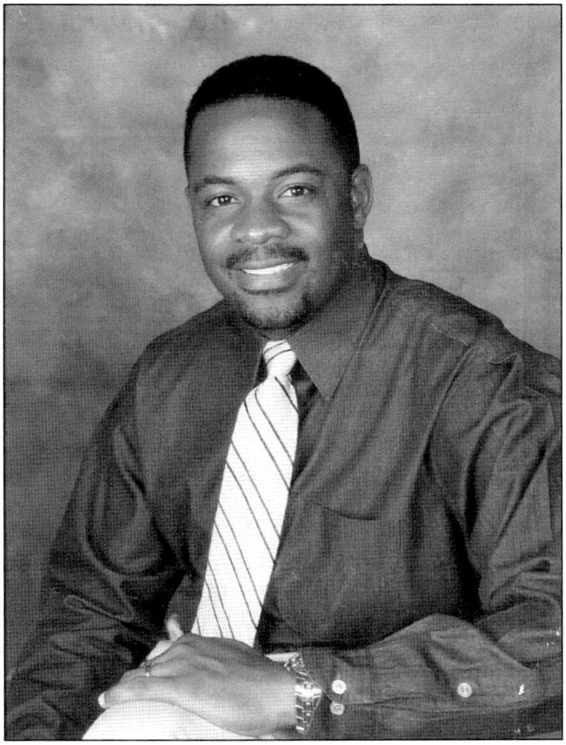

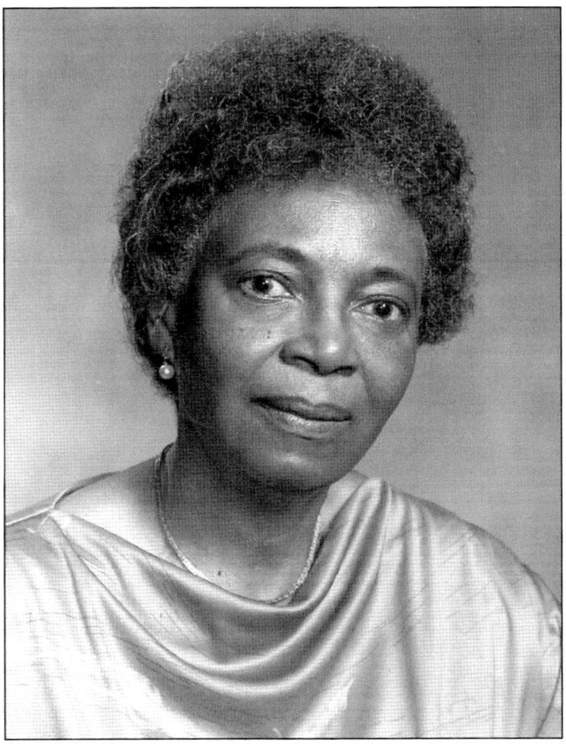

The first African-American mayor of West Palm Beach, Eva Williams-Mack (1915–1998) came to West Palm Beach in 1948. She was elected to the City Commission in 1978 and was elected mayor in 1982. She worked as a public health nurse for 26 years and taught at Florida A&M University. She was responsible for health classes, including sex education, and she worked to have pregnant girls remain in school. She also founded the Sickle Cell Foundation of Palm Beach County.

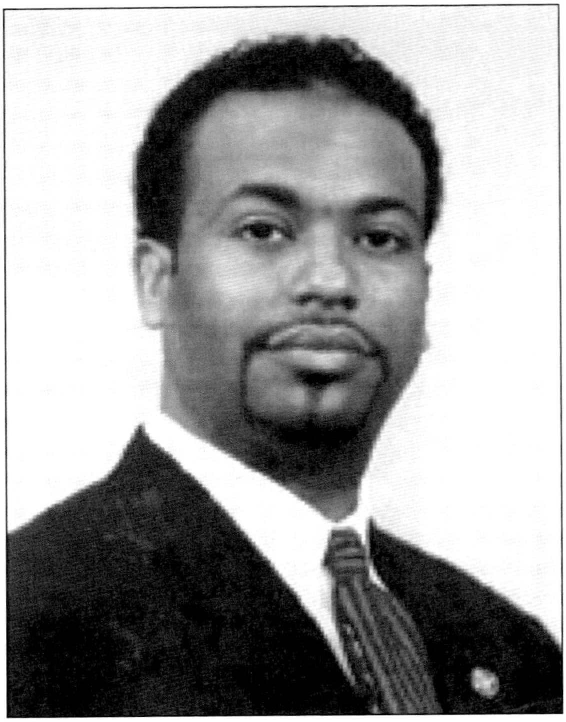

James "Hank" Harper Jr. is a member of the Florida House of Representatives, representing District 84. He is the son of Mr. and Mrs. James H. Harper Sr. and the great-grandson of Millie Gildersleeve, the first African-American pioneer in Palm Beach County.

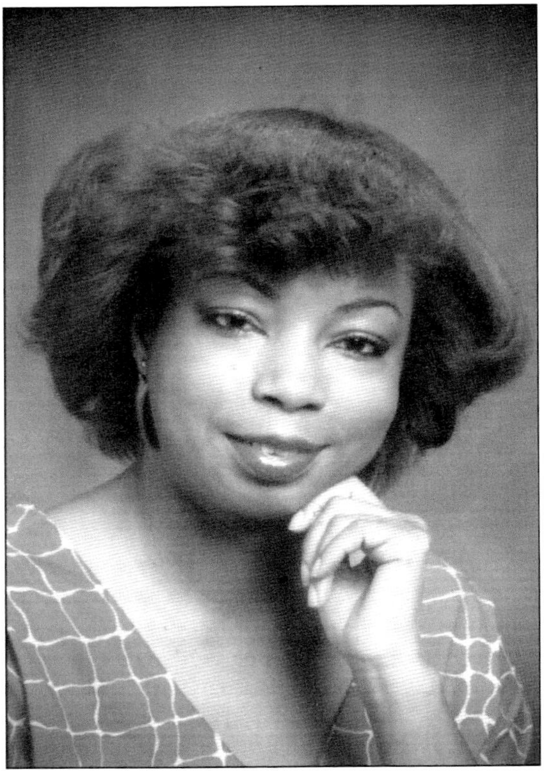

Cornelia Nikki Primous is a school counselor for the Atlanta Public School System. Presently, she is working on her doctoral degree in educational leadership at Nova Southeastern University. She is the daughter of Herman Jimerson and the late Dorothy Johnson and the granddaughter of pioneers Rev. William and Mrs. Cynthia Jimerson.

Prior to integration in the 1960s, African Americans could not use the main library downtown. A small branch library was set up on Tamarind Avenue to accommodate the African-American community, and Harriet Washington was the branch librarian. She and Ida Mae Young Burns were moved to the main library on Clematis Street after integration.

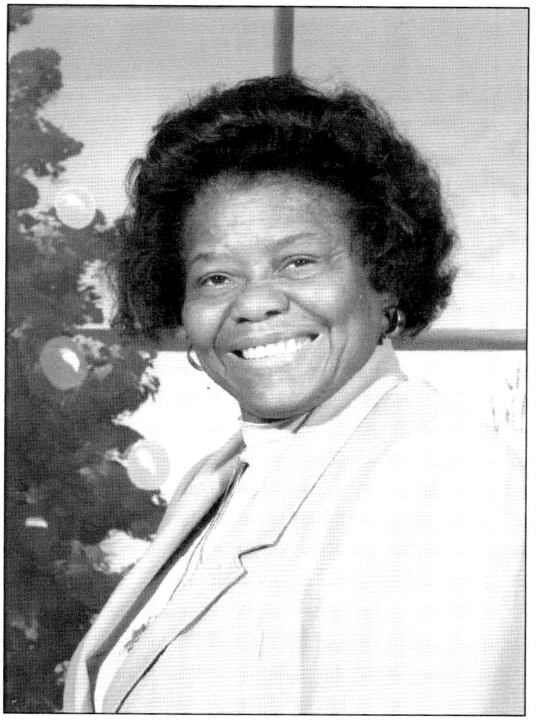

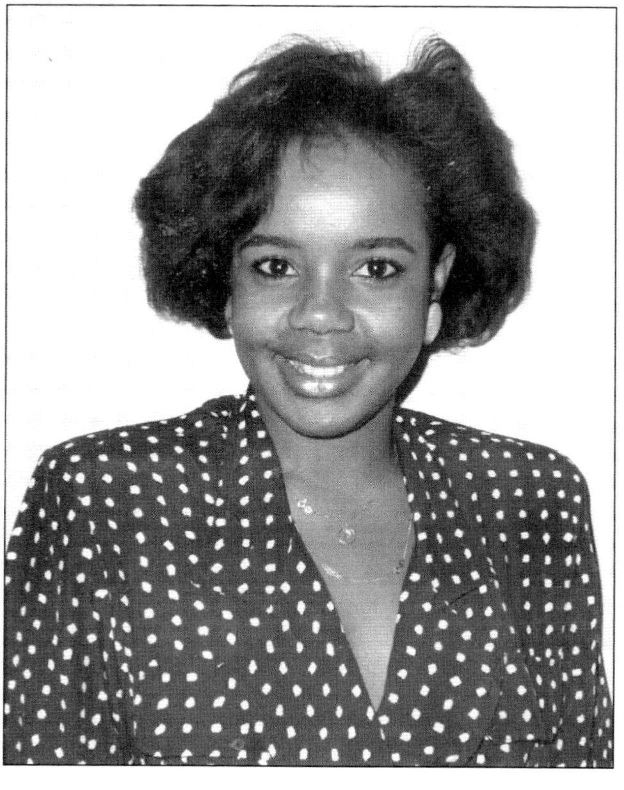

Frances Yvette Clarke is the granddaughter of pioneers Rev. William and Mrs. Cynthia Jimerson and the daughter of Everee Jimerson Clarke. She is currently a real-estate investor. She is a former director of affiliate marketing at Black Entertainment Television and a former manager of revenue operations at MCI WorldCom. Her professional affiliations include two terms as president of the National Association of Minorities in Cable and membership in the Cable Telecommunications Association for Marketing, National Cable Television Association, and National Exhibition Association.

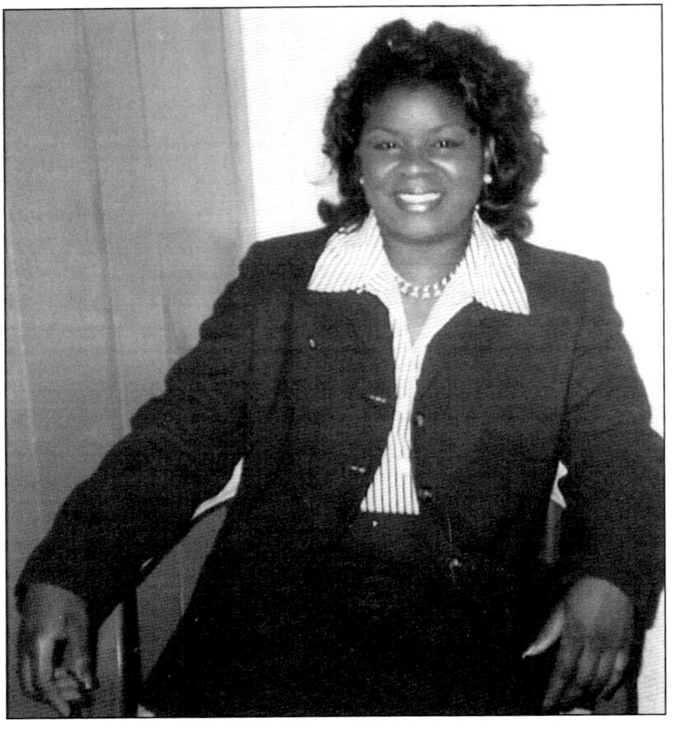

Dr. LaRhonda Brown is the assistant pastor of Greater Anointing Deliverance Ministries. She is the founder and CEO of From Glory to Glory International Ministries, Inc. and the director of public relations and events coordinator for Teen Spirits of the Greater Palm Beaches, Inc. She is a graduate of North Shore High School, Palm Beach Atlantic University, and Evangelical Bible Seminary, Greenacres, Florida. She was ordained in the United Christian Church and the Ministerial Association in Cleveland, Ohio, and through Interdenominational Ministries Association in Greenacres, Florida.

Janese Sampson has performed extensively throughout the Eastern United States and in Belgium and Holland, and she has completed a five-city, eight-concert tour of the People's Republic of China. She has also been a guest soloist with the Greater Palm Beach Symphony. She received her undergraduate degree from Florida State, is a member of Sigma Alpha Iota, received a Master of Music Degree in flute performance from the University of Maryland, and received Alpha Kappa Alpha Sorority's Outstanding Achievement Award.

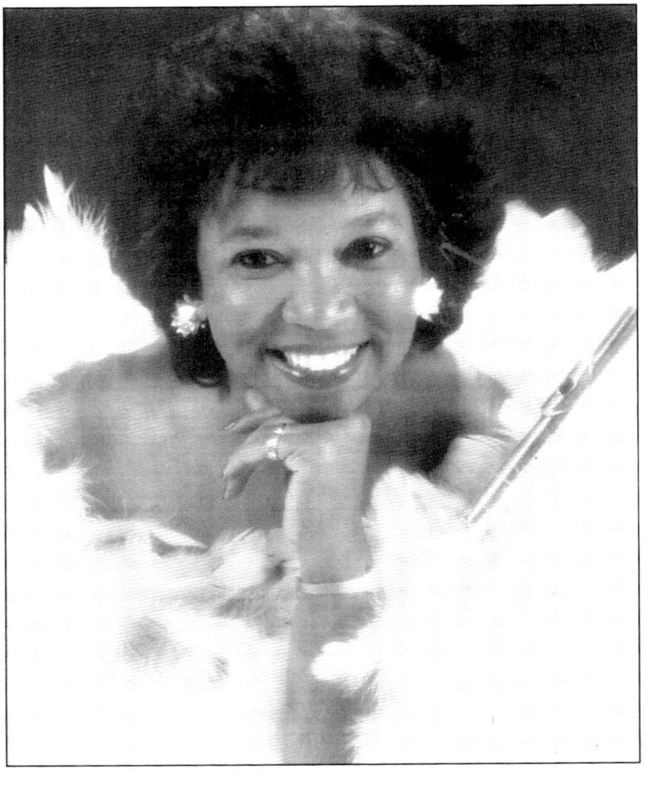

Mary Thompson Cleare, the youngest daughter of the late John F. and Nellie S. Thompson, graduated from Roosevelt High School in 1951 and attended Florida A&M University, receiving a bachelor's degree in elementary education. She taught for 35 years in the Palm Beach County School System. She is an active member of St. Paul A.M.E. Church, serving as chairperson for the Bread Ministry and for the Stewardess Board, and serving in the Missionary Society. She is the mother of Rev. James S. Cleare.

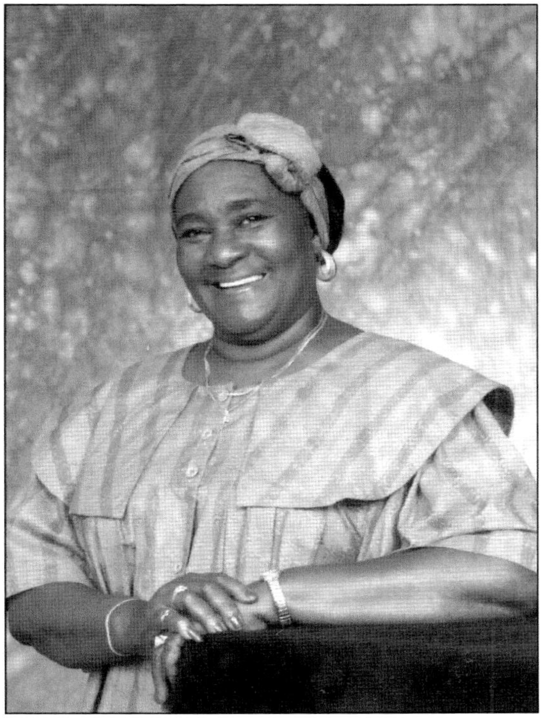

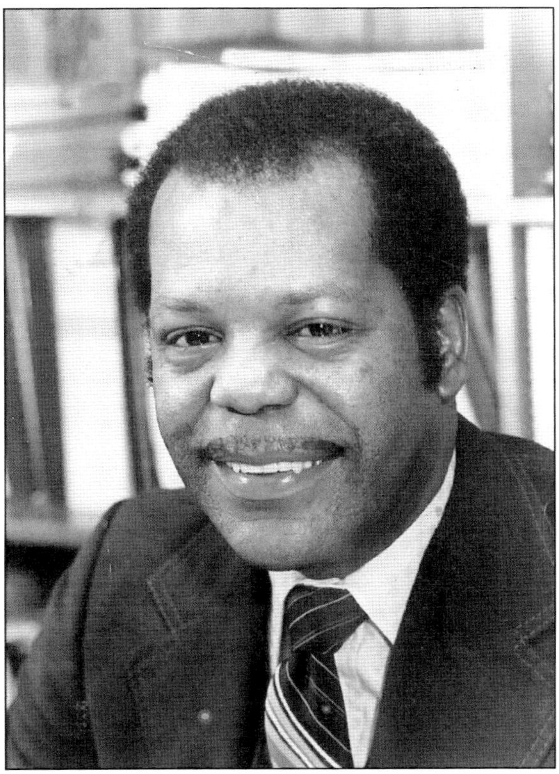

Edward J.White is the son of pioneers Edward J. White Sr. and Carmeta Ferguson White. A Pleasant City native, he attended Phillips Open Air School and Pleasant City Elementary School. obtained a bachelor's degree in industrial arts from Florida A&M University. He is a retiree from the Palm Beach County School System, where he taught industrial arts, vocational studies, and computer technology. He has been married to the former Marian Bacon for over 40 years, and they have two sons and six grandchildren.

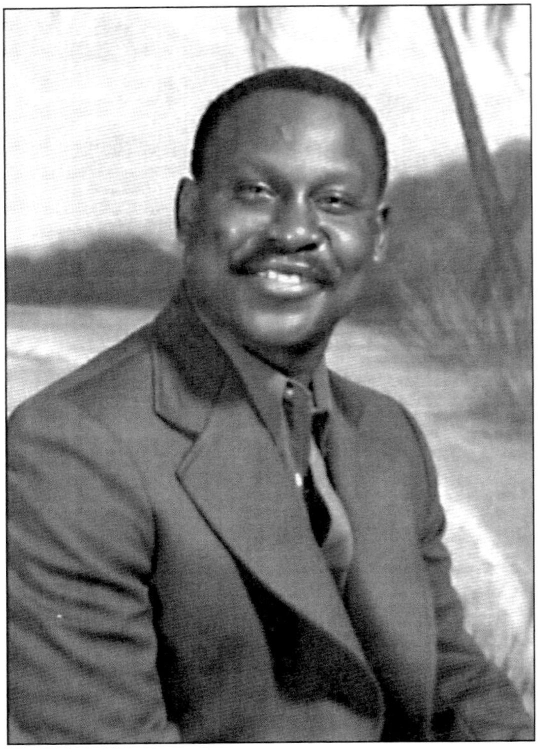

Donald Richard Wilson retired from the Palm Beach County School System after 35 years of service, including 17 years as an administrator. In 1999, he was elected to the Riviera Beach City Council. He chaired the Cultural Arts Committee that brought the signature event "Jazz at the Beach" to the city.

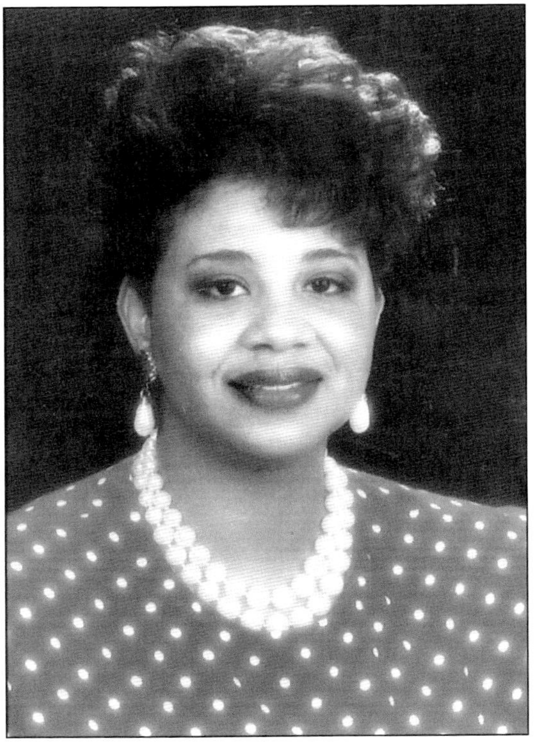

Frances Y. Francis is the vice president in the Small Business Banking Division at Bank of America. She specializes in small business loans in Palm Beach, Martin, St. Lucie, Indian River, Okeechobee, and Glades Counties. She is a graduate of Twin Lakes High School, Palm Beach Community College, Olympic College in Bremerton, Washington, and Palm Beach Atlantic College. She and her husband have three daughters and two grandchildren.

Charlie Lovett Ellington is the first African-American supervisor of special education in the northern part of Palm Beach County. She is the daughter of a great pioneer and educator, Mrs. Inez Peppers Lovett. She is a graduate of Industrial High School and Spelman College in Atlanta. She has master's degrees from Florida Atlantic, Nova Southeastern, and Florida A&M. She serves on both the Judicial Committee for the 15th Circuit Court of Florida and the board of directors of the Raymond F. Kravis Center.

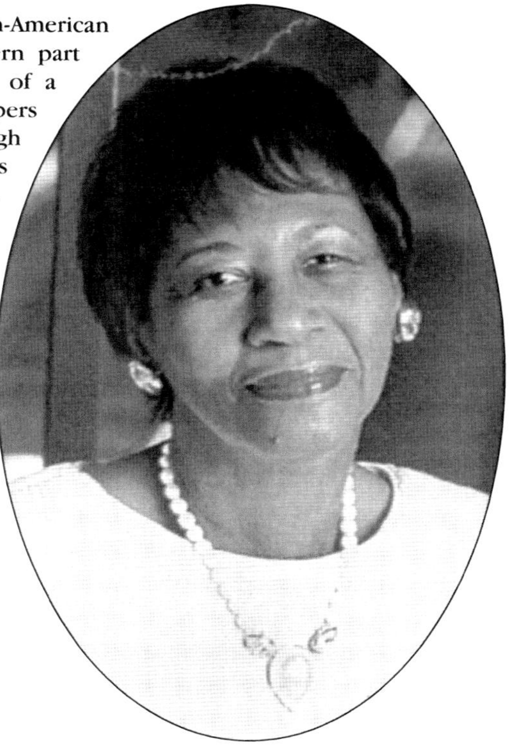

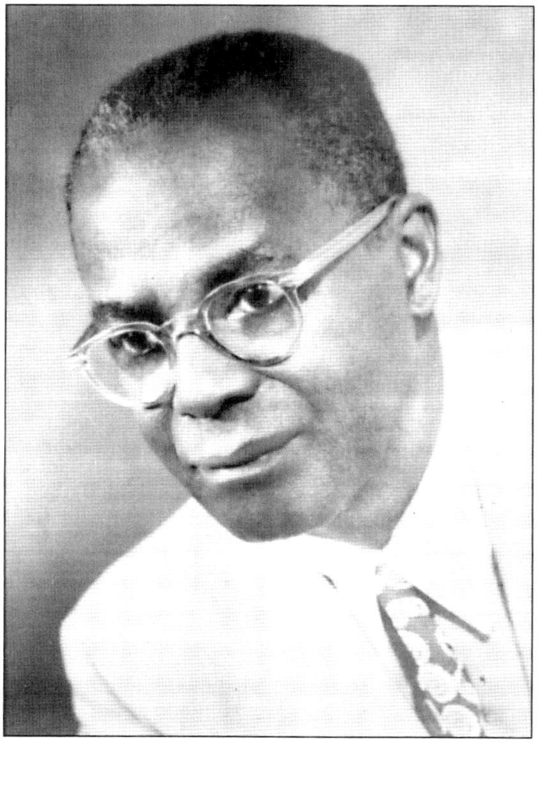

Dr. Russell Dyett, a pioneer and medical doctor, had an office at 528 Third Street. He was very active in civic and community affairs. He was a member of the prestigious Vanguard Club.

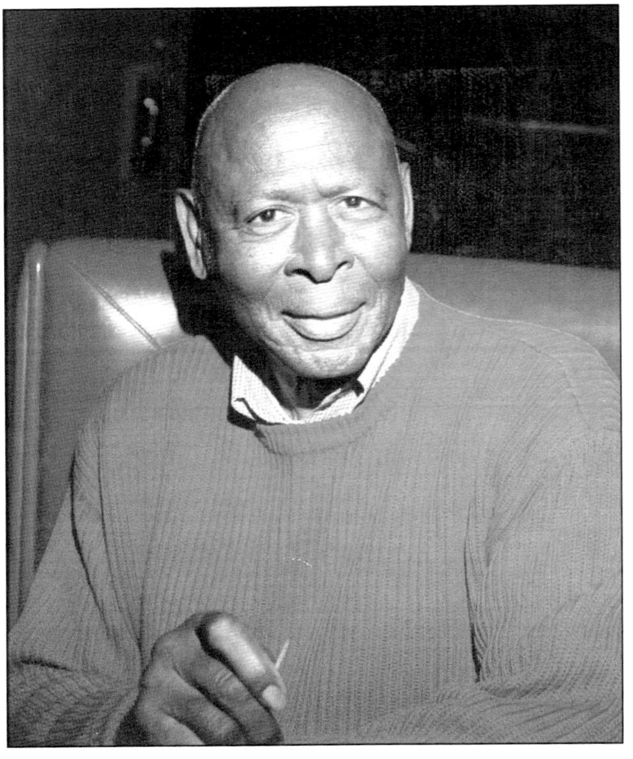

Oris Walker, a Tuskegee Air Force veteran, retired from the Palm Beach County School System, where he served as an administrator for many years. He served on the board of adjustment in Belle Glade.

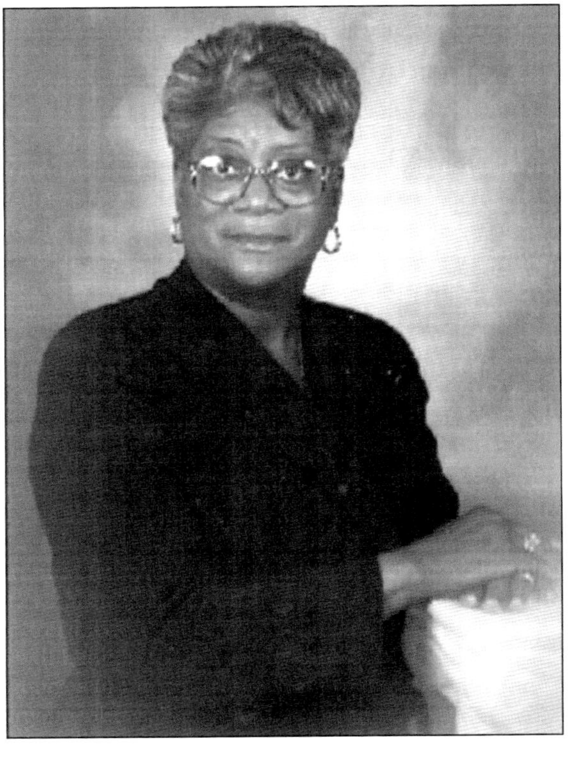

Marian Bacon White was the first woman president of the 11th Episcopal District Lay Organization of the African Methodist Episcopal Church (Florida and the Bahamas). A graduate of Roosevelt High School in West Palm Beach and Florida A&M University, with a bachelor's degree in elementary education, she retired from Palm Beach County Schools after 33 years. She has been a delegate to the General Conference for six quadrennials and served as lay leader of the delegation at the 2004 General Conference. Locally, she is a member of St. Paul A.M.E. Church (formerly of Pleasant City), where she served in many capacities for a number of years. She has been married to Edward J. White, grandson of pioneers Prince and Frances Ferguson, for more than 40 years. They have two sons and six grandchildren.

Ten

Is Paradise Lost?

Visitors to the Pleasant City area of West Palm Beach today cannot imagine what was ever so great about Pleasant City, with its shabby old houses, boarded up storefronts, multiple dwellings, uncollected trash, and crime infestation. Developers have seen the importance of the location, bordered on the east by Dixie Highway and only two blocks from Lake Worth, the proximity to downtown, and recently the prime location between City Place and the newly planned Northwood redevelopment.

Pioneers had problems holding on to this parcel of land ever since it was purchased from land developer George Curry in the early 1900s. More homes were burned on and around Dixie Highway than over in the Styx in Palm Beach, but the pioneers were not motivated to move

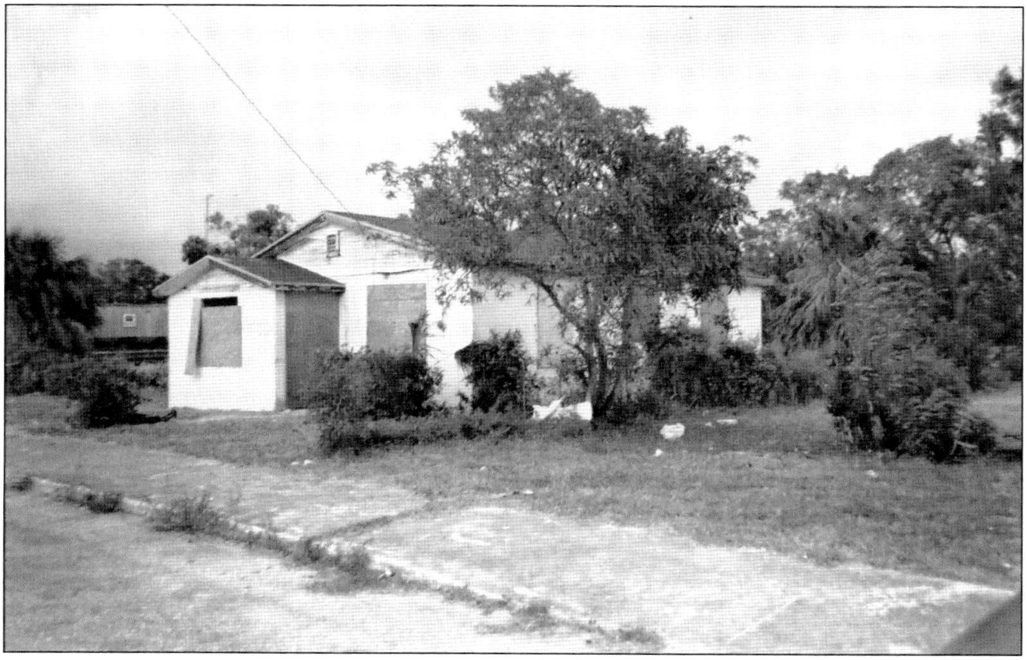

west across the railroad tracks. People born or raised in Pleasant City prior to the 1940s had a special bond with each other and the community that is often difficult for outsiders to understand. We were like one big family. In fact, many of us were relatives and friends from various parts of the South and the Caribbean who came to assist in the early building of the town of Palm Beach. Life was very pleasant in Pleasant City. We hardly had to go far out of our community, except for work, school, and major clothing and furniture shopping.

Services were conveniently located. We had three supermarkets within walking distance. On Northwood Road, between Dixie Highway and Spruce Avenue, was May's Market, which grew to be a family-owned business of three markets. The Northwood store and the Rosemary Avenue store, on the border of the community, offered unique services. Most families were not able to purchase groceries in large quantities, so the Mays conveniently packaged smaller quantities—if a customer could only purchase a half pound of sugar, one onion, even one cigarette, they provided it. The post office was located at the corner of Twenty-third Street and Dixie Highway, across from the Gulf Oil station and the Northwood Pharmacy. Most of the businesses on Northwood Road, Dixie Highway, and Spruce Avenue were larger and hired people from the community. If the residents were not working in Palm Beach or in the schools, they were working in Northwood, for the city, or for their own businesses.

Education was very important to our parents. In our homes, it was "go to school or go to work." There were not many dropouts. Those who attended the Fanny Phillips Open Air School on Twentieth Street got a solid educational foundation or else! They attended Pleasant City Elementary School and loved it. We all walked to Industrial High School, down the Florida East Coast Railway tracks to Fifteenth Street and to the top of the hill on Eleventh Street. We had great teachers who really cared about us. We had great non-academic programs, including drama, chorus, sports, and debating teams.

Although we have always had to go out of the community for recreation, we had so much at Roosevelt Park: shuffleboard, table games, dances, and parties. Baseball and football were

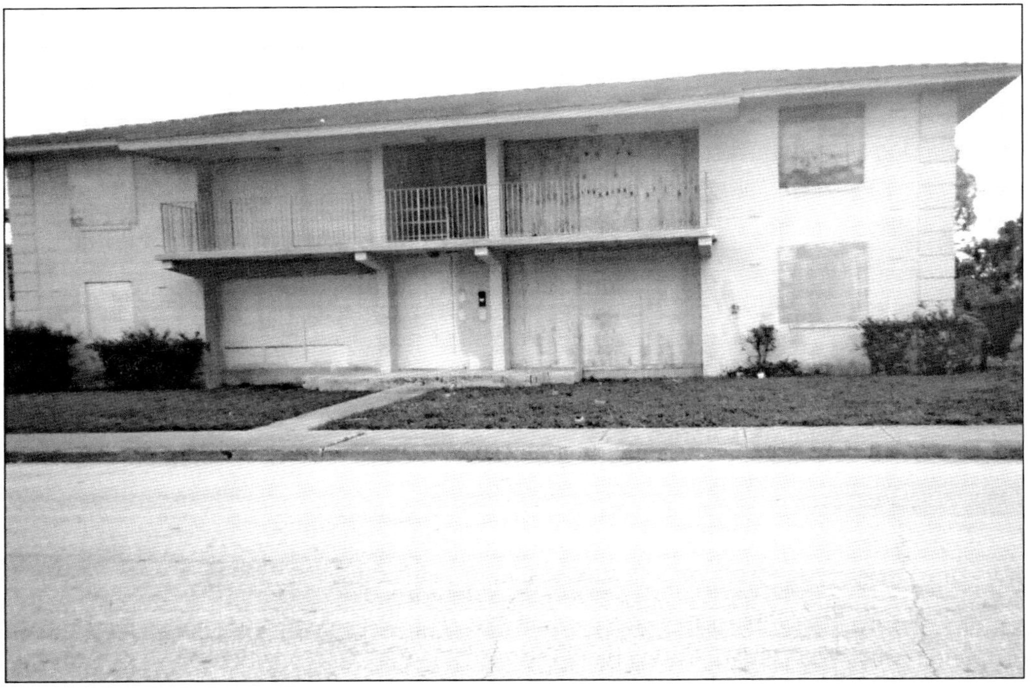

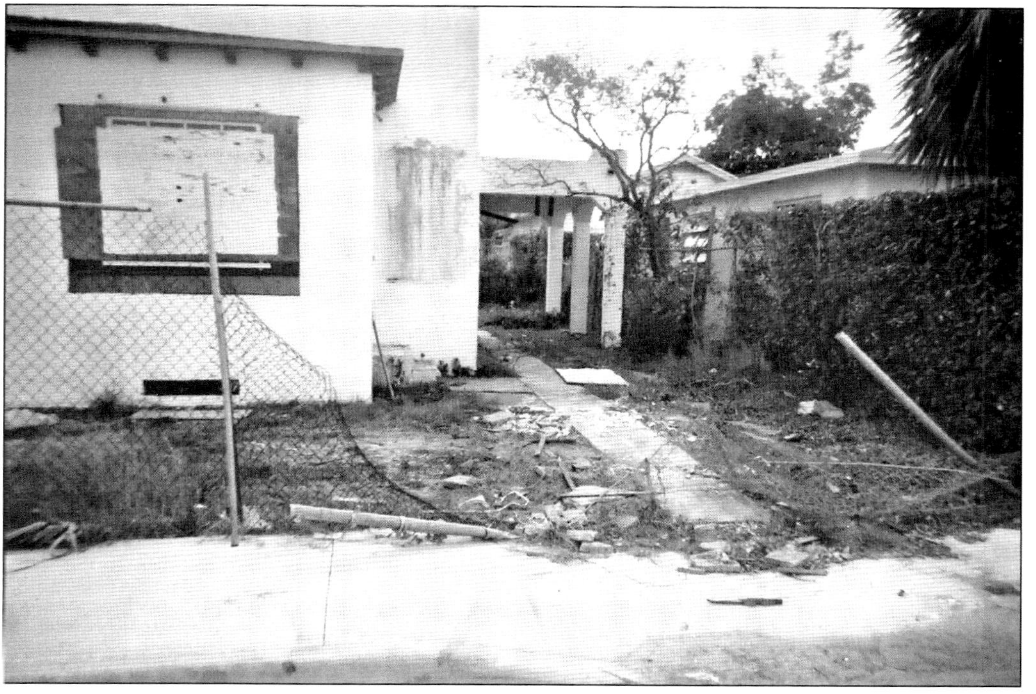

played at Coleman Park. We had two movie theaters on Rosemary Avenue. In the 1960s, we had an auditorium that meant much to the community. It was a place to see an ice show, concerts, or a circus. The auditorium gave our youth an opportunity to display their talent before a vast audience in school concerts and beauty and talent pageants. Youth need a place to go to enjoy those things again.

Back in Pleasant City, we found solace in our churches. They kept us busy with scouting and youth clubs and gave us a good religious foundation. Our churches can do more to help our young men and women who are out on the streets.

We once had beautiful single-family homes, and family life was so important. Today, we are wondering what will happen next. Developers decide they want the property for redevelopment, and all of a sudden the city codes change and residents have a few days to comply or their property is taken. It is rezoned or taken by eminent domain. Although Pleasant City is the oldest African-American community in the city of West Palm Beach and Palm Beach County, it has been refused historic designation because many of the properties that could have qualified have been torn down, the area has been rezoned, and the local residents have very little to say. Meetings have been called, but residents feel hopeless when they are told that whether they like it or not, eminent domain can be used to accomplish the city's goals.

It has been decided that a new project to be named Merry Place will have housing above stores and more multifamily dwellings. Most people would like to have a single-family home with a yard for the kids and pets.

A number of Pleasant City residents have retired from jobs up north, and would have loved to have moved back to Pleasant City. However, without decent housing, they went to North Palm Beach, Wellington, Riviera Beach, and other areas where there are single-family homes or small condos. We are still hopeful that something will happen to restore the beauty of this once-viable community. With all of the grants given to agencies in the past three years to improve the quality of life in Pleasant City, we should not have any problems. We should be living in Paradise.